The Buddha in the Tarot

Buddhist Reflections on the Major Arcana

Paul Greer

Createspace

Copyright © 2017 Paul Greer
All rights reserved.

Thank you to Michael Welton for his kind permission to quote an excerpt from his article "Can Buddhism Save the World?" at http://www.counterpunch.org/2016/01/15/can-buddhism-save-the-world/.

All extended quotations of Buddhist and Hindu materials were sourced from public domain sites, especially www.sacred-texts.com.

All Biblical quotations are from the Revised Standard Version.

Cover Image: *Taoist Sage in the Mountains* (stock image no. 117111903); license for commercial use obtained from stock.adobe.com.

Contact Paul Greer at **Augustine196785@gmail.com**

ISBN-13: 978-1542598101

ISBN-10: 1542598109

Contents

General Introduction	1
The Fool (0)	19

The Way of the World

Introduction	31
The Magician (1)	33
The High Priestess (2)	43
The Empress (3)	53
The Emperor (4)	65
The Hierophant (5)	73
The Lovers (6)	83
The Chariot (7)	93

Departure and Trials

Introduction	101
Strength (8)	105
The Hermit (9)	113
The Wheel of Fortune (10)	121
Justice (11)	131

The Hanged Man (12)	141
Death (13)	147
Temperance (14)	155
The Devil (15)	165
The Tower (16)	175

The Return

Introduction	181
The Star (17)	185
The Moon (18)	197
The Sun (19)	207
Judgement (20)	219
The World (21)	233
Notes	248

General Introduction

Buddha, Tarot and Me

From what I have read, it seems almost customary for Tarot authors to include some reflections on their own personal journeys with the cards; how the relationship began, and how it has developed over time. Not wanting to break with tradition I will do the same here; although I wish to start with some words on Buddhism before moving on to discuss the Tarot.

I was first introduced to Buddhism as a Religious Studies undergraduate in the 1980s, and despite forays into other areas of research and spirituality, it remains for me one of the most accurate, compelling and insightful accounts of the human condition that has ever been formulated. And, although I would not count myself as a card-carrying Buddhist, Buddhism remains a significant factor in my life, and continues to shape my ethical values and my understanding of humanity and existence in general. It has also been my privilege to teach Buddhism to A Level students for the last twenty years or so; although my discussions on impermanence and emptiness have perhaps generated more perplexity and angst than insight.

My relationship with Tarot is a different matter. My first recollection of the deck was as a youngster, watching a television series of fictional short stories entitled *Tales of the Unexpected*, where the cards appeared on a slowly revolving carousel during the closing credits, accompanied by images of a revolver, the silhouette of an erotically-dancing woman, a glowing African tribal mask, and a roulette wheel. This rather eerie but captivating vignette remains in my mind to this day.

As an undergraduate I decided to join an "Occult" mail-order book club, on the basis that they would send me three complementary gifts. The first was Doreen Valiente's *Natural Magic*; an early Wiccan work from the seventies, and one that still commands much respect today. Of particular interest was a chapter entitled "Magic of the Cards," which gave some background to the art of *cartomancy*. The second gift was a coffee-table tome, entitled, strangely enough, *Cartomancy*, written by Alessandro Bellenghi. Like most books of its kind, it was designed to provide the enthusiastic neophyte with a brief history of card divination, an introduction to Tarot symbolism, and a basic guide to a few commonly-used spreads. The book itself was paired with the third and final gift, and, if I am frank about it, the one I was really after – a 1983 *Carti Mundi* reproduction of the *1770 Vandenborre Bacchus Tarot* deck.

With Valiente, Bellenghi and the *Vandenborre* deck in hand, I set off into the mysterious world of the Tarot. To be honest, my first steps into this strange place were not as straightforward as I had hoped they would be. The *Vandenborre* deck is not the best to learn from, as it contains a number of significant departures from the more commonly-used images of the Major Arcana. The High Priestess card is replaced by a swaggering braggart by the name of *Le'Espagnol Captana Earcasse - The Spanish Captain*. The rather sober Hierophant is usurped by *Bacchus* himself, sitting on a cask, quaffing a huge carafe of wine. Other modifications include The Hanged Man shown standing on his feet, and The Tower transformed into a tree, re-titled *La Foundre* (Thunder). This, accompanied with a lack of imagery on the pip cards and the murky woodblock rendering, made for difficult reading. I persisted however, and eventually produced some insightful readings for my friends and family. Yet, I was always a little uneasy with the practice of divination, and felt a real desire to engage with *The Devil's Picture Book* in some other way.

Work and family life relegated the cards to the bottom of a dusty bookcase until, in 2012, I decided to commit myself to the Tarot once more. This time, I went about my task in a more rigorous and systematic fashion, reading as much as I could, and purchasing better decks. By this time my focus has shifted from divination to a more therapeutic and contemplative approach towards the cards, inspired in much part by Jungian opinions about what the Tarot was "really" about.

I began, quite casually at first, to notice some interesting parallels between Buddhism and the Tarot cards, particularly those of the Major Arcana. The life of the historical Buddha in particular seemed to mirror a surprising number of images found on the cards. Additionally, many concerns and attitudes which are central to the Buddhist worldview – such as wisdom, compassion, effort, resolve, renunciation, balance, and of course, enlightenment - also began to find some resonance with the deck.

My personal discovery of correspondences between Buddhism and Tarot provided one of the inspirations for writing this book, and my overall aim is to offer a series of Buddhist reflections on the Tarot, with particular attention given to the cards of the Major Arcana. However, before I delve into discussing other motivations behind this project, I feel it is necessary at this point to provide some background – especially for the uninitiated – into that strange and wonderful world that is Buddhism.

The World of Buddhism

The religion of Buddhism is founded on the teachings of *Gotama Buddha*, who lived and died two-and-a-half thousand years ago. Born the son of a northern-Indian King, *Prince Siddhattha Gotama* spent his youth surrounded by luxury and sensual delight. With a growing awareness of life's pains and hardships, and moved with compassion for others, he left his pampered life at the age of twenty-nine and set out on a quest to find a solution to the problems of suffering. After six years of intense spiritual struggle he had an experience of awakening, and was henceforth known as *The Buddha - The Enlightened One*. He spent the remaining forty-five years of his life teaching and engaging with any who would listen, and establishing a community (*Sangha*) that would practice and continue his doctrine of liberation (*Dharma*). He died at the age of eighty, perhaps as a result of unintentional food-poisoning.

There are two main branches of classical Buddhism. *Theravada* or the *Tradition of the Elders* is a branch that holds to the words and teachings of the Buddha found in the *Pali* scriptures, which many view as representing some of the earliest Buddhist teachings. This is a form of Buddhism still practiced in Thailand, Sri Lanka, and Myanmar, among other places. *Mahayana* or the *Great Vehicle* is an umbrella term applied to forms of Buddhism that display a number of doctrinal developments from earlier teachings. Some of these teachings are so unique that certain scholars make a further division between *Mahayana* and *Vajrayana* (*Diamond Vehicle*) Buddhism. *Mahayana* Buddhism is associated with the Buddhism of China, Japan, Vietnam, Bhutan, and Tibet, among other places.

For those new to Buddhism, its teachings may seem like an overly-pessimistic way of envisioning human life and the world. The bottom-line, according to the Buddha, is that everything is characterized by *dukkha* - often translated as "suffering" or "unsatisfactoriness." The Buddha's list is quite comprehensive:

> "This, brethren, is the noble truth of suffering: birth is suffering, old age is suffering, illness is suffering, death is suffering. Union with unpleasant things is suffering, separation from pleasant things is suffering, not obtaining what we wish is suffering ..."[1]

Moreover, this sense of suffering cannot be pinned on external factors outside our control, whether gods, fate, angelic despots or general randomness. The suffering originates from within. Buddhism traces our woes back to a number of afflictive mental states which condition our generally negative experiences of life, including the "three poisons" of greed, hatred and delusion, our selfish desires which generate harmful patterns of thought, speech and behaviour, and perhaps, most fundamentally, our ignorance. We are especially ignorant of the impermanent nature of the world and ourselves, and this creates strong attachments to things, whether our own sense of self, our thoughts, or sensory objects. These attachments can only bring us suffering in the long run; for, in spite of the illusion of permanency, life in reality is impermanent to the core. To add to our woes, this bleak scenario does not terminate with the destruction of the body. Our afflictive mental states condition new of forms of life which then inherit our delusions, and play out the same Shakespearean tragedy again and again, with new names and new faces. In Buddhism, this potentially unending cycle of folly is termed *Samsara* – literally, "wandering around." This however does not mean that Buddhism holds to the doctrine of reincarnation or transmigration. The Buddhist concept of rebirth (*punabbhava*) is not only different from the Hindu notion of reincarnation (*punarjanma*), but in some respects its opposite. The Buddha recognized the notion of an indwelling eternal *atman* or soul, moving from one life to another, as yet another example of delusional "clinging" to some imaginary essence outside the reality of impermanence. "Death" and "rebirth" in Buddhism are pervasive and constant; they are moments of change in a single stream of change extending over countless lifetimes. Delusion involves the belief that there is some eternal "self," "soul" or *atman* lying trapped underneath this process that can somehow "escape." In the unequivocal words of the Buddhist *Visuddhi-Magga* (*Path of Purity*):

> No doer is there does the deed,
> Nor is there one who feels the fruit;
> Constituent parts roll on;
> This view alone is orthodox.[2]

Given the Buddha's rejection of various ideas which were and still are highly cherished by many spiritual seekers, it comes as no surprise that he characterized his own teachings as *patisotagami* – "against the current."

The good news, according to Buddhism, is that human are capable of ending the cycle of Samsara, by eradicating "unwholesome" states of mind and cultivating "wholesome" and "beautiful" ones instead. This can be achieved by following the three trainings in Wisdom, Morality and Meditation which are encapsulated in the *Noble Eightfold Path*. One who has attained this is said to have gained *Nirvana* – the "blowing-out" or "cooling" of all afflictive mental states. What makes Buddhism unique as a world religion is its belief that this process requires no divine aid or grace, and is in fact achievable within the limitations of one's own body-mind complex. We ourselves create our suffering, and we ourselves can end it.

The awakened do not "glow" after enlightenment; they were, and are, still human. In the words of the well-known Zen aphorism: "Before Enlightenment chop wood carry water; after Enlightenment, chop wood carry water." The difference for one is who is awake is a total reconfiguration of the mind in relation to itself, the body, and the world. Can such inner change be accomplished by mere mortals such as ourselves? The Buddha thought so, and in the *Kusala Sutta* he reasoned with his followers that if it were not possible to develop that which is "skillful," then he would not have asked them to do so in the first place.

There are a number of features within Buddhist doctrine and practice which make it particularly attractive to a growing number of Westerners. These include its emphasis upon reason and investigation over faith; its optimism about the human potential for transformation; its apparent congruity with scientific understanding (especially in the areas of Physics and Ecology); its tolerance of other religions and lifestyles; and its experiential approach to truth. In the West, Buddhism's practical and pragmatic nature has prompted developments towards a "religion-less" form of practice, divested of what some view as "harmful" accretions that have attached themselves to the Buddha's original vision of transformation and liberation.[3]

Why the Buddha in the Tarot?

As stated, the aim of this book is to provide a series of Buddhist reflections on the Tarot, focusing on the cards of the Major Arcana. There have been a number of motivating factors behind this project. The first, as I have already said, is that connections between Buddhism and Tarot appear to exist, and this in itself serves as a reasonable justification for their elucidation. Uncovering such correspondences has been an engaging and compelling enterprise, although one that perhaps relates to no more (or no less) than the innate heuristic skill of *apophenia* – our naturally-evolved ability to see meaningful patterns in random data. While the cynically-minded might view this as something that undermines the integrity of any and all symbol-correspondence endeavors, others might be inclined to adopt a more positive perspective, recognizing apophenia as a useful and natural mechanism which provides a catalyst for profound and creative insight.

This leads on to another justification for this project which, to use Bradford Hatcher's words, may be described as "the most useful point" in enabling two formerly separate systems to communicate – to enrich, deepen, and enhance ideas and perspectives.[4] In this respect, I must acknowledge that my appreciation of both

Buddhism and Tarot has been enriched by the simple act of placing them side by side. On the one hand, the Tarot has provided me with an interpretative lens for looking at Buddhism, bringing into sharp relief ideas which I had never really considered important or worth investigating. Conversely, my acquaintance with Buddhism has prompted glimpses of some unusual yet nevertheless persuasive meanings in the Tarot; meanings that would otherwise be absent.

The final motivation for this project relates to an observation made by the Buddhist writer Sangharakshita. If Buddhism is to be fully-grounded in the West he argues, then it must remain genuinely Buddhist at its core, but at the same time learn to speak the "language" of the West, in terms of expressing itself in and through its literature, music, art, and mythology.[5] It is my view that Tarot provides a valuable resource by which Buddhism can do so; or, to put it another way, that Tarot can be open to and expressive of a Buddhist vision of the spiritual life.

Although Tarot has been defined as an ongoing-project characterized by openness, creativity and invention,[6] some may be of the opinion that a Buddhist-Tarot convergence is simply a step too far; an unlikely marriage of two very different and perhaps incompatible points of view. Some may therefore be surprised to learn that an attempt to unite these two seemingly odd bedfellows was made by Robert Place in his 2004 book *The Buddha Tarot Companion: A Mandala of Cards,* which served as a reference point for his uniquely designed *Buddha Tarot* deck. For Place, what brought Buddhism and Tarot together was the life story of the Buddha himself, which shared with Tarot's Trumps the same "archetypal pattern."[7] Although one can certainly agree with Place on this point, his approach raises two issues. First, his Tarot deck contains many significant departures from traditional decks and imagery, prompting the question of why such a major redesign was necessary if, as he says, the Buddha's life and Tarot share the same "archetypal pattern." Another issue relates to interpretation. Although Place makes much use of Buddhist terminology, he is keen to place Buddhism itself within the folds of neo-Platonism or the "Western Mystery Tradition."[8] In this book I have endeavored to let Buddhism speak more for itself; and when it does, it can often seem at odds with the *Perennial Wisdom*. More positively, this "bias" towards Buddhism permits us to see meanings in the Tarot imagery which would certainly be absent when viewed through a more-typically Western approach.

Although my own "Buddhist" interpretation of the cards differs from Place's in many instances, and quite dramatically at times, his insight that the Buddha's story and the Tarot conform to the same "archetypal pattern" is a useful and important one, and forms a foundation for my general approach to the cards, and how they relate to the story of the Buddha's life. In many ways, Place's approach is based upon a Jungian view of the Trumps, considered as a narrative sequence culminating in self-realization or *individuation*; or in the Buddha's case, enlightenment. Before we address the cards directly then, it is necessary to examine to some extent how Jungian thought has influenced Tarot interpretation, particularly in its view of the Major Arcana as both a "path" and therapeutic process towards individuation.

From Divination to Individuation, and the Hero's Journey

In popular thought and actual practice, Tarot continues to be associated with *divination*. This term derives from the Latin *divinare*, meaning to "forsee" or to be "inspired by a god," and generally indicates the acquisition of hidden knowledge by supernatural means. The classical Greek term for this practice was *mantike*, from which we derive a modern expression for Tarot divination itself – *cartomancy*. Despite the fact that some Tarotists have put forward sophisticated and compelling interpretations of what Tarot divination may actually entail,[9] in popular thought it continues to have strong associations with "fortune-telling" and other contentious practices, which hint at a degree of charlatanry and material expectation underscoring the whole process. Moreover, such practices have been criticized for encouraging a lack of self-responsibility and a certain degree of passivity towards the cards.[10] For Thomas Saunders, divination "debases" both Tarot and Tarotist. Tarot he argues is about taking responsibility in the here-and-now, and not about future hopes, fears or material expectations.[11] Additionally, given that the Buddha himself condemned the practice of divination as being one of the "lowly arts" (*Kevatta Sutta*), and that the renowned monk Thich Nhat Hahn censures the practice of fortune-telling by ordained Buddhists,[12] it may seem that a Tarot-Buddhist comparison is perhaps inappropriate.

Other practitioners, whilst not wishing to negate Tarot's divinatory dimension entirely, have sought to recontextualise it within a more intellectually-credible framework. Thus Tarot's occult connotations have been realigned with *Chaos Theory*, the *Implicate Order*, *Synchronicity*, *Morphic Resonance*, and other plausible theories suggesting "the sympathy of all things." There are others still who have shifted Tarot's focus almost entirely away from divination to therapeutic application, where the traditional relationship between reader/querent has been readjusted to that of counselor/client.[13]

There are however those who adopt a more solitary, meditative and contemplative attitude towards the cards, viewing them primarily as an aid towards self-understanding and self-transformation.[14] It is within this form of practice in particular that we find the most obvious influences of Jungian thought. Despite the view that the Tarot may be "doctrinally foundationless"[15] or the fact that Jung himself saw the Tarot images as being only "distantly descended from the archetypes of transformation,"[16] it is rare to find a modern book on Tarot that does not make some kind of nod to Jung, whether in terms of borrowed concepts (Archetype, Collective Unconscious, Anima, Animus, Masculine, Feminine, Shadow, Self) or in the generally personal and therapeutic flavor of what Tarot is seen to be about. Richard Roberts sums up the views of many when he says that Tarot is "above all" a system of self-development, similar to Jung's individuation process.[17]

What makes Jung popular is his attempt to make religion or "spirituality" intelligible and meaningful to contemporary individuals. Jung argued that our materialist culture had left us in a disenchanted world "bereft of gods";[18] a serious situation which threatens our "psychic balance."[19] Humanity needs to recover some form of spirituality said Jung, but can no longer find solace in the "metaphysical certainties" of the medieval world.[20] Spirituality now needs to engage both "sentiment" and "reason,"[21] and for Jung this meant extracting the old religious myths, doctrines and rituals from their original supernatural framework, and reinterpreting them within a more natural and therapeutic one. Religious "salvation" now only makes sense within the therapeutic perspective of personal transformation; or in Jung's words, "individuation." Individuation as Anthony Storr says represents a kind of "Pilgrim's Progress," aimed at personal unification and wholeness, as opposed to some post-mortem destination.[22] It was Jung's successful linking of religious myth and imagery with such a therapeutic and "this-worldly" process which continues to shape and inform much Tarot practice and interpretation.[23]

Of equal importance is the link made between the sequence of Tarot Trumps and Joseph Campbell's understanding of the *Hero's Journey* – the Jungian interpretation of the individuation process as an archetypal path through life. In his 1949 book *The Hero with a Thousand Faces*, Campbell argued that many of the world's hero myths shared the same underlying archetypal structure, which he referred to as the *monomyth*. The classic Hero's Journey he argued was a narrative magnification of an originally primitive rite of passage formula of separation, initiation and return. The journey is one is which the hero sets forth from the everyday world into a realm of wonder and testing. An important victory is won, and the hero then returns to his or her community, "to bestow boons."[24] Campbell's understanding of the Hero's Journey relied heavily upon Jung's theory of the archetype, and, although he did not actually use the term "individuation process," it is certainly implied. Of much relevance is the fact that Campbell saw this monomyth clearly reflected in the story of the Buddha's own journey to enlightenment and his subsequent return to the world, to bestow upon humanity his gift of the Dharma.[25] In his subsequent work, *The Masks of God: Oriental Mythology*, Campbell modified his analysis somewhat, and aligned the Buddha's life story with an *Archetypal Savior Biography*, within which he recognized numerous thematic correspondences between the life of the Buddha and other World Saviors, including Jesus.[26]

The notion that the Buddha's life story can be understood as an archetypal journey over (or at least alongside) actual events seems to match the historical record. The Buddhist tradition was never really concerned with preserving every detail of the Buddha's life, but only certain "critical" moments. Yet, when put together, these moments constitute a clear path or journey towards enlightenment, and a subsequent return to the world to teach and spread the Dharma. These key moments were regarded as being so central to the Buddhist message that from early on, artists, sculptors and poets sought to preserve them in statues, reliefs, and poetry. This archetypal focus continues to have appeal among modern Buddhists. According to Joseph Goldstein for example, the Buddha may have been an historical person, but we can also see his story as expressing a number of basic archetypal characteristics of human life, and thus one that "connects the Buddha's journey with our own."[27]

The notion of an equivalent *Fool's Journey* was first applied to the Tarot in 1970 by Eden Gray in her *A Complete Guide to the Tarot*. The Fool's Journey says Gray corresponds to our own journey though the twenty-one "life experiences" illustrated in the cards of Major Arcana, which she also considered as being "archetypes of the subconscious."[28] Gray's views illustrate a particular interpretive division adopted by most Tarotists today. Namely, that while the Minors reflect the more mundane aspects of the everyday, the Majors point to a number of "touchstone" events in our journey through life. For contemporary Tarotists, the Fool's Journey - or the *Twenty-One Doors* as it is sometimes called - is usually framed within the context of contemplative practice. The Fool is considered as representative of our potential, and is led through each card in turn, learning their lessons, and thereupon proceeding to the next. More complex interpretations involve separating the cards into different developmental phases or themes. Rachel Pollack for example applies a tripartite schema to The Fool's progress which clearly reflects the underlying structure of Campbell's monomyth - the *Worldly Sequence* of growth towards independence; *Turning Inwards*, signifying inner reflection and spiritual development; and finally *The Great Journey*, indicating social reintegration.[29]

The view of the Buddha's story and the Fool's story as similar expressions of the same archetypal journey serves as a basis for our investigation of the "Buddha in the Tarot." Yet, it is clear that links between Buddhism and (Jungian-influenced) Tarot practice exist at a more foundational level. What really unites the two systems is a belief in the human potential for positive change, and that humans have the innate capacities to affect such change. It is within this "fathom-long body," declares the Buddha in the *Rohitassa Sutta*, that we find both the origins of the world of suffering, and its end. In fact the Buddha insists that enlightenment can only be found through our own efforts; there is no easy way to awakening; no grace-dispensing savior to carry the burden for us. As the *Dhammapada* states: "Purity and impurity belong to oneself, no one can purify another."³⁰ Buddhism, as Dzogchen Ponlop argues, is fundamentally at odds with religious concepts such as "original sin," which view human nature as essentially contaminated and corrupted. Within Buddhism humans are regarded as "primordially pure"; replete with many "positive qualities" which sit alongside those more negative potentials.³¹ These "positive qualities" form the basis for the Buddhist vision of self-development. Although it would be naïve to suggest that the concept of individuation is identical to the Buddhist concept of enlightenment, many of Jung's general ideas, as Adrian Chan-Wyles has pointed out, pass "very close" to the Buddhist model of self-transformation.³²

The Structure of this Investigation

Our investigation of "The Buddha in the Tarot" will begin with an analysis of The Fool; that mysterious figure regarded as being both within and outside all other Trumps. The subsequent inquiry is divided into three parts, corresponding to the three elements of Campbell's monomyth, and similar sequences found in the Buddha's journey towards enlightenment and his ensuing return to the world. The first has been termed *The Way of the World*, and comprises cards 1-7 - from The Magician to The Chariot. This mirrors Pollack's "Worldly Sequence," and relates to the growth of personal consciousness and factors which allow for life to be lived in society – parental influences, education, relationships, and growing independence. In the Buddha's own story, this sequence culminates with his chariot ride into the city of *Kapilavastu*, and his encounter with the *Four Sights*. The second has been termed *Departure and Trials*, and comprises cards 8-16 – from Strength to The Tower. This sequence reflects a "turn away" or within to the world of spiritual reflection, and includes the many trials to be found along the way to individuation. In the Buddha's story, this sequence extends from his departure from his father's palace, to his enlightenment under the Bodhi tree. The third has been termed *The Return*, and comprises cards 17-21 – from The Star to The World. This sequence reflects the issues of social engagement and reintegration; a return to the world to "bestow boons." In the Buddha's story, this sequence relates to his decision to return to society, to teach and spread his new Dharma.

Each card itself will be discussed under three sub-headings. The *General Overview* will examine traditional and popular interpretations of the card in question, but will also include what I consider to be relevant insights from other disciplines and spiritual paths. The second is entitled *In the Story of the Buddha*, and discusses a relevant episode or event from the narrative accounts of the Buddha's own journey. The third sub-heading is termed *A Buddhist Reflection*, and discusses Buddhist ideas that I feel are pertinent to the overall theme of any particular card. For example, The Lovers card addresses the issues of sex and relationships within Buddhism, while The Hermit explores the practice of renunciation.

Our investigations in the main should be considered with a Standard or Universal *Rider-Waite-Smith* (*RWS*) deck in mind. This is a deck which continues to hold a foundational role within contemporary Tarot reflection and interpretation. In this respect it is assumed that the reader will have access to images from the *RWS* or a similar deck (the *B.O.T.A.* deck for example). Both the black-and-white images from Waite's *The Pictorial Key to the Tarot* and the colored ones from Pamela Coleman

Smith's 1910 (PAM-A) deck can by accessed at www.sacred-texts.com.

Any attempt to reduce the complexity of the Major Arcana to a purely linear storyline, as I have done here, must take onboard Arthur Rosengarten's criticism that it may impose unwarranted restraints on "experience and possibility."[33] A similar point is made by Joan Bunning, who highlights the fact that our own journey through life might not move as smoothly as that of the Fool's.[34] I agree, but our investigations here are first and foremost about the Buddha's story, not ours. One feature about such an archetypal narrative is that it is, well, "archetypal." Its very attraction, persistence and appeal are in its conformity to patterns of development that resonate with millennia of human experience. So, we may find that this story does resonate with our own experiences in a somewhat identical fashion; and if it does not, this neither detracts from the appeal of the story itself, nor invalidates our own spiritual adventure.

However, before we enter *The Way of the World*, it is necessary to begin our investigations with The Fool – after all, it's his or her journey.

The Fool (0)

General Overview

We begin our investigations of the Buddha in the Tarot with The Fool. The *RWS* version of this card shows a young man in boots and garish clothing walking towards the edge of a precipice. With his right hand he carries a rod with a bundle attached, while with his left he holds a white rose. A small dog on its two hind-legs is shown at his left-hand side. The sun is depicted shining at its zenith.

The Fool is a unique card in that it is numbered with a zero (0). For many interpreters this indicates that it stands outside the normal sequence of cards, representing both the individual's potential before commencement on the path, and his or her spiritual fulfillment at its completion, symbolized by The World. In this respect Roberts draws our attention to the color of The Fool's boots – he is the only character in the *RWS* deck with golden footwear. For Roberts, this suggests that he has already traversed the "golden path" of spiritual development.[1] It is also interesting to note that if we place The Fool at the end of the Trumps we can observe the Sun rising from its lowly position in Death, to its zenith in our wandering vagabond. Generally speaking, The Fool is considered to be not only outside all cards, but within all cards too, representing the challenges and transformation at each stage of the process. As a prequel to the path, the Fool is often viewed as representing a sense of spontaneity, levity, innocence, naivety, and perhaps even childishness; all suggested by his playful gait and lack of self-concern. As a conclusion to the path, The Fool is linked with a sense of awakening and freedom, grounded in the accumulation of experience, reflection, and wisdom.

Of note too is the little dog at his side, which in some interpretations indicates an element within The Fool's own nature, attempting to draw him away from danger, or preventing him from engaging in some perilous new experience.[2] Another useful interpretation is offered by Place, who links the dog with the Fool's status as *outsider*. Place draws our attention to the fact that the beggars, troubadours and religious mendicants of the medieval world had to contend with wild dogs and other savage creatures as they wandered through the countryside.[3] This is an insight perhaps shared by older renditions of the card – for example the *Tarocchi of Venice, Mantegna,* and *Marseilles* versions - where dogs are depicted tearing at The Fool's clothing. His outsider status is further suggested by his beggar's stick and tied bundle of belongings, which he holds casually over his right shoulder.

In the Story of the Buddha: The Narrative Itself as Skillful Means

The Fool represents no single episode from the life of Gotama Buddha. In fact, he represents the enlightened reality to which the narrative points. To understand this rather abstract idea we need to be aware of two Buddhist concepts relating to the meaning of the term "Buddha." One of these is *Dharmakaya* ("Truth Body" of the Buddha), and the other is *Nirmanakaya* ("Manifest

Body"). The Dharmakaya indicates the eternally awakened mind that, according to the Mahayana tradition, resides within all things. The Nirmanakaya represents that same mind as it spontaneously manifests itself in the world, and whose purpose is to awaken all to their true nature. The Nirmanakaya, to use Yeshe's words, represents the enlightened mind's appearance in the world in ways to which "unenlightened beings can relate."[4] The relationship between both is discussed in an important Mahayana text called the *Lotus Sutra*. Here, the Buddha tells his followers that he has been teaching the Dharma to many beings for "countless eons." His followers ask how this can be possible, and he then proceeds to tell them the parable of *The Good Physician*. We are told that a wise doctor with many sons left home to go on business. On his return, he found that they had all taken some poison that had been left in the house. He provides an antidote, but only a few take it. The others, in their agonized and delirious state, refuse. The father devises a plan to make them better – he will leave, and pretend that he has died. This he does, and news quickly spreads about his "death." The remaining sons in their grief take the medicine to honor their father's memory, and are cured. The father then returns home, and is reunited with his sons. His "death" was a "skillful means" (*upaya*) which motivated his dying children to take the medicine that would heal them. In the same way, says the Buddha, the story of his own birth, enlightenment and death is not to be taken at face value – it is primarily a skillful means of motivating those lost in Samsara. Its real purpose is to provide the impetus for action, the motivation to engage with ourselves. In truth, "I am always here teaching the Dharma."[5]

This is an understanding of the Buddha's story which is implied in a well-known Mahayana version of his life called the *Lalitavistara Sutra* – a title which literally means *The Play in Full*. If we reflect on this title, we realize that the Buddha's "manifest form" is not even a "person" within the story called "Gotama," but is in fact, the narrative itself. The story of a young prince, his discovery of suffering, his renunciation, and his journey to enlightenment, *is in itself* the manifest form of the eternal Buddha nature, "teaching the Dharma" in such a way that the unenlightened may comprehend and respond to its transformative message.

The Fool and the other twenty-one cards of the Major Arcana represent two different perspectives on enlightenment. As Stephen Batchelor says, enlightenment is both an "ever present possibility" and "a linear process ... over time."[6] Another way of putting this is in Lama Yeshe's differentiation between the "resultant" and "causal" approaches to enlightenment. The "resultant" or *Tantric* approach is based on the view that we already possess that which we seek, and therefore we should learn to "think, speak and act" as if we were already awakened. By contrast, the "causal" approach is a gradual one which entails following prescriptive guidelines – ethical, meditative, and wisdom-related – for the realization of enlightenment at some future time.[7] This causal vehicle reflects in many ways the path to awakening found in the other twenty-one Trump cards.

The fundamental message of the Buddha's "manifest body" is that the way to enlightenment can be apprehended in the "stuff" of the world – which may be a person, or more simply, a story. As Reeves says, the Buddha can be found in "anybody and anything at all"[8] -

perhaps even in a Tarot deck. In our next card, The Magician, we begin our "causal" journey to enlightenment though the Nirmanakaya of the Tarot; the *Play in Full*.

A Buddhist Reflection: The "Fool" as an Issue of Perspective

The Fool is perhaps the most enigmatic and ambivalent symbol of the Tarot deck. On the one hand, we all seem to share a similar view about what a "foolish" individual is – one lost in naivety, immaturity, recklessness, and daydreams. On the other hand, we are simultaneously aware that "foolishness" is often a matter of personal perspective and opinion. The card as Pollack recognizes is essentially "faceless" and perhaps even "distorted" – especially when its status as "fool" is conferred upon it by others.[9]

It is clear that those trapped in Samsara – "uninstructed worldlings" (*puthujjana*) to use the Buddha's terminology – will have a particular angle on what constitutes "foolishness." It will be the person who turns his or her back on all that this world has to offer in terms of wealth (*artha*), pleasure (*kama*) and social order (*dharma*), for navel-gazing and other pointless "spiritual" pursuits. This "worldling" perspective is highlighted by Deepak Chopra in his novelization of the Buddha's life. When the Buddha's father King Suddhodana discovers from *Asita the Seer* that his son may become a great spiritual teacher rather than a mighty ruler, he clutches himself with horror, and declares that only "a fool" would exchange kingship over the world for such a pointless vocation.[10]

Yet, we must not forget that the Buddha himself had his own perspective on "foolishness." A foolish worldling is one who tries to find lasting happiness by clinging to things that perish. One who is driven by greed, hatred and delusion. One who is unaware that his or her actions have consequences. As these verses from the *Dhammapada* reveal:

> "These sons belong to me, and this wealth belongs to me" – with such thoughts a fool is tormented. He himself does not belong to himself; how much less his sons and wealth? ... Fools of poor understanding have themselves for their greatest enemies, for they do evil deeds which must bear bitter fruits.[11]

The perspective-derived ambiguity of The Fool is captured brilliantly by Pamela Colman Smith in her rendition of the image. The Fool's eyes are not focused on the movement of his body – is he lost in ignorance and delusion; or is this an enlightened outsider who has given up self-cherishing? Are his overstated boots simply part of his garish costume, or do they represent freedom, given, as Cirlot points out, that in ancient times only slaves walked barefoot?[12] Or what about the feather in his cap – is this some *Yankee Doodle* tomfoolery, or indeed *Maat's* feather, conveying wisdom and truth? He walks towards the cliff edge – are these the steps of a deluded worldling, or the fearless and compassionate strides of a *bodhisattva* – an *enlightenment being* who chooses to immerse him or herself once more in Samsara?

The inherent ambiguity of foolishness is exploited to great effect in the stories of the Zen Buddhist tradition, where the apparently "foolish" and irreverent behaviour of the wise is set against the deluded mindscapes and expectations of the truly foolish. A well-known Zen story which illustrates this is that of the two monks and the woman at a river. In the story, two monks, one senior and one junior, are travelling together when they come across a young beautiful woman, attempting to cross a river with a strong current. The woman asks for assistance, but the junior monk is reluctant, given his monastic vow never to touch a woman. Without any thought, the senior monk lifts her up, carries her across, and places her gently on the other side. The two monks continue in silence for many hours. Finally the junior monk cannot control himself any longer, and demands of his companion why he acted in the way he did. The older monk looks at him and replies: "I placed her down by the riverbank - why do you still carry her?"

This little story provides some useful insights into the nature of both the enlightened and the "foolish" mind. The foolish mind equates righteous action, perhaps even "enlightened" action, with perfect adherence to proscribed rules, whether social standards or, in this case, obedience to the monastic code of conduct. This sets limits on the nature and level of compassionate action that can be provided; action always takes place within the context of self-monitoring and self-protection related to a field of expectations. By contrast, the enlightened mind is not bound by such a self-imposed prison. This does not mean that actions here are immoral – it means they are spontaneous, natural, fearless, devoid of self-observation, "skillful." Second, the foolish mind does not operate in the present; it ruminates over the past or the future; or more accurately, clings to them. The foolish monk was still clinging to the woman; still clinging to the past. By contrast, the so-called "Fool" as Greer observes experiences all that life may bring in the present, "without opinions."[13]

Buddhists use a special term for the awareness of the present moment – "suchness" (*tathata*). An interesting exploration of this takes place in the so-called *Flower Sermon*, where, as in Smith's rendition of The Fool, the Buddha reveals all through the simple twist of a flower held lightly in his hand. In the *Flower Sermon* the Buddha is depicted as being near the end of his life, and has gathered his disciples to listen to what perhaps might be one of his final teachings. The disciples sit, waiting patiently for the Buddha's words of wisdom. Instead he simply sits, twirling a flower in his hand. Most of the monks grow impatient, but the Buddha simply sits as before. Within the assembly, the monk *Kasyapa* smiles.

Kasyapa's smile is regarded as the starting point of Zen Buddhism. It is the first transmission of awakened consciousness, outside scripture, outside tradition. By means of the flower, the Buddha conveys to Kasyapa the "suchness" of reality. Enlightenment, in other words, cannot be "attained" or "learned," whether through books or tradition. "Suchness" can only be experienced directly and intuitively. We may catch a glimpse of it during any mundane experience; such as in the smile of a child, the rustle of the wind in the trees, or, in this case, in the simple twist of a flower. Within that moment, we see a thing naked, as it truly exists; recognising both its beauty and impermanence without it being overlaid with our usual projections and preconceptions.

Within the Mahayana tradition, to be aware of the suchness of the present moment is at the same time to be aware of the fullness and emptiness of all things. At the relative level of truth, Buddhism recognizes that separate phenomena exist – me, you, tree, flower, the world. Yet, at the absolute level of reality, all such objects are "empty" (*sunyata*) of "separate existence" (*svabhava*). This does not mean that they do not exist. It means that they are full of everything else.

Thick Nhat Hahn explores the relationship between "fullness" and "emptiness" through the example of a simple flower, recalling once more our Fool, walking with the flower held lightly in his left hand. Hahn notes that if we look deeply enough into a flower, we can see that it is full of many other things – the wind, the soil, the rain, the clouds, and the sunshine. The "flower" simply cannot "be" without them. We could pursue this much further – the flower contains the hill on which it grew, the life-history of the person who picked it, the birth of the sun, and so on. In fact, looking deeply enough, we can see that it contains the entire cosmos. At the same time, if we remove these "non-flower" elements, the flower magically disappears. The "flower" in truth reveals itself to be a particular nexus of all other things, lacking only one thing – *own existence*. This, concludes Hahn, is "the meaning of emptiness."[14] The interdependence of all phenomena is again expressed in the well-known *Indra's Net* analogy of the *Flower Garland Sutra*. Here we are asked to image an infinite net with a polished jewel at the center of each node. When we look into each jewel, we see nothing but the reflections of all the other gems in the net. In the same way, the self is empty of own existence, but reflective of everything else. As a matter of interest, within Zen, the recognition of the "empty but full" nature of all things is sometimes conveyed with the painted symbol of an empty circle – the *Enso* –reminding us of the Fool's zero. The center is empty, and yet, at the same time is contained within the fullness of the circumference.

The importance of this insight into emptiness is that it forms the basis for genuine compassion within Buddhism. Compassion here is not simply based on feelings of pity for others, or merely on a lack of attachment to self. It is grounded in the recognition that the self is contained in the other, and the other in the self. This puts an added perspective on the actions of the compassionate monk at the river. In carrying the distressed woman he is in fact carrying himself. Interestingly, a link between The Fool and interdependence/compassion was recognized by Richard Gardner in 1971, in one of the first examples of Tarot *channeling*. According to Gardener's channeled Fool, his "true face" will never be revealed until we recognize that our own welfare is "the welfare of all."[15]

According to some forms of Zen, awakening to the suchness and emptiness of reality is not something that requires years of practice, nor only achievable by a few. All creatures contain the *Buddha Nature*, and this can be realized suddenly. *Buddha Nature* is a central concept within both Mahayana and Vajrayana Buddhism. It indicates the eternally-awakened nature of mind which lies within each one of us. It simply has to be uncovered rather than developed through any rigorous "path" that we may wish to pursue. In his *Sermon on Sudden Awakening*, the 8th-Century Chinese monk *Shen Hui* argues that followers of the Dharma should reject as ineffectual all they have learned before, even those who have spent decades in meditation. In its natural state, he says, everyone's mind is serene and unpolluted, and conforms to the nature of a Buddha. Thus, our efforts should not focus on the gradual accumulation of wisdom through some arduous training regime, but on "salvation by Sudden Awakening."[16] Similarly, according to the 9th-Century Zen master *Huang-Po*, those who strive solemnly to attain enlightenment are unaware that "Mind is no other than Buddha"; instead, they wrongly imagine "a mind beside Mind itself and seek Buddha outwardly after a form." The rigorous and misplaced discipline that such an endeavor involves "is not the way of enlightenment."[17]

The ignorance of The Fool – whether he or she is an "uninstructed worldling" or someone pursuing the eightfold path to "attain" or "grasp" Nirvana – lies in the fact that we already possess that which we seek. The "secret significance" of The Fool card, as Katz and Goodwin suggest, is that we are, and always have been, free.[18] We wander like fools - as the *Lotus Sutra* implies in the parable of *The Concealed Gem* - destitute and forlorn, unaware that a priceless jewel is sewn into the seams of our clothing.[19]

The Fool, it seems, remains as enigmatic as before. From one perspective he or she is the enlightened individual as perceived by those living in delusion – an outsider, a dreamer, a veritable "Fool on the Hill"; a "Zero." From another, he or she is the Samsaric worldling, ignorant of their true nature and potential, unaware of their predicament. Yet, The Fool also indicates the pure, natural, and spontaneous nature of the awakened mind; a mind which sees in the twist of a simple flower both the suchness and emptiness of all things.

The Fool (0)

The Way of the World: From The Magician to The Chariot

Introduction

As stated in the General Introduction, the following sections are built around three sequences, wherein we will investigate each of the Trump cards in some detail. The first sequence – *The Way of the World* – concerns those factors and forces which allow for life to be lived in society – parental influence, education, relationships, and growing independence. These concerns are especially evident in cards 3-7 - The Empress, The Emperor, The Hierophant, The Lovers and The Chariot. However, as Pollack has argued, cards 1 and 2 – The Magician and the High Priestess – correlate to much more fundamental qualities and forces that influence our lives – the "masculine" forces of will, action and creation; and the "feminine" forces of receptivity, intuition, mystery, and wisdom. For Pollack, these fundamental but oppositional energies intermingle together in our lives to create our personal perceptions of the world and influence our interactions with it. At a more general level they also serve as foundations for the creation and continuance of society as a whole.[1]

Tarot's distillation to the forces of nature and psyche to a gender-related dyad has received some criticism, from feminists in particular. The "feminine" within Tarot is often associated with a cluster of related qualities – passivity, intuition, nurture, fertility, and so on; while the "masculine" is linked with oppositional qualities such as control, independence, organization and movement. For Tarotists, as within the New Age in general, the "feminine" connotes a set of repressed values which must be reclaimed in the causes of psychological, environmental and social healing. For feminists by contrast, the "feminine" constitutes patriarchy's "ultimate ideology."[2] To extol the "feminine," as Rosemary Ruether argues, is to reinforce projections onto women of those universal human capacities and qualities which men simply refuse to acknowledge as their own.[3] Given this, there is something to be said for the view amongst some Tarotists that a truly liberating practice is one which consciously walks away from this binary dualism.[4] My own opinion on the issue is that the concepts of "masculine" and "feminine" can still be usefully retained within Tarot, at least in a provisional and pragmatic sense. However, it is important that we remember to disengage them from any sense of value or importance relative to each other; also, that they represent a range of universal human qualities that can be actualized by everyone.

The Magician (1)

General Overview

Our journey through *The Way of the World* begins with the commanding figure of The Magician. The Magician is often considered alongside The High Priestess, together representing the fundamental forces and energies that hold sway over our lives. The *RWS* image shows a magician standing behind a table at dawn, his upraised right hand holding a wand, while his left is shown pointing downwards to the earth. On the table before him lie a pentacle, wand, cup and sword; representing the four Tarot suits and the four elements. A *lemniscate* appears in the air above his head.

In traditional Tarot interpretation, The Magician is a symbol of masculine power, determination, intention, and action. He represents our ability to transform ideas into reality through the act of will, shown by his hands extending simultaneously to both the heavens and the earth. In this respect he is often associated with the well-known Hermetic declaration of will: "As above, so below." The ideas of creative potential and manifestation are also suggested by the card's dawn background – this is a new day, a new expression of creative endeavor. The lemniscate above his head may likewise symbolize his participation in the never-ending creative energy and drive of the universe. The objects on his table and in his hand represent the only available materials with which to work his magic – the *Four Great Elements* of the phenomenal world – earth, air, fire and water. In this card we see a clear progression from the inherent latency of The Fool. His bundle has now been opened and its contents spread on the alchemical table, ready for transmutation. Likewise, his beggar's stick has now become the masculine symbol of directed will and determination – the wand.

In the Story of the Buddha: The Birth of the Future Buddha

It is customary to think of the Buddha as a distinct individual, and perhaps as someone almost "superhuman." This is inaccurate on two counts. First, the Buddha was as human as you or I, and like us, had at his disposal no more than this "fathom-long" body comprised of the four great elements of being – solidity, fluidity, heat and motion – the four elements on our Magician's table. Second, it would be more accurate to describe a "Buddha" as a causal process than a distinct person. In Theravada Buddhism especially, no event – including the appearance of a Buddha – occurs except in relation to previous conditions and causes. This causal process extends through countless lives, but moves in a particular direction – towards the cultivation of the "wholesome" (*kusala*) and the "beautiful" (*sobhana*) by means of the application of skillful will (*cetana*). This is a process mirrored in the symbolism of The Magician. With his right hand pointing to that which has been, the Magician gathers to the present all that has been achieved; and here, with steady eyes on the four elements of being, and under the direction of *cetana*, he manifests the shape of his future. When directed by less than skillful cetana, this process results in the appearance of all forms of Samsaric life, from godlike beings to hungry ghosts.

The understanding of the Future Buddha as "causal process" was so natural to early Buddhists that they placed his birth within the context of 547 previous lives devoted to skillful living. As a process, the birth of the Future Buddha begins in the Introductory section to the *Jataka* (*Birth*) narratives with the story of *Sumedha*, an ascetic who lived in the town of *Amara*, "[a] hundred thousand cycles vast/And four immensities ago." Sumedha, a "master of the Vedas three,"[1] honored a previous Buddha called *Dipankara* by placing his body on the muddy ground to allow him to step on it as he passed by. Sumedha vows to become a Buddha himself and Dipankara, discerning the monk's thoughts, confirms that "'he, unnumbered cycles hence,/A Buddha in the world shall be.'"[2] The hundreds of stories that follow document Sumedha's long route towards the development of those virtuous potentials called the *ten perfections*: generosity, morality, renunciation, wisdom, energy, patience, truth, determination, loving-kindness and equanimity. These qualities are all contained in or are reflective of the "beautiful" or "wholesome" aspects of mind. Finally, the *bodhisattva* is reborn in the realm of the *Tusita* gods. After some time, the gods declare that the conditions for his birth have arrived; and so, the Future Buddha makes the "five observances" concerning his birth (time, continent, country, family and mother), dies, and for the last time is reborn.

The birth of Siddhattha Gotama is described alongside a number of supernatural events which are reminiscent in part of the birth stories of other World Saviors, including Jesus. His birth is accompanied by gifts, songs, devotions, streams of water from the sky, and salutations from half the *Vedic* pantheon. The narrative here is designed to stress the uniqueness of the Future Buddha's past accomplishments, his importance in establishing the Dharma, and in sectarian terms, Buddhism's supremacy over Hinduism.

But there is another dimension to the story and it is one that accords well with our reflections on the Magician. The narrative is principally concerned with highlighting a Future Buddha's mastery and correctly-directed will over the materials of the world; the elements of human identity. The infant, we are told, is born by emerging from his mother's side. He takes seven steps, and with each step a lotus appears out of the ground. When he has finished, he turns to the four cardinal directions and declares that he is the "highest in the world" and that never again will he experience a "new existence."[3]

Being born from his mother's side clearly indicates the Future Buddha's victory over the constant cycle of rebirth within Samsara. The seven steps may indicate mastery over the seven kinds of suffering in the world outlined in the *Path of Purity*, or knowledge of the *Seven Factors of Enlightenment* described in many Buddhist texts. The lotus blossoms are themselves significant, indicating not only purity, but the view that spiritual development may only arise from the muddied conditions of embodied life. The act of turning to each of the four cardinal directions suggests mastery over the four elements, over the aggregates of human nature. In Buddhist and Hindu thought, each cardinal point is associated with a particular "guardian" or "heavenly king" (the four *lokapalas*), who are in turn each associated with one of the four Great Elements.[4] The Future Buddha's mastery over these elements is further confirmed in Chinese versions of the narrative where, as he addresses the four cardinal points, he places his arms in a pose identical to that of our Magician - a pose which remains popular in Chinese Buddhist iconography – and declares that in both the heavens and the earth he is honored above all, and that he has come to set all beings free from suffering – from birth, old age, sickness and death.[5] Such a precocious utterance is in fact a revelation concerning the causal parameters of enlightenment – hard-won mastery over the elements, directed by a skillful and determined will, aimed at the cultivation of *The Beautiful*. This sense of determined striving is even suggested by the child's name itself – *Siddhattha* – "He who has attained his goal." But we also perceive something else within the child's proclamation - the view that one's enlightenment cannot be neatly disentangled from the suffering of others. The magician's left hand it seems points to more than personal liberation.

A Buddhist Reflection: Karma and the Alchemy of Identity

The fundamental and revolutionary starting point of the Buddha's message in not just that we are capable of enlightenment, nor that we are exclusively responsible for it, but that it can be achieved solely through the limitations of our own body-mind complex. In this body, with this mind, and at this very moment, says Lama Yeshe, we have everything we need for "blissful liberation."[6] So, like The Magician, let us take a look at what we have at our disposal. Let us, as the Buddha says in the *Kayagata-sati Sutta*, sit like a butcher over a cow that is about to be cut up, and reflect upon this human frame.

We begin by emptying The Fool's bundle and placing its contents on the table before us. What do we see? We find the Four Great Elements (*mahabhutani*) of Solidity, Fluidity, Heat and Motion - the actual qualities found in earth, water, fire and air. From these four elements are derived the five basic aggregates (*khandhas*) from which everything in the world is fashioned. The first and most fundamental aggregate – "form" (*rupa*) – connotes the basic physicality of all objects in existence. For humans, form also includes the six sense organs (eyes, nose, tongue, body, ears and mind) and their corresponding objects in both the exterior and interior worlds (visible objects, odor, taste, tangible objects, sound and thoughts).

The other four aggregates are interdependent processes which arise in relation to contact between a sensory organ and its corresponding sensory object. One of these is "consciousness" (*vinnana*) which is our basic "awareness" of the world. There are six types of consciousness according to Buddhists, based upon the particular sense organ and sense object in question. Thus, a blind person lacks "eye consciousness." Consciousness only arises out of and is dependent upon sensory objects and the other aggregates. If someone were to speak of a "consciousness" that existed apart from the other aggregates, says the Buddha, then that person would be referring to something that does not exist.[7]

The aggregate of "feelings" (*vedana*) signifies the physical and mental sensations which arise through contact with objects, and these are described as pleasant, unpleasant or neutral. "Perceptions" (*sanna*) is the aggregate that recognizes and understands the particular qualities of objects and experiences, and discriminates between them; it is therefore also linked to the formation of memory.

The aggregate of "mental formations" (*samkhara*) describes our mental tendencies, habits and inclinations, of which Buddhists enumerate either 51 or 52, including some that are universal and intrinsic to life; for example "will" – the urge to decide and act. "Unwholesome" mental formations include delusion, a disregard for consequences, restlessness, greed, hatred, envy, and laziness. "Occasional" formations include energy. "Beautiful" tendencies include mindfulness, tranquility, compassion and wisdom.

Although no aggregate stands by itself, it is primarily within the aggregate of mental formations that many of our problems most obviously appear. For example, a mind conditioned by delusion considers that there is some kind of permanent self either within, between or behind the impermanent and constantly fluctuating aggregates, and this results in clinging and suffering. Yet, what is the source of our suffering is also at the same time the source of our liberation. Through wisdom, energy and determination, we can eradicate the unwholesome and cultivate The Beautiful.

Of fundamental importance to this magical transmutation is an appreciation of the part played by the will in its ability to either enslave or liberate us. Once a particular sense object creates a sensation, whether pleasant, unpleasant or neutral, the function of the will is to move the mind in a particular direction in order to actualize a goal in relation to that object. For example, if I see, smell, taste, hear, or feel an object that creates a pleasant sensation, my mind settles on it, is attracted to it, and is urged forward as if to possess it. Conversely, if the object creates an unpleasant sensation, I am repulsed and urged away from it, as if to escape. This process applies to all sensory objects that arise through contact – including thoughts. Liberation is made possible through skillful use of this natural quality of will.

This brings us on to another important issue – the relationship between will and *karma*. As will is concerned with achieving a particular goal, it is viewed as the most significant component in the generation of karma. In fact, for the Buddha, the two are virtually synonymous.

In its most fundamental sense karma simply means "action," but within Buddhism it properly indicates "willed action." Karma however is also viewed more broadly in terms of a "law" of cause and effect. In this, Buddhism recognizes that our willed actions have consequences – they generate implications which we cannot escape. In the Buddha's words: "The evil-doer mourns in this world, and he mourns in the next; he mourns in both. He mourns and suffers when he sees the evil of his own work."[8] It would however be wrong to consider such effects in terms of divine rewards or punishments. Karma is an entirely natural process. To see it as retributive justice would be tantamount to suggesting that falling down is gravity's punishment on the wicked.

Karma basically conditions our experiences of life within the world, whether in terms of strengthening existing mental habits and responses, or in terms of affecting the environment we inhabit. This is known as the "fruit" (*phala*) of karma. Karma generates the basic conditions from which we presently act and experience the world, which in turn, under the direction of will, shape our future. We are, as the Buddha says, "inheritors" of our deeds.

The High Priestess (2)

General Overview

The *RWS* deck depicts The High Priestess enthroned between two pillars labeled *B* and *J*. She holds in her hand a scroll entitled *TORA*, while a crescent moon lies at her feet. The lunar symbolism is also reflected in her crown, which shows the waxing, full and waning phases of the moon. She sits in front of a veil adorned with closed pomegranates, which obscures a blue, watery expanse that lies beyond. The High Priestess' robes are blue and white, suggesting a sense of purity and spirituality. The lower section of her robes appears like a rippling extension of the water from beyond the veil, perhaps signifying that she is a manifestation of it. In traditional interpretations the card is said to symbolize the qualities of passivity, darkness, depth, secrecy, intuition, mystery and wisdom. Within a wider spectrum of possibility[1] however, it may also connote dreaming, illusion, and ignorance.

While the Magician represents life in the everyday world of elements, action, will and creation, this card brings intimations of another world either behind or within that same realm of phenomena. This is suggested by the twin pillars and the veil, which were said to stand at the entrance to Solomon's Temple and before the *adytum* or *Holy of Holies* within – God's dwelling place on earth. The pomegranates - unlike those of The Fool's attire - are closed, suggesting mystery and the unmanifest. Whatever lies beyond is obscured, signifying a lack of knowledge on our part. This necessitates the need for a mediator; one who can lead us from ignorance into the depths of reality itself – The High Priestess. Smith's depiction suggests the figure of *Isis*, Goddess of the Moon and Mysteries; the one who declares that "no man has ever lifted the veil."

Yet there are other candidates. One is the figure of the *Shekinah*, which means to "inhabit," and represents God's feminine presence in the world. According to *Rabbinic* literature, the *Shekinah* was thought to be present in the Tabernacle and behind the veil at the Temple. She was even thought to reside within the very words of the Torah itself. The 2nd-Century Rabbi Hananiah ben Teradion declares that if just two people sit together discussing the Torah, then "'the Shekinah is in their midst.'"[2] The Torah itself lies partially obscured in The High Priestess' right hand, suggesting either intimations of a deeper comprehension of the divine, or our own limited understanding.

Another candidate is the Gnostic figure of *Sophia* - the mediatrix between spirit and matter. She is the one who "fell" into this world, and yet at the same provides us with the correct *Gnosis* that will facilitate self-remembering, and liberate us, or so the Gnostics thought, from the "prison" of matter. Sophia is the one "through whom you will be delivered."[3]

In the Story of the Buddha: The Wisdom of Asita.

An episode from the Future Buddha's early life which captures the sense of wisdom inherent in The High Priestess is that of the sage *Asita* before King *Suddhodana* and Queen *Maha-Maya*. Asita is sometimes referred to as the "Buddhist Simeon," given the number of striking similarities between both figures. Both possess the wisdom which allows them to see beyond what others see, and recognize the unique lineage and promise of the infants before them. Both regret that they will not live long enough to hear what these World Saviors have to say, or witness what they will accomplish.

There are various versions of this story. In the Pali account from the *Jataka* narratives, Asita is called *Kaladevala*, although both names are related to the color "black," suggesting his ascetic background. The *Jataka* account informs us that the sage was a close friend of King Suddhodana, and was skilled in meditation. One day, while taking his rest in the *Heaven of the Thirty-Three*, he notices the gods in joyful celebration, and learns that "a son has been born to king Suddhodana, who shall sit at the foot of the Bo-tree, and become a Buddha, and cause the Wheel of the Doctrine to roll ... and we shall hear the Doctrine."[4] In Asvaghosa's *Buddhacarita* (The *Life of Buddha*), Asita is depicted as the King's own priest, and learns of this wonderful birth through "signs and the power of his penances."[5] Asita arrives at the palace to look upon the face of the Future Buddha. Recognizing that the young prince displays the auspicious marks of the *Great Person* (*Mahapurusha*), he turns to the King and smiles. His joy quickly turns to sadness, in the realization that he will not live long enough to hear him teach. The king, troubled by such strange behavior, inquires of Asita concerning any possible misfortune that may await his son:

> "No misfortune is to happen to him. He will become a Buddha without any manner of doubt ... I wept at the thought of my own great loss; for, also, I am not

to have an opportunity of seeing this marvelous person after he has become a Buddha."6

In Asvaghosa's account, Asita is said to remark that the child will one day "shine forth as a sun of knowledge to destroy the darkness of illusion in the world." He will "proclaim the way of deliverance to those afflicted with sorrow, entangled in objects of sense, and lost in the forest-paths of worldly existence, as to travelers who have lost their way."7

In his wisdom, Asita sees that the child displays the thirty-two auspicious marks of the *Mahapurusha* and is thus destined for greatness. The marks themselves are derived from *Brahminical* thought, and were originally associated with the physical qualities of one who was qualified to teach spiritual truths to others or read and interpret the *Vedas*. This is perhaps why the *Ambattha Sutta* records the story of an arrogant young *Brahmin*, sent to ascertain if the Buddha has all the requisite marks to teach. The actual marks are described in the *Lakkhana Sutta*, and include such things as long toes, a thousand-spoked wheel on the soles of his feet, a golden complexion, an immense torso, and long eye-lashes. Such features may appear somewhat odd, but have been central in shaping and defining the appearance of the Buddha in Buddhist iconography for millennia.

Should they be taken literally? It seems not. According to the *Samannaphala Sutta* for example, when King *Ajatasattu* went to meet the Buddha to ask about the benefits of the contemplative life, he was unable to distinguish him from his disciples. The Buddha himself rejected the notion that a "Great Person" could be recognized from physical characteristics alone. In the

Mahapurisa Sutta, the monk *Sariputta* asks about the qualities of a Great Person; to which the Buddha replies that it is the act of freeing the mind that makes one great or not.

There are of course symbolic interpretations of the thirty-two marks. One such interpretation can be found in the Mahayana *Abhisamayalankara Sutra*, associated with the Future Buddha *Maitreya*. Here, the author links the thirty-two Marks with inner attitudes relating to compassion and wisdom. The Buddha's long fingers and toes for example are said to relate to him having saved animals from slaughter.[8]

There is also a relationship between the concept of the Mahapurusha and that of sacrifice. In early Hindu thought, the Mahapurusha is linked to the idea of a primal *Cosmic Man* (*Purusha*) - the physical embodiment of the divine. According to the *Rig Veda,* the universe comes about through the self-sacrifice of Purusha, whose death generates all the qualities of the phenomenal world. In other words, it is self-sacrifice that makes one a "Great Person." This is recognized within Buddhism too, not simply in its concern with the sacrifice of ego, but in its desire to cultivate a level of generosity that offers all of one's self to others. Thus the 8th-Century monk *Shantideva* reflecting on his own body declares that he has "surrendered" it "indifferently for the weal of the world," becoming "a spy for the service of others."[9] In this respect it is perhaps possible to interpret Asita's recognition of the "marks" as indicating his awareness of the generosity and self-sacrificing nature of the infant Mahapurusha before him; a recognition which recalls the gift of *Myrrh* made by another wise man to another infant.

A Buddhist Reflection: Ignorance, Wisdom and Perfect Wisdom

Wisdom cannot be separated from ignorance. One presumes the very existence of the other. But what is "ignorance" (*avidya*)? For Buddhists it may imply many things – a lack of understanding of the impermanent nature of the self; clinging to objects and ideas that change; living in the memories of the past or in the expectations of the future; a disregard for the consequences of our actions; a general unawareness of the endless round of Samsaric life. At the bottom line, ignorance is to exist in a fabricated dream-world of our own creation that we believe to be real. It is to live in "delusion" (*moha*). Yet, within the parameters of Buddhism's non-dualistic understanding of reality, "awakening" is not the Gnostic flight from matter to spirit, nor the neo-Platonic ascent of the soul. It means changing our perceptions of the only world we have. As Ayya Khema puts it, we only really have to change ourselves because there is "nothing to change out there."[10] Thus in Buddhism, the realization of the spiritual world that exists "behind" the High Priestess' veil is nothing more or less than that which Thich Nhat Hahn describes as "the removal of wrong perceptions."[11]

In Theravada Buddhism especially, the removal of wrong perceptions is achieved through the practice of *Wisdom* in tandem with *Morality* and *Meditation*. These three are the conduits through which skillful cetana is centered and directed. In the Theravada tradition, Wisdom is concerned with the cultivation of *Right View* and *Right Intention*.

Right View means ultimately to see things as they really are. To begin with, this entails reflection upon the core aspects of the Buddha's teachings; for example, the *Three Marks of Existence* that are said to characterize all aspects of the phenomenal world – suffering (dukkha) impermanence (*anicca*) and no-self (*anatta*). Analysis of the so-called "self" leads to awareness of the aggregates from which our sense of self arises. Reflection upon dukkha leads to an appreciation of how suffering or unsatisfactoriness arises through thirst, craving, and attachment to objects that turn out to be impermanent. Reflection upon thirst (*tanha*) leads to insights concerning how our grasping attitudes are conditioned by sensations that arise through our sense organs. Yet Right View means more than a mere intellectual understanding of these ideas. A reasonably-intelligent person is well-aware that this thing we call our "self" is often more elusive and insubstantial that we sometimes like to think; but this basic appreciation will not make much of an impact upon our lives. Right View, as Rahula points out, is not merely having an intellectual grasp of something (*anubodha*), but "penetration" (*pativedha*) into that thing, which can only be developed properly through meditation.[12] Khema concurs, and points out that there is a real difference between an intellectual understanding of impermanence and no-self, and "knowing" and "feeling" these truths in meditation.[13]

In Theravada Buddhism, Wisdom is also linked to Right Intention. This constitutes the type of ethical outlook that must be cultivated alongside Right View, but to some extent arises naturally out of it too. Right Intention involves the cultivation of attitudes of harmlessness, detachment, and renunciation. What Buddhism recognizes here is that most of our unskillful actions are based upon the opposite kinds of mental attitudes – hatred, attachment and greed. Right Intention is therefore linked with skillful actions in the world, whether of body, speech, or mind. These actions are enmeshed in the ethical requirements of the path – *Right Speech*, *Right Action* and *Right Livelihood*. Here, Buddhism recognizes that our actions, and even the very professions we pursue, are not simply indications of a "good" or "bad" character, but reflections of our wisdom or lack of it.

The general message of Mahayana Buddhism is that the earlier Buddhist perception of Wisdom was appropriate for a particular time, but it is not as penetrative as it might be. The suggestion voiced in texts like the *Lotus Sutra* is that in his skillful means the Buddha did indeed "hold back" insights that could only be divulged when the time was right. This approach is explained in a variety of parables, including that of the *Phantom City*. Here, the Buddha is depicted as a guide, leading his followers through the wilderness of Samsara to the *City of Jewels*. His followers, too tired to go on, feel they must head back. In response, the Buddha conjures up a "Phantom City" in which the explorers can rest until they have gathered enough strength to carry on. The earlier view of *Wisdom* is just this very Phantom City. By contrast, the Mahayana or "Great Vehicle" offers what it considers to be the *Perfect Wisdom* (*Prajnaparamita*); the Wisdom that goes beyond the limited and provisional scope of the *Hinayana* ("Little Vehicle") perspective.

This Perfect Wisdom was encapsulated in a type of literature of the same name, and includes such texts as the *Prajnaparamita*, *Diamond* and *Heart Sutras*. At the same time, the notion of Perfect Wisdom became personified as a goddess, who, like our High Priestess, stands as a mediator between wrong and right perceptions of the world. Her unsurpassed status is captured in an invocation from the *Prajnaparamita Sutra of 8000 Lines*, in which she is described as "Emptiness," the "wisdom of the Buddhas," and the one who "turns the wheel of the dharma."[14]

Prajnaparamita as goddess is usually depicted with four arms, two of which are in a meditation gesture, suggesting that penetrative wisdom cannot be attained through knowledge alone. Like our High Priestess, she also holds a book in her hand, representing the teachings which reveal the reality she embodies – emptiness.

One of the key insights of the *Prajnaparamita* sutras is that since no beings truly exist as separate, substantial realities, then ultimately, no "beings" actually experience Nirvana. Nor can it be said than any "beings" actually experience the sufferings of Samsara. One jarring feature of the texts is placing such penetrative insights alongside the conventional wisdom of the earlier teachings. Thus we read in the *Heart Sutra* that there is no ignorance and no end to ignorance, no suffering and no path.[15] Similarly, according to the Buddha in the *Diamond Sutra*, although "I have thus delivered immeasurable beings, not one single being has been delivered."[16]

Another insight of the *Prajnaparamita* perspective, and a counterpoint to the view expressed in The Magician, is that enlightenment cannot be conceived of as the end result of a causal process. If it was, it would be dependant upon something for its existence, making it Samsaric. Nirvana simply *is*. This insight is expressed in the *Diamond Sutra*, in its denial of the thirty-two marks as indicators of enlightenment. In his commentary on this text, Edward Conze notes that the marks are traditionally associated with the accumulation of positive qualities gained from "a hundred acts of merit." This, as we have seen, was certainly Asita's view on things. From the perspective of Perfect Wisdom however, enlightenment is "not produced by anything."[17] All beings carry within themselves the Buddha Nature, and the potential to actualize it. As the 13th-Century monk *Nichiren* reasoned - even a heartless rogue loves his wife and children, and in this way, manifests to a certain degree that "bodhisattva world" within.[18]

In Theravada Buddhism, Right View gives birth to Right Intention – the cultivation of harmlessness, renunciation and detachment. In a similar way within Mahayana Buddhism, Prajnaparamita gives birth to compassion (*karuna*). True compassion in Buddhism as we have said is not just based upon feelings of kindness or generosity, but upon identification. It originates from the abandonment of the self, and a subsequent expansion into wider fields of identification. As Shantideva puts it:

> By constant use the idea of an "I" attaches itself to foreign drops of seed and blood, although the thing exists not. Then why should I not conceive my fellow's body as my own self? ... I will cease to live as self, and will take as my self my fellow-creatures. We love our hands and other limbs, as members of the body; then why not love other living beings, as members of the universe? By constant use man comes to imagine that his body, which has no self-being, is a "self"; why then should he not conceive his "self" to lie in his fellows also?[19]

The Empress (3)

General Overview

As a pair, The Empress and The Emperor suggest more "earthy" reflections of those abstract ideas presented in the previous two cards. There are though a number of ways in which this Empress-Emperor relationship can be conceived. From a Jungian perspective, the pair represent a complementary dyad, symbolizing those forces and qualities involved in personal development, whether familial or social. The Empress here conforms to the "mother archetype"; the idealized depiction of the "feminine" and the "motherly" qualities of nurture, relationality, sensuality, sexuality and fecundity. Such qualities are often projected onto some divine figure, illustrated in the card's associations with various Earth Mother goddesses, including *Cybele*, *Demeter* and even *Venus*. The Emperor here conforms to the complementary "father archetype," associated with authority, law, order, structure, reason, and emergent identity. Divine figures associated with this archetype may include *Zeus* and the "Heavenly Father" of the *Abrahamic* faiths.

Another way to envisage the relationship between both is in terms of a cultural "transition," reflecting the popular view of a prehistoric shift from matrifocal to patriarchal culture. In the movement between the cards we find, says Sallie Nichols, the shift from a "matriarchal realm" focused on communality and the celebration of natural cycles, towards the masculine world of *Logos*, reason, and the dominion of "spirit over nature."[1]

A third approach is to view the two cards in relation to philosopher Owen Barfield's developmental model of human consciousness and its relations with nature. In the era of *Original Participation*, humanity engages with nature in a pre-rational unconscious manner. The era of *Separation* indicates the rise of rational thought, of science and technology, in which humanity becomes separate observers of the world around. In the era of *Final Participation*, humanity moves once more towards a position of reconciliation with nature, grounded in a new holistic synthesis of reason, imagination, and creativity. Such reconciliation, I will argue, is suggested in the final cards of the Trumps.[2]

In the *RWS* deck The Empress reclines on an opulent throne with the symbol of Venus emblazoned on a nearby shield. She sits open-legged and pregnant, surrounded by images of a fecund world. As in The High Priestess, she holds dominion over an expanse of water; except here, it is the running waters of life, as opposed to the still, dark and deep waters of mystery and wisdom. She wears a three-tiered crown composed of twelve stars and a necklace of seven pearls, representing her presence within the entire cosmos.

In contrast with the notions of intuition, passivity and wisdom evoked by The High Priestess, The Empress represents the more earthy aspects of the feminine principle. In her presence we are reminded that the word "mother" is perhaps etymologically derived from the sound "ma," the simplest cry of a child, and one from which we obtain many words connected with the processes of birth, life, and nurture – *matrix, maternal, manifest* and *matter.*

For Pollack, the earthiness of The Empress connotes a sense of "passion" - a life lived within the body, the world, the senses and our emotions; which, she argues, form the prerequisites for authentic spiritual development.[3] Her views echo those of many contemporary Neopagans, like Starhawk, who places the true locus of spiritual value within bodies, nature, sensuality and sexuality, rather than some "abstract otherworld."[4]

Yet, within the spectrum of possibility, The Empress evokes darker and more ambivalent connotations. This is a point recognized by Hajo Banzhaf, who sees a "wild, destructive" element within the dark and wooded background of this card.[5] This neglected or hidden side of The Empress is more-readily seen in a number of "darker" stylizations; for example, in those of the *Deviant Moon* and *Dark Grimoire* Tarot decks. In Jungian interpretations, this is the "cruel" shadow of the mother archetype; the neglectful, uncaring, and distant parent. At a more metaphysical level, we are reminded that the Great Goddess of the Earth has a darker side too. In Egyptian mythology we find it in *Sekhmet*, the *Powerful One* - the ferocious side of *Hathor* who takes the form of a lioness to devour and butcher humans and drink their blood. In Celtic lore we find it in the figure of the *Morrigan* or *Phantom Queen* – the crow goddess of war, strife, and violent death. Campbell also reminds us that the rituals associated with the goddesses of the past were not all of the "nurturing mother" variety. There was as much sacrificial blood and gore in the twilight groves of the ancient Minoans it seems as there was "spiral-dancing."[6] According to feminist philosopher Simone de

Beauvoir, the rites of the ancient Mother Goddess were ambiguous in character, suggesting not only a sense of awe and marvel at nature's fecund powers, but that of dread in relation to her more mysterious, chaotic and chthonic processes. If men worshipped the Goddess, or by reproductive association, women, it was because they "feared nature."[7]

By the time of the Babylonian *Enuma Elish* in the 7th-Century BCE, and its description of the hero *Marduk's* victory over *Tiamat*, it is clear that the Great Goddess of the Earth had become linked with a sense of chaotic violence and disorder. The subsequent centuries witnessed a profound shift in religious thinking, now concerned with spiritual deliverance above and out of nature, which by now had become associated with the notions of distortion, deception and enslavement. In some forms of ancient Gnosticism for example, this world of ours is viewed as a distorted reflection of a perfect Heavenly World; a counterfeit reality regulated by various celestial rulers (*archons*) who govern the stars and heavenly spheres above the earth. In Gnosticism, the "divine spark" within humanity is viewed as being "imprisoned" in matter, and subject to the harsh laws of a false god. These laws are designed to keep the spirit in a state of ignorance concerning its divine origins. The spirit is left to linger in a world of sensuality, deficiency, darkness, ignorance, illusion and terror. For many of the ancients, the uncertain qualities of nature prompted what Hans Jonas calls a "revolt against the world"; a "violent denunciation" of physical existence.[8] For the Gnostics and other spiritualities of the time, nature, as Ruether says, became viewed as an "alien reality" and not our "true home."[9]

Such observations seem to confirm the view discussed above that the shift from Empress to Emperor may reflect a shift in sensibilities regarding our bodies and the natural world. Many feminists and Neopagans would concur, and describe the history of Western spirituality in terms of a transition from an earth-based matrifocal culture, to a patriarchal one focused around attempts to control and transcend the confines of matter, the body, and the world.[10]

In the Story of the Buddha: The Death of Queen Maha-Maya

The Buddha's mother, Queen *Maha-Maya*, makes for an interesting but enigmatic figure within the Buddha's biography. According to Asvaghosa, she is "chosen" to be the Buddha's mother on account of her piety, excellent stewardship over her subjects, and for her outstanding beauty and radiance among women:

> Verily, the life of women is always darkness, yet when it encountered her, it shone brilliantly; thus the night does not retain its gloom, when it meets with the radiant crescent of the moon.

On account of her qualities as "the most eminent of goddesses to the whole world," the Future Buddha, assuming the form of an elephant, "entered the womb of the queen of King Suddhodana to destroy the evils of the world."[11]

As if the conception were not strange enough, the Future Buddha is said to have emerged from his mother's side "unsmeared by any impurity," like "a jewel thrown upon a vesture of Benares cloth."[12] Despite the fact that his mother delivered "without pain and without illness,"[13] she dies mysteriously, seven days later, only to be reborn in the Tusita Heavens.

Perhaps the most enigmatic aspect of the story is the Queen's name itself – *Maha-Maya* – which literally means the *Great Illusion*. Sometimes the texts refer to her as *Maya-Devi* – the *Goddess of Illusion*. The name immediately calls to mind a darker and more ambiguous dimension to The Empress just discussed – that of deception and distortion.

The concept of *maya* has a long evolutionary history within Indian thought. In the early *Vedas*, it was associated with a magical power which allowed the gods to assume material form and create the phenomenal world. This sense of the term is even found in the *Bhagavad-Gita*, where it is related to the power which allows Vishnu to assume the form of an avatar. In Vedantic thought from the *Upanishads* onwards, maya takes on a more abstract and negative quality, viewed as an obstruction which prevents direct penetration into the nature of reality. In more mythological and theistic forms of Hinduism, the concept is associated with *shakti* – the feminine aspect of the divine which creates the world, but at the same time obscures its underlying nature. Of interest is the fact that this feminine principle became personified as Maha-Maya or Maya-Devi, sometimes linked with the Hindu figures of *Kali* and *Durga*.

Within Buddhism the concept of maya became internalized and psychologized, associated with the illusory nature of the ego and with our wrong perceptions of the world. This is especially evident within Mahayana Buddhism. Here, maya indicates our inability to grasp the reality of impermanence; the fact that life is no more than "stars, darkness, a lamp, a phantom, dew, a bubble."[14] Thus, the removal of maya in Buddhism, as it is in the *Advaita Vedanta* of the Hindu philosopher *Sankara*, is really a shift in our perceptions of the reality which is ever before our eyes. Maya is a perceptual error arising in the human mind, not a description of the world outside us. Unlike Gnosticism, Buddhism aims at clarity, not transcendence. Sankara's well-known snake analogy, in which a person mistakenly projects the appearance of a snake onto a piece of rope, and believes it to be real,[15] could equally-well apply to the Buddhist view of Samsaric experience.

In the story of Queen Maya, the Buddha's birth from her side suggests that his teachings are a means of removing this veil of maya; of removing our wrong perceptions of the world; perceptions which keep us locked into an endless cycle of suffering and rebirth. Maya's death, seven days later, again suggests a removal of obscurations. Seven is an auspicious number within Indian thought, and suggests in this context an end to the maya of the *Saptha Matrika* – the *Seven Divine Mothers* or celestial manifestations of Devi who were also associated with the seven stars of the Pleiades. These goddesses, like the seven pearls around The Empress' neck, emanate from the Great Mother, and represent the cyclic forces which, for those living in delusion, generate Samsara – the endless round of suffering and unsatisfactoriness produced by desire and ignorance.

A Buddhist Reflection: From Samsara to Tara

Within Buddhism, the material world as both a system of cyclic processes and the stage of human passions, sensuality and rebirth, is regarded with understandable ambivalence. On the one-hand, the Zen tradition places emphasis upon suchness and *wabi-sabi* – an intuitive appreciation of the beauty and yet the sadness inherent within each fleeting moment. Within Zen, such moments are caught in the sparse but sensuous words of the *Haiku*. We are also reminded that it was in his darkest hour, when he was most alone with himself and on the verge of awakening, that the Buddha touched the earth, and asked it to bear witness to his efforts. Here, we are reminded that the earth - abused, neglected, and often seen as a source of opposition to our spiritual endeavors - is still our home. Yet, as discussed earlier, this "mother" embraces more shadowy connotations, and there are elements within early Indian Buddhism and Indian religious thought in general which reflect an element of uncertainty towards our "Great Goddess."

All life may spring from the world, but she is at the same time both the actuality of creation and destruction, and for many a symbolic representation of enslavement and delusion - the endless round of birth and death known as Samsara. This darker side of The Empress is realized in the Hindu image of *Kali Ma*, the *Dark Mother*. In her most benign aspect she is viewed as a preserver and the creator of all life. She is the unfathomable generative matrix from which all life pours forth. Yet, in her darker aspect she represents the frenzied entropic powers of death and destruction. She is the one who consumes her own children. These two sides are brought together in a meditative vision experienced by the Hindu mystic and Kali devotee Ramakrisha, in which he saw Kali emerge from the Ganges, give birth to a child, nurse it, and then consume it. Kali then returned once more to the Ganges, where she disappeared.[16]

In its earliest monastic forms, According to Lambert Schmithausen, Buddhism was never really interested in the beauty and fecundity of the world, but on its more negative aspects, especially the "ubiquity of decay and impermanence." Buddhism's aims were that of spiritual "detachment."[17] This quest for detachment is rooted, not only in general observations of decay and death in the world, but in the view that our cravings for sensory experience tie us to Samsaric rebirth. Indeed, the Buddha named sensory desire (*kamacchanda*) as the first of five hindrances to enlightenment.

It comes therefore as no surprise that Buddhism has drawn its fair share of ire from the Neopagan community; a community focused on the celebration of passion, sensuality and sexuality, along with its understanding of the divine within nature. Witchcraft, says Starhawk, rejects the First Noble Truth of Buddhism that all life is suffering or is unsatisfactory. The attempt to escape or transcend sickness, old age and death "is not the optimal cure."[18] This however is a misrepresentation of Buddhism. Buddhism does not deny human happiness, nor does it seek to transcend life lived in nature. Instead, it points out that sensory contact with the world generates cravings, which, given the reality of impermanence, eventually turn to feelings of unsatisfactoriness and suffering. In regard to the natural world, Buddhism adopts the middle way of "detachment" – not pantheistic immanence, nor Gnostic negation. It does not seek transcendence of the world, but instead, the removal of wrong perceptions about the world. The middle way of Buddhism is, as Robert Thurman succinctly puts it, the way of "deglamorized awareness."[19]

In his book *Up from Eden*, transpersonal psychologist Ken Wilbur criticizes some elements of the Neopagan movement for failing to move beyond a "chthonic" interpretation of the Goddess, with too much focus upon birth, death, female biology and reproduction. He reminds us that goddesses such as Isis were also envisaged as Wisdom, and viewed as the divine ground of all space and time.[20] Yet within Buddhism, one vision of the goddess need not be abandoned for the other. This is seen especially in those *Tantric* practices related to *Tara*.

Tara is often conceived as the gentle, compassionate savioress of Tibetan Buddhism; one who was born from a single tear from the Bodhisattva of Compassion, *Avalokitesvara*. Yet Tara actually embraces twenty-one different emanations or aspects, some of which appear extremely wrathful. A good example is that of the Red Tara, *Kurukulla* ("She who is the cause of knowledge"); goddess of enchantments and sexuality, who wears a garland of fifty severed human heads and dances upon a male corpse within a circle of flame. Despite her fearsome and chthonic appearance, her presence within Tantra pertains to a wisdom that is positive and transformative. As John Reynolds explains: her garland of fifty severed and bloody heads relates to the fact that she is capable of subduing the "fifty negative emotions," while the human corpse that she dances upon represents the destruction of ego.[21]

Like most Tantric deities, Kurukulla represents a particular manifestation of enlightened awareness, and by invoking the wisdom and energies she represents, the practitioner, it is said, accelerates spiritual liberation. A central concern within Tantric meditation is that of subduing and transmuting negative energies. In this respect the wrathful deities, as Thubten Chodron says, demonstrate that there are many ways of working with "our afflictions," whether gently, or more aggressively. Those fearsome and chthonic manifestations represent a more forceful though nevertheless compassionate form of wisdom, enabling us to deal more effectively with our "disturbing emotions."[22] In Tara Kurukulla, we see that a chthonic representation of "the Goddess" need not be abandoned for something that appears more subdued or transcendental. The blood, skulls, rage, and general gore of life lived within the four elements can still be skillfully transmuted in the service of penetrative wisdom.

The Emperor (4)

General Overview

The Emperor personifies the masculine forces of will, reason and order as applied to the realms of nature and social relations. He delineates, categorizes and defines experience in the world, in much the same way that the ancient Babylonian hero Marduk fashioned time and measurement from the body of the Great Goddess Tiamat. We have, as Nichols says, well and truly left behind a mentality based upon communality and natural cycles, and entered the masculine world of *The Logos*.

In the Emperor, The Empress endures, but only as life directed, managed, and controlled – this is signified by the *ankh*, which The Emperor now clutches firmly in his hand. The water of life has in fact receded to the background, and lies far in the distance behind the principal subjects of this card – The Emperor and his four-sided throne. The number four is a symbol of both wholeness and ordering – the four directions, seasons, elements, and so on. (Of interest is that some versions of this card actually have the Emperor sitting on a cube; for example, the *Waite-Trinick* and *B.O.T.A.* decks.) The square throne itself sits atop a rugged landscape – the perceived "chaotic disorder"[1] of nature. Such control over chaos is also suggested by the four rams' heads on the throne, representing *Aries*, the zodiacal symbol of leadership. The rams' heads also recall the views of the

12th-Century monk *Joachim of Fiore*, who equated the *Age of the Father* with the God of the Old Testament – the One who demanded a ram's sacrifice from Abraham. This is an age characterized by obedience to God's commands revealed in holy writ. In sociological terms, the figure represents social order and stability maintained by strong leadership and adherence to rules. In psychological terms, he represents the emergence of what Jung described as the male's "logos-oriented" psyche[2] – discriminating consciousness which both fashions and maintains a particular perception of the world and a distinct sense of self.

At one extreme within the spectrum of possibility, the Emperor represents the lopsided elevation of reason, rationality, selfhood and rule over the feminine qualities of intuition, nurture, compassion, and connection. From an Ecofeminist perspective, this signifies the conceptual values of patriarchal culture – systems of power and control characterized by value-hierarchical dualisms that elevate and maintain the "realities" of male domination.[3] From this lopsided perspective, The Empress as both spontaneous womb of life and bringer of destruction comes to be viewed with much distrust - as foreign, alien, *maya*; a threat to the maintenance of the ego and thus that which must be tamed, controlled, or even transcended. As Jung said, "matricide" is complementary to ego-development.[4] The Emperor, as male ideal, takes his ultimate projected form as the separated, self-existing God of the Abrahamic faiths. This is William Blake's demiurgal monstrosity, *Urizen*: "Lo, a shadow of horror is risen in Eternity! Unknown, unprolific, self-clos'd, all-repelling."[5] This "self-clos'd" ideal is clearly indicated by the Emperor's armor, which makes its first appearance here in the Trumps. The armor forms an impenetrable barrier of protection, delineating and separating the self from others. While the Emperor retains and enforces this seperative male ideal of self without connection, the other side of "selfhood" is projected upon the Empress and her female representatives – connection and nurture without self.[6]

This dualistic and lopsided view of both the self/other and masculine/feminine are for many the defining hallmarks of patriarchal culture, and have it is argued contributed in no small way to the unbalanced social and spiritual life which many now experience. The rise of patriarchal culture, as Edward Whitmont suggests, has appeared alongside the development of an egoic, heroic, self-disciplined will, bound to maintain the laws of its divine "liege lord." Yet negatively, this has seen the fragmentation of reality into a collection of "mutually exclusive opposites," and the separation and devaluation of "the feminine."[7]

In the Story of the Buddha: The Ploys of King Suddhodana

The Emperor card clearly relates to the story of King Suddhodana, and his stratagems aimed at preventing his son from following a course that would foster any form of spiritual development. In some versions of the story, we are told that the omens point towards his infant son becoming either a great king or a great spiritual teacher. Suddhodana, desirous that his son should attain the former, and exercise "sovereign rule and authority over the four great continents,"[8] indulges the young prince with delights of every sort. If he is surrounded by pleasure, reasons the king, he will not be troubled by the more spiritual and problematic aspects of life.

Suddhodana builds his son three palaces, and smothers him in opulence and sensual delight:

> And the Future Buddha, with his gaily dressed dancers, was like a god surrounded by hosts of houris; and attended by musical instruments that sounded of themselves, and in the enjoyment of great magnificence, he lived, as the seasons changed, in each of these three palaces.[9]

Joseph Campbell compares Suddhodana here to the figure of King Herod within the gospel narratives; both represent hostility towards a more spiritual and balanced understanding of "kingship" - renunciation and service.[10] To be fair though, both the Theravadin texts and the *Buddhacarita* convey very positive images of Suddhodana. The *Buddhacarita* for examples states that he was the "very best of kings ... intent on liberality yet devoid of pride; sovereign, yet with an ever equal eye thrown on all, - of gentle nature and yet with wide-reaching majesty."[11] Moreover, Suddhodana wishes that his son attain nothing less than the position of *Chakravartin* – a mighty yet benevolent ruler of the world. His apparent disappointment at the prospect of his son becoming a mere "teacher" might well then seem understandable, perhaps even justified.

Yet, despite his beneficence as a ruler, and his good intentions as a father, the texts imply that Suddhodana had his shortcomings, particularly as regards to issues of a spiritual nature. Asvaghosa for example points out that his main concerns were "duty, wealth, and pleasure."[12] These three pursuits are regarded as legitimate ones within the context of Indian religiosity. But there is also a fourth which appears missing from Suddhodana's leadership – *moksha* or "spiritual liberation." *Kama* or "pleasure" is one of the ways by which Suddhodana attempts to steer his son away from the spiritual life. Yet *dharma* or "duty" (not to be confused with the Buddhist Dharma) is another key concern within Indian thought. To this day, *dharma* within Hinduism is tied to the concept of the caste *varnas*, where one's "duty" is to remain faithful to the obligations of one's social group. The prince's "duty" was to remain faithful to his calling as a member of the warrior or *kshatriya varna*; a calling which Suddhodana attempts to instill in his son through a proscribed programme of princely education. Thus, Suddhodana's attempts to shield his son from spiritual matters are not just based on a sense of vocational guidance, but upon the view that his son becoming a mere "teacher" is a challenge to the eternal *dharma* of caste duty itself.

A Buddhist Reflection: The Chakravartin

While Buddhism places emphasis upon an individual's responsibility for changing his or her own mindscape, it nevertheless puts some weight on the notion of the inspired and enlightened leader who can help facilitate such transformation. Such a person is expressed in the idealized figure of the *Chakravartin* – the "wheel-turning" monarch who rules with responsibility, wisdom and compassion. In the *Cakkavatti Sihanada Sutta*, the Buddha, by means of a fictional tale, outlines the duties of those in positions of social leadership. Relying upon, honoring and respecting the Buddhist Dharma, says a Maharaja to his princely son, a king should protect his people and his animals, eradicate "wrongdoing," and provide help to the destitute. The text goes on to offer a vision of what happens when the monarch's duties are cast aside; a vision which seems to strike a note of contemporary relevance. When no provision is made for the poor, poverty becomes widespread; and from this stealing and violence are nurtured, eventually leading to an extensive "destruction of life."[13]

When Buddhist kings eventually came to power in India and elsewhere, such discourses were taken as fact, and initiated an era of responsible kingship. An excellent example is that of *Ashoka* of the *Mairya* dynasty, responsible for a war against the state of *Kalinga* which resulted in the deaths of many thousands. After his conversion to Buddhism, *Ashoka* initiated a number of staggering religious and social reforms. These developments, if true, justly challenge even current notions of social welfare. The "Edicts of Ashoka," as Phelps comments, document one of the rare times in world history where animals were afforded a measure of state-protection commensurate with its human citizens.[14]

A more contemporary example of such enlightened leadership is to be found in the Kingdom of Bhutan. Since 1971, and under the leadership of its fourth and fifth kings, this tiny Buddhist Kingdom has rejected GNP as an indication of progress, and has championed instead the notion of "Gross National Happiness" – the "spiritual, physical, social and environmental happiness of its citizens and natural environment."[15] This has involved some startling reforms, including placing environmental protection at the center of the kingdom's constitution. Over the last two decades, the state has doubled the life expectancy of its people, and has made education provision almost universal. Such changes, as a statement from Bhutan's *Gross Happiness Commission* confirms, are firmly grounded in skillful cetana in pursuit of wisdom and compassion, which recognizes that "true abiding happiness cannot exist while others suffer."[16]

There are few today could claim for themselves the title of *Chakravartin*. Yet, at a more general level, The Emperor raises important questions for many in the West - especially for those who occupy a position of authority or guardianship over others. Moreover, it directs our attention to the issue of our own "lordship" over the plentiful resources we now have at our disposal– an issue we will return to in our reflections upon the Justice card.

The Hierophant (5)

General Overview

In traditional interpretations The Hierophant represents religious institutions, doctrines, teachings, or more simply, education. The term "Hierophant" literally means "holy teacher," and this is reflected in the card's imagery which shows a Pope or some other figure of ecclesiastical authority sitting on his throne, instructing two novices. His three-tiered crown and rod suggest mastery over Christian doctrines relating to mind, body and spirit, or Heaven, Earth and Hell. In the usual *RWS* interpretation, the card represents the *exoteric* teachings of religion – those which provide morals, stability and social cohesion. The Hierophant sits between two dreary grey pillars; and, unlike the pillars of The High Priestess, there is no veil to penetrate - for none is recognized by those who administer "The Truth." To put it in Waite's eloquent words: "it may so happen that the pontiff forgets the significance of this his symbolic state and acts as if he contained within his proper measures all that his sign signifies."[1] The "Keys to Heaven" which lie at the base of the card are both golden, indicating a lack of insight and wisdom (a silver key) beyond the merely doctrinal. Overall, The Hierophant, as Waite says, is "the ruling power of external religion" and "not inspiration."[2] This of course does not mean that traditional teachings have no meaning or value. A broad education, as both Pollack and

Banzhaf recognize, may go far in preparing our Fool for the "world outside."[3]

At one extreme within the spectrum of possibility, The Hierophant may indicate a slavish adherence to proscribed rules and religious dogma. Thus, in Waite's interpretation the card also connotes "captivity" and "servitude,"[4] represented perhaps by the two doting novices. Fenton-Smith agrees, and equates the card with "narrow-mindedness" and an unwillingness to move beyond the "pillars" of traditional beliefs into personal insight and responsibility.[5]

In a feminist reading of this extreme, The Hierophant is the institutional and theological extension of The Emperor's rational, ruling ego; enforcing the ethical and doctrinal parameters within which admittance to Heaven is granted, and promoting a distinctly sterile vision of humanity's spiritual destiny. It is an ethical and doctrinal standard which allows no room for diversity. It is the "one-for-all" standard of Blake's Urizen:

> One command, one joy, one desire,
> One curse, one weight, one measure,
> One King, one God, one Law.[6]

It is a standard set towards an all-consuming apocalypse revealed in scripture, where those who diverge from the One Law are demonized and damned: "the fornicators, sorcerers, idolaters, and all liars, their lot shall be in the lake that burns with fire and sulfur" (*Rev.* 21: 8). It is a vision of a purified, crystalline, spiritual destiny within - most appropriately - a <u>cube</u> described as *The New Jerusalem*, where all traces of the feminine - organicism, darkness, and even the sea itself, the source of all life - are removed: "the first earth had passed away, and the sea was no more" (*Rev.* 21: 1). Apparently, the descending cube, "clear as glass," has "no need of sun or moon to shine upon it" (*Rev.* 21: 18, 23). For feminists, this imposing, sterile, crystalline *Ka'bah* marks the terminal point of patriarchal imagination and spirituality, which with some justification has been termed "necrophilous."[7]

At the other extreme within the card's spectrum of meaning we find the call to non-conformity, to rebellion. This may range from issues self-trust and heresy to the much darker limits of licentiousness and moral nihilism, where "do as thou wilt shall be the whole of the law." This is perhaps a neglected dimension of the card, but one that is certainly recognized by Richard Gardner's channeled Hierophant, who admits that he has only offered "masculine knowledge," and demands of his "poor sheep" why they never think to look for themselves.[8] Similarly, Pollack argues that The Hierophant may represent a new but "heretical" form of religious understanding, based upon personal insight and a growing sense of connectedness.[9] Within New Age thought, this emerging cosmic religion is sometimes viewed as reflecting Joachim of Fiore's *Age of Spirit*, or in astrological lore, the *Age of Aquarius*.

In the Story of the Buddha: Siddhattha's Education

The traditions report that after his mother's death, Siddhattha was looked after by *Pajapati Gotami*, Queen Maya's younger sister, who became the infant's stepmother. He began his formal education at an early age, under the tutelage of a teacher by the name of *Sarva Mitra*. Although the texts are quite general concerning the specifics of his education, it is presumed that he received one befitting a child of his status – a broad curriculum that perhaps included reading, writing, mathematics and history, and princely pursuits such as archery and wrestling. According to the texts, he excelled at his studies, and "learned in a few days the various sciences suitable to his race, which generally took many years to master." Yet, we also learn that his father was keen to shield him from speculative and philosophical musings, or any sight "which could disturb his mind."[10] This strategy however did prevent his son from gaining spiritual insights from the world around him. Nature, the neglected world of The Empress, became his teacher; his gateway to comprehension and wisdom.

One incident in particular that stands out is his first experience of meditation under a rose-apple tree. This incident seems particularly significant as it was the one which the Future Buddha, many years later, recalled to mind as he engaged in deep reflections under the *Asvattha* tree just prior to his enlightenment. The incident took place during an annual ploughing festival which celebrated the first furrowing of the fields, and was attended by all and sundry. The young prince was sitting under the tree, observing a ploughman as he furrowed the ground. He noted the struggle of the ox as it moved with the plough, and the sweat on the man's back as the sun beat down mercilessly. He also observed the tiny insects that emerged from the earth as the plough cut through their homes, and the lacerated worms that wriggled and struggled to get away from the birds that tried to consume them. At this point, according to the text, he instinctively put himself into a cross-legged position, and began to focus his mind. He found himself entering a trance-like state or *jhana*, which produced a sense of deep calm and bliss; and, at the same time generated insight concerning the realities of life within the world.

The young prince learned three things from nature that day. First, that meditation produces a sense of calm detachment that can lead to insight. Second, that all living beings are caught up in a web of interdependent conditions that generate suffering. Third, that as one modern version of the story puts it - reciting the ancient Vedic texts will not help the worms very much.[11]

A Buddhist Reflection: Taking yourself as an Island
The Buddha had many positive words for teachers, and it is certainly instructive that immediately following his enlightenment his first thoughts were for his two former meditation instructors, and where he might find them. In the *Sigala Sutta* the Buddha marks out both teachers and priests as two of six "directions of worship." We should honor our teachers by being conscientious and attending to their teachings, and priests through kindness in thought, speech and deed. By way of reciprocation, we shall receive a detailed foundation in "all skills" and thus find the way to "heaven."[12] In both Zen and Vajrayana Buddhism, the *roshi*, *guru*, or *lama* commands the complete and unquestioned obedience of his or her students, to the point where they are regarded as a "fourth" refuge after the Buddha, Dharma, and Sangha. Within Zen, the pupil is expected to demonstrate absolute trust towards their teacher, and respect them as much as their own father.[13] In the Vajrayana practice of *Guru Yoga*, the teacher as Powers notes is viewed as providing a model of that enlightened state one is striving to attain. The teacher not only transmits the Dharma, but provides an example of enlightened living in practice. Thus, the pupil's relationship with the teacher is more intimate than his or her relationship with any Buddha.[14]

This close relationship between teacher and student is founded on the view that enlightenment cannot be discovered through mere ritual or intellectual study. It is, as the ancient Zen master *Bodhidharma* puts it, "outside tradition, outside scripture." It is a "direct pointing to the heart," achieved only through the guidance of one who is already awakened. As the teacher opens awareness to one's own nature, in the same way, the pupil may one day do the same for others. Thus enlightenment becomes not just an individual experience, but an ongoing process of awakening that spans centuries; an unbroken "transmission of awakened consciousness" from teacher to student, that goes back to the Buddha himself. Accordingly, the pupil, particularly within Vajrayana, is encouraged to see his or her own efforts as being part of a "lineage" of transmission that contains the very essence of the awakenings of all previous teachers. In Tantric "empowerments," the pupil visualizes his or her meditational deity surrounded by the many teachers of that particular lineage, up to and including the present one. The pupil then asks them to bestow their inspiration and blessing. In response, as Lama Yeshe explains, they merge together as one within the pupil's own heart, where all dualisms end in the "clear space of emptiness."[15]

At the same time, Buddhism recognizes the inadequacy of certain teachers and teachings, particularly those based on dogmatic tradition, hearsay or popularity. A good example of this is discussed in the well-known *Kalama Sutta*. The *Kalamas*, much like many spiritual seekers today, had been beset by a number of compelling and competing teachers, gurus, doctrines, and speculations, and had turned to the Buddha for advice. He advised them that they should reject the ten traditional sources of authority and belief – including the reputation of teachers, scriptures, hearsay, and attractive speculation – and instead adopt practices that made for common sense, and were conducive to the universal good.

The Buddha recognized that the path to enlightenment, ultimately, must be walked alone, with oneself as the only true master of transformation: "A man is his own helper; who else is there to help?"[16] Shortly before his death he encouraged his followers not to mourn his passing, nor to panic about who would be their new teacher. Instead they should adopt a stance of self-reliance:

> "Therefore, O Ananda, be ye lamps unto yourselves. Rely on yourselves, and do not rely on external help. Hold fast to the truth as a lamp. Seek salvation alone in the truth. Look not for assistance to any one besides yourselves."[17]

It is clear from the suttas that the Buddha, like many other wandering *shramanas*, had little respect for the teachings of the established religion of his age – *Vedic Brahmanism*. The time of the Buddha was, as Ling points out, one of "spiritual malaise," where the teachings and rituals of the old order were being challenged and rejected.[18] This sense of discontinuity and dissolution is expressed in the distressed cry of one seeker from the *Maitri Upanishad*:

> Oceans dry up. Mountains sink down. The positions of Dhruva (the Polar Star) and of trees change. Earth is drowned. The Suras (angels) run away, leaving their (respective) places. ... Thou art able to extricate me (out of this Samsara). I am drowned like a frog in a dry well.[19]

The Buddha had some harsh words for the Brahmanic priesthood. Their rituals and teachings were elitist, and full of esoteric pretensions. Three things are conducted in secret he said: affairs with women, wrong views, and "the mantras" of the priesthood.[20] The Buddha was also critical of their ritual practices, which appeared not only incomprehensible, but wasteful and cruel. In the *Kutadanta Sutta*, we hear of a Brahman about to offer a "great sacrifice" to the gods, involving the slaughter of many hundreds of animals. The Buddha insists that there is a better type of sacrifice: "abstinence from destroying life; abstinence from taking what has not been given; abstinence from evil conduct in respect of lusts; abstinence from lying words."[21] The Buddha was especially critical of the Brahminical doctrine of caste. The *caste-varna* structure was, and remains, an enforced system of social stratification and control, which legitimates itself through appeal to Vedic texts, natural order, and social cohesion. One of its Vedic manifestations - which we have already alluded to - was the myth of the Mahapurusha, the Cosmic Man who sacrifices himself to create the cosmos; but also, more negatively, social division:

> When they divided Purusa how many portions did they make? What do they call his mouth, his arms? What do they call his thighs and feet? The Brahman was his mouth, of both his arms was the Rājanya (Warrior) made. His thighs became the Vaisya [Merchant], from his feet the Sudra [Servant] was produced.[22]

Another contributory to caste stratification is the doctrine of the three *gunas* or "strands" that are understood to be the basic building blocks of reality, or the three "modes" of existence. These strands - which recall the three tiers on the Hierophant's crown and notches on his rod - are *sattva* (goodness and light), *ragas* (energy and fire) and *tamas* (dullness and darkness). Goodness, it is said, reflects the nature of the Brahmins; energy, that of the aristocratic warriors; the merchant class and the commoners are a blend of both energy and dullness; while the servants and slaves embody dullness and darkness, and are thus, according to the *Bhagavad-Gita*, only fit for "service."[23]

A corollary to the doctrine of caste is that of "duty" (*dharma*). As discussed in relation to The Emperor, it is incumbent upon every member of each *varna* to remain faithful to the duties and responsibilities of his or her social group. This obligation is given much consideration in the *Bhagavad-Gita*. In chapter two, the young prince *Arjuna* inquires of *Krishna* why he must slaughter his cousins in battle. Surely, he reasons, such a terrible deed cannot be justified? Krishna offers these words in response:

> "Having regard to your own duty also, you ought not to falter, for there is nothing better for a Kshatriya [Warrior] than a righteous battle ... But if you will not fight this righteous battle, then you will have abandoned your own duty and your fame, and you will incur sin."[24]

The Buddha rejects these traditional notions of caste and duty; but he does not abandon them entirely. Instead, he does something more creative – he re-envisions them in terms of wisdom and ethical conduct, as opposed to natural birth-right. All humans, from whatever walk of life, are equally capable of developing spiritual insight and compassion. It is not the prerogative of some self-congratulatory karmic elite. As the *Dhammapada* states: "A man does not become a Brahmana by his platted hair, by his family, or by birth; in whom there is truth and righteousness, he is blessed, he is a Brahmana."[25]

The Buddha's ethical re-envisioning of caste has not fallen on deaf ears. The contemporary *Dalit* (oppressed and untouchable) Buddhist movement in India, which centers itself around the teachings of B. R. Ambedkar, has been responsible for the conversion of many thousands of lower-caste Hindus. Ambedkar formulated twenty-two vows for new converts to Buddhism. Like the twenty-two Tarot keys, these vows form the foundation for a new way of being and living in an age that has moved beyond blind adherence to institutionalized doctrines that divide and oppress. Many of these vows – which aim to "establish equality" and generate "compassion and loving-kindness for all living beings"[26] - may help us re-connect us with The Hierophant in a more positive and appropriate way.

The Lovers (6)

General Overview

The Lovers card lends itself to many interpretations. As one which belongs to the "worldly" sequence of the path, it is sometimes interpreted as representing love, romance, emerging sexuality, passion, and new relationships. Yet it can also refer to "choice," a fact noted in the name given to earlier versions of this card - *The Crossroads*. In the *Marseilles* version, we are shown a man about to make a choice between an older dark-haired woman and a younger blonde woman. In Jungian interpretations this has been linked to a young male's developing ego, attempting to extricate itself from the regressive pull of the unconscious, his "mother"; seeking fulfillment instead in women who conform to the image of his own "inner feminine" – his "other half," the *anima*.[1] For Nichols, The Lovers is also concerned with "growth" beyond the limitations and challenges of the previous cards, which together represent the forces of nature, society, parents, and education. The Lovers says Nichols indicates the challenge of integrating these forces with our emotional side, through which we gain further insight and knowledge about ourselves and the world around.[2]

The imagery on the *RWS* version of the card clearly relates to the story of Adam and Eve in the Garden of Eden. They stand between the Tree of Knowledge and the Tree of Life, while above, an angel presides over a choice that must be made. In mainstream Christian theology, derived particularly from Augustine, this scene is linked with the doctrines of "The Fall" and "Original Sin." In Augustine's interpretation of the *Genesis* story, the couple are commanded by God that they must not eat from the Tree of Knowledge lest they bring sin, disorder and death into the created world. Adam and Eve disobey, falling from perfection and corrupting the entire human race, which now stands as a *massa damnata*; incapable of change, and reliant upon the atoning sacrifice of Christ for the remission of sins.

However, a more upbeat and evolutionary interpretation of this same scene was given by the earlier theologian Irenaeus. Irenaeus focused on one verse from *Genesis* in particular: "Then God said, 'Let us make man in our image, after our likeness'" (*Gen.* 1: 26). From this Irenaeus theorized that human nature is not a finished business; it is an ongoing journey. First, humans are made in God's image, possessing a soul, a moral nature, and freewill. The second part - where we acquire God's likeness - is in fact an ongoing process of evolutionary development. Adam and Eve's decision to eat from the tree was, admittedly, a mark of immaturity; yet their expulsion from the garden was something that permitted growth in human character. It is only through a life lived in a world of good and evil, says Irenaeus, where humans are forced to make choices and face the demands and limitations of embodied existence, that true "maturity" can be won. This indicates the radical difference between the Irenaean and mainstream Christian concepts of human "perfection." In mainstream Christianity, it is a long-lost state of pre-experiential innocence married to obedience to God's laws. For Irenaeus, it is a future product of growth through personal decision-making. There is no "fall" into depravity in Irenaeus' view; there is only the naivety of children who still need to develop, to grow up. Irenaeus' *End of Days* is a vision of *theosis* or "divinization." "Our Lord Jesus Christ" says Irenaeus "became what we are, that He might bring us to be even what He is Himself."[3]

At the same time, any movement towards maturity brings into sharper focus a growing sense of self, especially in its incompleteness and isolation. How is such duality to be overcome? One answer according to Nichols is to immerse oneself in a world of sexual passion, by which our yearnings for completeness are allayed, at least temporarily.[4] This passionate option is clearly suggested in Adam's wistful gaze upon Eve's naked form, and by the flames which ignite the tree behind him.

Yet the card suggests that there is an alternative choice, and we recognize this in Eve's eyes, which are drawn, not to Adam, but to the world of wisdom, symbolized by the angel. Although Waite was quite unspecific about the issue, in many interpretations this heavenly figure is seen to represent *Raphael*, the archangel of healing. This interpretation has its roots, not in ancient scripture, but in Milton's *Paradise Lost*, where Raphael is sent by God to warn Adam about the dangers of eating from the Tree of Knowledge. Yet, an equally deserving candidate is the figure of *Gabriel*. In Jewish lore the Tree of Life was also known as the *Tree of Souls*, where latent souls developed before being placed in the *Treasury*, to await the hand of Gabriel who implanted these seeds of pure potentiality within an embryo. According to I *Enoch* 20: 7, Gabriel is also the angel who stands guard over Eden, thus preventing Adam and Eve's return to their original state of childish bliss. While prohibiting any return, Gabriel is simultaneously responsible for leading humans onwards in terms of wisdom and insight, a role confirmed by his identification with the Kabbalistic *sephirah* of *Yesod* (*Foundation*) - the bridge between the worlds of the Divine and *Malkuth* (*Material Creation*) – and his manifestation in the Judgement card, appearing before humanity with the promise of resurrection into new life. His important role confirms the central theme of the Irenaean theology – that the transition from "image" to "likeness," from child to adult, is made via engagement with the world of "soul-making." It demands conscious choice and commitment; not a return to pre-experiential womb-like ecstasy. This may of course involve sexual passion in which we lose our ego-centered perspective for a time; but the journey will also involve confrontation and struggle - with others, and with ourselves. It may also, as Eve's eyes suggest, involve a temporary removal from the ways of the world and the delights of sensory entanglements (the fruits shown on the Tree of Knowledge in the card[5]), and the quest for greater wisdom and understanding.

In the Story of the Buddha: A Life of Sensual Delight
Given has father's insistence upon a course of sensual indulgence for Siddhattha, it comes as little surprise that the young prince found himself immersed in a world of sexual activity, surrounded, we are told by "hosts of houris."[6] "Within the Royal apartments," writes Asvaghosa, "the women delighted him with their soft voices ... their playful intoxication." So intense was the pleasure, says Asvaghosa, that the young prince even fell from the roof of a pavilion, "[b]orne in the arms of these women well-skilled in the ways of love."[7] "Gotama's life," says John Stevens, consisted mainly in removing women's clothing, caressing their breasts, and "devouring them with love."[8] To "seal the deal" as it were, the king

arranged for his son to marry his beautiful cousin, *Yashodhara*, "a bride possessed of beauty, modesty, and gentle bearing, of wide-spread glory."[9] In addition to Yashodhara, the young prince had several other official wives, and, according to Stevens, "an army" of the most beautiful, skillful, and appreciative women in the kingdom.[10]

In a sense though, it was only through this initial immersion within a world of sensuality and passion that the prince was able to explore its limited value in depth, and reflect upon other possibilities. As Yeshe Gyaltsen's version of the narrative puts it, the songs and music of the many houris began to "emit verses" that reminded the young prince of the true nature and purpose of his life.[11]

In time, Yashodhara bore Siddhattha a son, *Rahula*, cementing, or so his father hoped, the young prince to a life of caste duty and family responsibility. Yet, the very name *Rahula* - which literally means "fetter" - gives us an indication that perhaps Siddhattha was starting to reflect more deeply on the course of his life so far; upon the restrictions placed over him by his father, and by the teachings and expectations of his society at large. Like Eve's eyes in The Lovers card, the prince's eyes were slowly being drawn to a different order of knowledge, experience and possibility.

A Buddhist Reflection: Sex and Relationships

The connection between Buddhism and the world of romantic love and sexual intimacy is a complex one. The *five lay precepts* advise only that lay Buddhists should not engage in "sexual misconduct," which would include rape, incest and adultery. The joys that a partner and family life may instill are recognized in the *Sigala Sutta* where they are hailed as two of the six directions of worship.[12]

It is a very different story for committed monks and nuns however. In the monastic code of conduct, sexual intercourse is named as one of the four *Great Offences* or *Defeaters* which results in expulsion from the Sangha. A monk is also forbidden from touching or caressing a female in a provocative manner. A monk or nun should never be alone with a lay person of the opposite sex, or be in a compromising situation that would cause rumors or gossip of a sexual nature to spread. During the alms round, monks and nuns to this day carry a small cloth to prevent any accidental contact between themselves and lay practitioners. Monks and nuns are also not permitted to act as "go-betweens" or romantic "match-makers" for others, and this explains why they do not preside over marriage ceremonies, other than to offer blessings.

Such prohibitions may appear to verge on the puritanical, the "ascetic." Yet they are grounded in two reasonably-sound Buddhist insights. First, that the world of love, passion, relationships and ultimately, children, involves a level of devotion and dedication that would make complete commitment to spiritual development well-nigh impossible. At a deeper level, Buddhism recognizes that romantic love and sexuality create deep attachments and desires for sensory phenomena. The Buddhist view is that while such sensual experiences may be pleasant, passionate, or even blissful at first, they will fade, due to their intrinsic impermanence, leaving one with the bitter taste of dukkha, and cravings for new and more intense delights and encounters.

The Buddha is no shrinking violet when he comes to elucidate on the "danger of form." In the *Mahadukkhakhandha Sutta* he asks us to contemplate a young woman at the height of her attractiveness. He then asks us to contemplate that same woman in her old-age, wrinkled and almost bald. Then, we should consider her as a corpse, distended and "oozing matter"; and finally as a mass of bones, scattered to the winds. This, he concludes, is the "danger" of form.[13]

An amusing incident that highlights Buddhist detachment from form occurs in the *Therigatha* (*Poems of the Elder Nuns*) where a beautiful young nun called *Subha* is accosted by some amorous Reynardine, hoping to woo her into bed, with the additional promise that "I would live but to serve thee." He proceeds to describe her loveliness in great detail, and how he is particularly captivated by her gorgeous eyes, "which feedeth the depth of my passion." At this point the young nun plucks out one of her eyes and hands it to him, commenting that he "chasest a sham, deluded by puppet shows." "Straightaway," the text notes, "the lust in him ceased."[14] From the viewpoint of the uninstructed worldling, such detachment from form and passion, sexual intimacy and family life, seems unreasonable and extreme. From a Theravadin Buddhist perspective, it forms the foundations for liberation and bliss; and this was particularly true for women, who, by joining the Sangha, were given the opportunity to remove themselves from lives centered around the sexual passions and desires of men.

An alternative approach to sex and passion is proposed in the Tantric practices of Vajrayana Buddhism. The basic premise of Tantrism is that the energies generated by the passions and desires which bind us to Samsara should not be dissolved, but instead, utilized. Such energies it is argued can be transmuted and channeled by practices that generate great spiritual insight and transformation. As the *Hevajra Tantra* puts it, the world is both "bound" and "released" through passion.[15] Such transmuted passion forms the basis of *Karmamudra Yoga*, which involves literal or symbolic sexual union between a *yogi* and *yogini* or "seal." This practice it said to generate bliss, but also insight into the emptiness of all phenomena.[16]

Such practices may seem very appealing to many in the West, especially for those who have been influenced by more puritanical notions of what the "spiritual life" might entail. Yet within Buddhism, they are reserved for very experienced practitioners; those are free from sexual desire based upon sensory attachment. Those who may be tempted to mimic such practices without the proper training are, as Powers warns, plainly deluded, and may bring upon themselves "great harm."[17] Such warnings are especially apposite for those involved in the burgeoning market that is *Neotantrism* - the repackaged New Age version of the practice. The term *Tantra* is one that continues to have many exotic and erotic connotations, and has thus been appropriated by those seeking financial gain through sexual desire; from its promotion in sex education courses, or even by sex-workers to increase sales. Such repackaging has not led to much insight, and indeed, its main appeal, as Georg Feuerstein reports, has been the promise of "sexual excitement" clothed in an "aura of spirituality."[18] Such practices are fraught with psychological dangers, including, as one practitioner relates, re-traumatization in victims of sexual-abuse.[19]

There is, thankfully, far more to "love" in The Lovers card than simply sexual attraction and passion. Of equal importance are our general attitudes towards those we form relationships with as we make our journey through life. In this respect, the simple Buddhist practice of *Metta Bhavana* (*Training in Loving-kindness*) may do more to transform our relationships with others than the more exotic practices of Tantra. Metta Bhavana is principally a Theravadin training, although variations on it can be found in both Mahayana and Vajrayana texts.

Paramananda divides this meditative practice into five stages.[20] In the first stage we bring to mind ourselves, and radiate feelings of loving-kindness towards our own center. This is an important element of the practice, based on the view that if we cannot love ourselves, then we will find it very difficult to love others. In the next stage we bring to mind someone we feel especially friendly towards or attracted to. From our center again, we radiate thoughts of loving-kindness towards that person. This process is then repeated for people we neither like nor dislike, and then perhaps most importantly, for someone we dislike intensely. Finally, we bring to mind all four, radiating thoughts of loving-kindness to all. While in this stage, we start to expand our thoughts to embrace all sentient beings in the world, and finally, all sentient beings in existence.

The purpose of the practice is twofold. First, it helps us realize how much of the love we offer towards others is based upon self-interest. As Thubten Chodron reflects, often the love we extend to others is based upon how they treat us. The second aim therefore is to move ourselves beyond such a self-centered view, where love is only conferred upon those whom we think have earned it in terms of their compliance to our expectations. True love, as Chodron says, is "totally unconditional."[21]

The Chariot (7)

General Overview

The Chariot is traditionally associated with success, conquest and victory, originating in the fact that the *Triumphal Car* was often employed in colorful processions by the victors of war. In our analysis, The Chariot is also the final card of the *Way of the World* sequence, and brings to fruition all that has been acquired in The Fool's journey through the previous cards – will, wisdom, nurture, society's rules and conventions, education, new relationships, and emerging sexuality. For Waite, the idea of "revelation" is also relevant to this card, arguing that the charioteer's epaulettes represent *Urim* and *Thummin* – the Hebrew tools of divine communication.[1]

In Jungian terms, the Fool has left behind the paradise world of childhood – a world represented by the city in the card's background - and entered one of emerging independence and personal ego. The card indicates a sense of growing self-discipline and self-control; of mastery over conflicting tendencies, suggested by the charioteer's ability to steer the two mismatched sphinxes. Our Hero, in short, has reached the point in his maturation where he can, as Nichols says, "ride out" into life to investigate his boundaries and ascertain new possibilities.[2]

Although the card is usually seen in a positive way, indicating success, mastery and will, feminists may beg to differ, arguing instead that it represents only the world of the heroic male ego; a world that is off-limits to many women, and simultaneously one which posits a lopsided view of the self and its social relations. Yet, conversely, the card may generate a sense of motivation and inspiration for women, indicating attitudes and values which for many, at least in the West, are now up for grabs. As an "Irreverent Feminist" says on her blog-post, the world of The Chariot is the world of "Boudicca," and the world "I want."[3] Such readings indicate that the development of a strong, willful ego is as pertinent to women as it is to men. Nonetheless, within the full spectrum of possibility the card does have negative connotations, suggesting an over-bearing ego-driven mentality. Such a position find its extreme form in what Nichols perceives as the sin of *hubris* - an over-reaching pride in which the self imagines it has transcended the very limitations of embodied life.[4] The precarious, ludicrous, and ultimately self-defeating nature of such imaginings find expression in the myth of *Phaethon* (*Shining One*), Apollo's son, who was unable to control his father's sun-chariot. To prevent disaster the inflated youth was smoothly dispatched with a thunderbolt from Zeus.

At the opposite pole of the spectrum the card may indicate a complete lack of mastery or an inability to move forwards. Here, one is drawn to the image of the two sphinxes which, despite the Charioteer's impressive wand, are clearly not moving, or perhaps moving in different directions, and do not appear to be reined or yoked. We are also reminded that The Chariot card itself may owe it origins to Renaissance *carousels*, in which various allegorical figures, including the Triumphal Car, were led round and round, going nowhere.

In the Story of the Buddha: The Four Sights
"Now on a certain day," so the texts recount, the Future Buddha wished to leave the confines of his palace and visit the park, and so, he "told his charioteer to make ready the chariot." The chariot itself was "sumptuous and elegant," and harnessed with the finest horses. And so the Future Buddha mounted his chariot, "which was like to a palace of the gods," and headed towards the park. The gods, realizing their opportune moment had arrived, decide that they must provide the prince with a revelation; they must "show him a sign."[5]

First, one the gods transforms himself into a decrepit old man. The Future Buddha spies him, and inquires of *Channa* his charioteer about the old man's appearance. When the prince learns of the inevitability and universality of old age, he reflects thus: "Old age thus strikes down all alike, our memory, comeliness and valor; and yet the world is not disturbed, even when it sees such a fate visibly impending." On his second outing, the prince witnesses "the calamity of diseases," and yet reflects that the world "can yet feel tranquility." On the third outing he learns of the reality of death, and is filled with horror: "Is this end appointed to all creatures, and yet the world throws off all fear and is infatuated!"[6] Up to this point, the young prince reflects what Thurman describes as the countless "kings" and "queens" of today's developed world; waited-on by the other half, oblivious to or in denial concerning life's grimmer realities. We simply do not want to hear that there is no real self, nor that all things are impermanent. However, this as Thurman says, is something those in the West need to hear - "and hear it well."[7] The young prince does "hear it," and is therefore sent one more revelation from the gods. He spies a monk, and inquires of Channa whom this person is, "so carefully and decently clad." His charioteer replies that this is one "who has retired from the world."[8]

The prince returns to the palace and broods over all that he has witnessed. Immediately, he is beset by numerous dancing girls, who attempt to rouse him from his melancholy, but to no avail. The Future Buddha falls asleep on his couch, and when he awakens, he looks at the sleeping girls surrounding him: "Some with their bodies wet with trickling phlegm and spittle; some grinding their teeth, and muttering and talking in their sleep." At that moment, the palace seemed to him "like a cemetery filled with dead bodies impaled and left to rot." His mind, says the text, "turned ardently to retiring from the world."[9]

A Buddhist Reflection: Dukkha

The Chariot may indicate self-mastery to the point of hubris, but it also as Pollack suggests points towards a growing awareness of life's limitations; of the conflicts we experience with the external world and within ourselves. The development of individuality has as its corollary a growing awareness of old age, sickness, and death.[10] This awareness of life's limitations is voiced in Gardner's channeled Charioteer, who demands to be freed from incessantly circling this "arena of death."[11] We are reminded at this point of the sphinxes on The Chariot card, and of the riddle posed by one of these creatures to *Oedipus* concerning the nature of humanity: "What is the creature that walks on four legs in the morning, two legs at noon and three in the evening?" This riddle indicates, as Pollack argues, that if we cannot comprehend and come to terms with the limitations of our embodied and finite existence, then it will destroy us.[12]

In Buddhism, likewise, the quest for enlightenment begins with the apprehension of *dukkha*; the awareness that life is characterized by suffering and unsatisfactoriness. It is an amusing coincidence here that the word *dukkha* is derived from the negative prefix *dus* and the root *kha* meaning "hole," and in its original context may have been used in reference to a chariot with a faulty wheel. Such a chariot may assist us in our travels, but the journey will certainly not be smooth nor enjoyable.

In his first teaching – *Turning the Wheel of Dhamma Sutta* – the Buddha differentiates between three forms of *dukkha* – ordinary suffering, suffering caused by change, and suffering as conditioned states. Ordinary suffering describes the suffering or unsatisfactoriness we experience at the everyday level, including being associated with people and phenomena we would rather not be with, and conversely, being separated from people and phenomena we are attracted too. Ordinary suffering also embraces our experiences of ageing, sickness, and death, not only in ourselves, but in those we love. These are the most visceral and potent pointers to the inevitable demise of our ego, and therefore, the most denied and suppressed by a society of heroic charioteers. Suffering caused by change derives from the reality of impermanence, both internally and externally, and how this affects us. We may find ourselves enjoying an excellent vacation, which, inevitably, comes to an end, and this generates dukkha. Or, we feel in love with someone - and yet suddenly wake up one day to find that this is no longer the case. The person may not have dramatically changed, but our internal appreciation of them has.

The third form of dukkha – as conditioned states – relates to the previously discussed view that the individual is comprised of five aggregates that generate and condition a sense of self, but that there is ultimately no "self" either between, behind or within these five constantly fluctuating and impermanent components. This idea of no-self is comprehensively explored in a well-known text called *The Questions of King Milinda*, where the curious but confused King asks the monk *Nagasena* to explain to him how he can not possibly have a self if he is plainly standing before him. The monk obliges, and uses the rather appropriate example of a chariot to do so. The chariot appears more than once within Indian thought as an analogy of human existence. In the *Katha Upanishad* the immortal "Self" as taken to be the chariot's "passenger." Nagasena's "Buddhist" chariot by contrast seems somewhat less metaphysical. Nagasena begins by asking the king to reflect upon the chariot by which he arrived. "Is the pole the chariot?" asks Nagasena. "No." replies the king. "Is the axle, wheels, chariot-body, yoke, or reins the chariot?" the monk inquires further. "No" comes the reply. In the same way, concludes Nagasena, the "person," like the chariot, is a convenient designation for a certain gathering of components that when examined separately, or taken apart, reveal no underlying "self." Terms such as "living entity" and "Ego" are in reality "a mode of expression," but in the absolute sense, "there is no living entity there to form a basis of such figments as 'I am,' or 'I.'"[13]

For Dominique Side, dukkha as conditioned states indicates "the background dissatisfaction" and insecurities we experience when we begin to confront, as the charioteer may, a dawning sense of our limitations and our general powerlessness; and, importantly, the apprehension that the fixed identity that we carve out for ourselves is perhaps "not who we really are."[14]

Departure and Trials: From Strength to The Tower

Introduction

For a significant percentage of Western individuals, it is fair to say that besides Death, The Chariot represents the terminal point in their journey through the Tarot. It is quite understandable why this is so, given that the card's heroic qualities – youthfulness, will, adventure, self-determination, control, sexual prowess, success and victory – are not considered to be mere life options for Westerners, but self-evident ideals to be pursued to the bitter end. In the West they have become fetishized guarantors of one's status as a successful, "complete," human being.

Thus, for many, a growing awareness of our intrinsic limitations, of *dukkha*, tends not to produce reflection, but instead, denial. Such denial has as its main goal the maintenance of the chariot-ride for as long as possible, and may manifest itself in a variety of forms; reflected particularly in the burgeoning profit margins of the cosmetic, pharmaceutical, and alcohol industries, or any other purveyor of mask and medication.

Any refusal to join in the fun results in one's emerging status as *outsider*, whether this be a title conferred upon us by others, or one that originates from our own dawning apprehension of society's ideals as "conjurer's trickwork."[1] For the outsider, like the Future Buddha on the night of his departure from the palace, there is the distinct impression that the world and everyone in it is asleep; that one stands as some solitary foreigner in a strange land. For some outsiders, like the *pneumatikos* of ancient Gnosticism, or the Romantic outsider in Byron's *Manfred*, there is a felt need to move "beyond the dwellers of the earth":

> My spirit walk'd not with the souls of men,
> Nor look'd upon the earth with human eyes;
> The thirst of their ambition was not mine,
> The aim of their existence was not mine ... [2]

For the outsider there are really three options available. First, he or she can attempt to get "back on the wagon" as it were, and learn to live a life of inauthenticity, in which "ignorance is bliss" – or at least better than the alternatives. Second, the outsider may choose to stay as an outsider, to forever occupy a position of savvy disengagement; masking their own fears and disappointments by throwing scorn at the general ignorance of the world. The third option is the path of spiritual reflection and awakening – the "call to adventure"; the path of the *seeker*. This is the path upon which answers are sought to life's deepest mysteries and questions. – Who am I? Can death and suffering be transcended? How is happiness to be attained?

The title which Pollack gives to this aspect of the Fool's Journey is *Turning Inwards*, as the Fool has now moved beyond the outer concerns and challenges of the *Worldly Sequence*, and has turned to the world within; to the issues of "the self." It is a sequence which begins with a withdrawal from society, and ends with a figurative death and rebirth, which Pollack equates with the Temperance card.[3]

My personal opinion is that Pollack ends this second sequence prematurely, and does so principally to create a balanced tripartite structure consisting of seven cards over three sequences. My own view is that the themes of cards 15 (The Devil) and 16 (The Tower) relate more clearly to the concerns of this second sequence. The cards up to and including The Tower seem to suggest the Fool's ongoing journey into what Banzhaf calls the "Arc of the Night,"[4] rather than something new. Indeed, Pollack's third sequence appears to carry too many themes, and even she admits that it may appear "too vague and fanciful."[5] For these reasons The Devil and The Tower are retained within the second sequence, despite the fact that the division of cards now appears slightly unbalanced (7, 9 and 5 cards respectively).

I have termed this second sequence *Departure and Trials*, reflecting Campbell's understanding of the "initiation" element of the monomyth, in which the Hero set off on his or her adventure, encounters a series of trials and ordeals, before finally receiving "the boon." Campbell saw this primarily as a mythological representation of psychological dynamics, in which the personality confronts the inner world of archetypal forces on his or her journey towards individuation. In terms of the Buddha's own story, this sequence extends from the night of his departure to his enlightenment under the *Bodhi* tree.

Strength (8)

General Overview

In conventional interpretations Strength is linked with a sense of endurance, courage and determination, and with confronting inner forces and conflicts with gentleness and compassion, rather than "subjecting them to your will."[1] In the *RWS* deck, the card shows a woman gently holding or shutting a lion's mouth, its powerful neck leashed with a chain of roses, which extends to the woman's dress. Like The Magician, the woman stands under a lemniscate, indicating the start of a new sequence of creativity, determination and directionality.

In older renditions of the card, the virtue of Strength is depicted in a more forceful and aggressive form, or what Amber Jayanti describes as the now-obsolete masculine principle of "domination by force."[2] For example, the *Morgan-Bergamo Tarocchi* version shows Heracles about to kill the *Nemean lion* with his club. Likewise, the *Mantegna* deck shows a woman holding a broken temple pillar, recalling the story of another lion-killer - Samson.[3] As with the *Marseilles* deck, Waite wished to link this virtue with a gentler and more elegant understanding of strength, connoting the more feminine qualities of introspection, acceptance and compassion. The woman, says Waite, represents "the strength which resides in contemplation." For Waite, the lion represents the animalistic and instinctive aspects of human nature, whose raw, impulsive energies are tamed, controlled and transformed through the gentle powers of contemplation and love. In Waite's words, the lion "signifies the passions," while the woman is "the higher nature in its liberation."[4]

According to Nichols in her Jungian interpretation of the card, the woman again corresponds to the Hero's *anima* – his unconscious feminine side which acts as a "mediator" between the ego and darker elements within the psyche.[5] Here, the card signifies revealing, confronting and taming the darker aspects of human nature. But, this entails doing so in a way that is contrary to dualistic forms of spirituality, which, as Banzhaf says, usually tackle our "sinful" impulses through more brutal means.[6]

Waite, as *Master Magus*, is quite guarded in his explanation of why he changed the traditional placement of this card (11), other than to say that he did so for "reasons which satisfy myself," and that for the general reader, "there is no cause for explanation."[7] Perhaps one explanation is his recognition that the card's associated qualities are necessary prerequisites for any advancement on the spiritual path beyond that of The Chariot. As Pollack observes, by placing Strength directly after The Chariot we become conscious of a type of power that lies beyond heroic will; one that allows us to engage with our inner turmoil "calmly and without fear."[8] In relation to this, Banzhaf highlights the rather unfortunate ends for those two mythic heroes – Samson and Heracles – who attempt to subdue and defeat their own "wild lions" through more aggressive means. Samson loses his strength, his sight, and is crushed to death by falling masonry. Heracles, more amusingly, is sentenced to dress and serve as a woman for a year in the court of Queen

Omphale, while she wears the skin of the lion he defeated, and carries his wooden club.[9]

In the Story of the Buddha: The Resolve of a Bodhisattva.

Siddhattha's vision of the "cemetery" we are told "further increased his aversion for sensual pleasure," and he resolved within himself to "go forth on the Great Retirement."[10] Asvaghosa is keen to elaborate upon this cemetery scene and does so in a way that whilst never purely Gnostic is its execution, comes close. The young dancing women unfortunately take the brunt of Asvaghosa's contempt for the sensory entanglements of nature. Siddhattha, says Asvaghosa, was "moved to scorn" at the sight of these women, "with every limb distorted," and declared to himself:

> "Such is the nature of women, impure and monstrous in the world of living beings; but deceived by dress and ornaments a man becomes infatuated by a woman's attractions."[11]

Siddhattha arose from his couch, and asked Channa his charioteer to saddle his prize horse *Kanthaka*. The horse *Kanthaka* is given some attention in the texts, described as being "eighteeen cubits long ... strong and swift, and white all over like a polished conch shell."[12] Such details are not without significance to the themes of the Strength card. The name *Kanthaka* itself is derived from the ancient *Marathi*, meaning "possessed of fortitude, enduring, patient."[13] We are also reminded that the white horse has a particular symbolic role within many religious myths, representing new birth from evil and stagnation. In Hindu mythology, we read of Vishnu's final incarnation as *Kalki*, the *Destroyer of Filth*, who will return on a white horse at the end of the *Kali Yuga*. In the myth of *Perseus* and *Medusa*, the white and winged steed *Pegasus* emerges from the blood of the decapitated priestess who, like the poor sleeping dancers, represents once again the male ego's demonization of female sensuality – alluring and captivating, yet chthonic and paralyzing.

Before leaving however, the prince desired to look upon his son and his wife once more, and opening their chamber door, "he paused, and gazed at the two from where he stood." He felt an intense desire to hold his son in his arms, but recognized that should he do so, his wife "would awake, and thus prevent my departure." "I will first become a Buddha," he reflects, "and then come back and see my son."[14] Unlike the Gnostic *pneumatikos* who desires to transcend the phenomenal world, to move "beyond the dwellers of the earth," the young bodhisattva yearns to return to his family some day, but realizes that this desire must take second place to a more compassionate one. "[W]hen thanks to you I have become a Buddha," he whispers to Kanthaka, "I will save the world of gods and men."[15] Having thus uttered his great *Bodhisattva Vow of Aspiration*, he mounts his horse, and with Channa holding on by the tail, he makes for the main gate of the city.

A Buddhist Reflection: Taming the Elephant and the Monkey

While the lion remains a useful symbol of the animalistic and unruly nature of the mind within Western mythology, the elephant and the monkey occupy a similar role within Buddhist thought. The association is detailed in a well-known pictorial aid to meditation, sometimes known as *The Elephant Path*. This teaching tool graphically explains how a meditator's mind is tamed and transformed through the two meditation practices of "calming-abiding" or "stabilization" (*samatha*) and "insight" (*vipassana*).

The diagram shows a monk at the start of his meditative journey on the path to enlightenment. At first, he is shown running, attempting to lasso a stampeding black elephant on the path ahead, which is being led hither and thither by a black monkey. The monkey, which represents the distractions of the mind, moves about entranced by various objects which lie to the left and right of the path. These objects – a piece of cloth, a mirror, fruit, perfume, and cymbals – represent the five sensory entanglements of touch, sight, taste, smell and sound. The black elephant, representing the mind itself, cannot be controlled at this point, and races ahead, oblivious to the hard work of the poor monk behind. Eventually, the monk gains some control with his lasso, the elephant slows down and its color being to whiten. Eventually the monkey disappears, and the elephant now completely white, is led by the monk at his own pace. With the monk finally in full control of the elephant, and sitting on its back, he brandishes a flaming sword – representing wisdom cutting though delusions – and gains penetrative insight into the nature of emptiness.

Of note is the bright flame which sits at every turn on the monk's path. This is of particular relevance to the theme of the Strength card, representing the effort, energy and potency that must be developed and maintained in order to control, tame and lead the mind towards enlightenment. As Shantideva says: "he who is patient will seek for strength, for in strength lies Enlightenment. Without strength there is no righteous work, as without the wind there is no motion."[16] *Right Effort* constitutes one element of the *Eightfold Path*, and signifies an ongoing and persistent undertaking to develop beautiful or wholesome mental formations. Similarly, "energy" or *virya* is regarded as one of the *Six Perfections* within Mahayana Buddhism, and one of the ten within Theravada. *Virya* can also be translated as "enthusiastic perseverance" or "zeal," and is etymologically linked with such words as "vigor," "vitality," and "virtue." Its root, *vir*, actually means "hero," and therefore also denotes a sense of courage and fearlessness – the qualities with which our Hero needs to begin his or her journey.

Buddhism recognizes a number of characteristics that contribute towards the cultivation of energy and enthusiasm, perhaps the most important being that of *bodhichitta* or "mind of enlightenment." This is the conscious effort to arouse within oneself a Buddha's own compassionate perspective on things. For many, the development of bodhichitta is regarded as perhaps the most important Buddhist practice; the means by which one stimulates the emergence of all beautiful qualities, and is transformed into "the priceless jewel of a Conqueror's form."[17] According to the Buddha in *The Collection of Pure Dharma Sutra*, those who seek enlightenment have no need to pursue many disciplines, but should unify themselves through the single practice of compassion, by which all other virtues spontaneously arise.[18]

The cultivation of bodhichitta is regarded as a defining trait of the *bodhisattva* – the "enlightenment being" who aspires to become a Buddha. The *Path of the Bodhisattva* begins with the solemn *Vows of Bodhichitta*, in either aspiration (for the initiate) or engagement (for the practitioner). Such vows, reflecting the one the Future Buddha made as he left the palace, are focused on strengthening one's resolve and determination to bring the mind of enlightenment into this world, "for the sake of all beings."[19]

The Hermit (9)

General Overview

The *RWS* rendition of The Hermit shows a solitary old man in a cowled habit, looking down from his isolated and bleak vantage point on a mountain peak. His right hand holds a lantern with a light inside, and his left grasps a staff for support. The card is associated with a number of related themes, including retreat, isolation, introspection, and self-reliance; but also the quest for direction and guidance.

The card is usually linked with a withdrawal from the everyday world to search for wisdom within ourselves; of creating a space where we can, as Lorelei says, seek out answers to the dilemma of "life's purpose."[1] The withdrawal itself may be a psychological rather than a literal one; a figurative departure from the values and beliefs of the "mass mind" in the pleasant vale beneath the mountain.[2] The way of the vale, to use the words of Gardner's channeled Hermit, is the "way of safety" and leads to nothing but "age and death." [3] Whether a real of symbolic withdrawal, the Hermit according to Saunders represents an attitude of self-reliance; of turning towards our "own inner light."[4] It denotes the call and guidance of the deeper aspects of ourselves, which if heeded, promise as Waite says that "[w]here I am you also may be."[5] Yet the journey to the interior may not be as revealing as we first hoped; the world within holds as much darkness, danger and peril as it does illumination. This is a point clearly suggested in the *Thoth* deck's rendition of the card, which shows The Hermit bowed down with *Cerberus* – the guardian dog of the Underworld – at his heels.

According to Pollack and Wen, The Hermit may not only indicate a turn to the world within, but a desire for guidance from a teacher or some other external source.[6] Banzhaf disagrees, and argues that the wisdom of The Hermit never arrives from a mentor, even when we think that to be the case. It would be futile, he insists, to actually try to find some "wise old man" to experience that to which The Hermit points.[7] Nichols concurs, and also highlights the problem of projecting such power onto others. Such projection leaves one vulnerable to abandoning our personal journey to find peace at the feet of some "ready-made guru."[8] Given the possible catastrophic results of such a venture, it is perhaps wisest as the Buddha himself advised to "be ye lamps unto yourselves."

In the Story of the Buddha: The Great Retirement

With the young prince on Kanthaka's "mighty back," and with Channa holding on by the tail, the three arrive at the city's great gate, only to find it shut fast. King Suddhodana, in order to prevent his son from leaving, had "caused each of the two leaves of the gate to be made so heavy as to need a thousand men to move it." The prince, full of resolve, declares to himself that should the gate remain shut he will "leap up and carry them both with me over the wall, although its height be eighteen cubits."[9] There was however no need, as the spirit within the gate opened it for him, allowing safe passage out of the city. His horse "went forth, planting his hurrying steps at full speed," his very hooves borne up by heavenly *Yakshas*: "O best of steeds, by thy speed and energy, strive for thine own good and the good of the world."[10] At that point the demon *Mara*, the enemy of spiritual striving, appears to the prince and urges him to turn back, promising that soon he "shall rule over the four great continents." The prince however casts this promise aside with indifference, "spewing it out as if it were but phlegm," and "turned Kanthaka in the direction in which he meant to go."[11] "Till I have seen the further shore of birth and death," he shouts, "I will never again enter the city called after Kapila."[12]

The three eventually arrive at the *Anoma* or "Illustrious"; a broad river which seemed impossible to cross. Once again *Kanthaka* comes to the rescue, and "sprang over the river ... and landed on the opposite bank." Then dismounting, and standing on the sandy beach "that stretched away like a sheet of silver," Siddhattha gives his jewelry to Channa and exchanges his fine clothing for monk's robes, which had been provided for him by the Brahma-god *Ghatikara*. Grabbing his own hair, "he seized the top-knot with his left hand," and with his scimitar, he "cut it off."[13]

The prince bids Channa farewell and asks him to take his jewelry and horse back home, and tell his family that he is well. On the journey back, *Kanthaka* dies of a broken heart, and is reborn in "the Heaven of the thirty-three." Channa, now oppressed even further, "came weeping and wailing to the city."[14] The prince, unaware of these events, heads for a tranquil forest and the "hermitage of the son of Bhrigu." Then, "he who by whom all objects are accomplished," entered the hermitage.[15]

An obvious feature of this narrative is the central role played by the horse Kanthaka in the Buddha's renunciation. Of significance in this respect is Kanthaka's association with the number eighteen - his length in cubits, and also the height of the city wall that he passes through, or in some versions, leaps over. Eighteen is an auspicious number within Indian thought because it can be reduced to nine (1 + 8 = 9) – symbolic of *Brahman* (ultimate reality), and also, coincidently, the number of The Hermit. It is a number especially apparent in the *Mahabharata*, which is divided into eighteen books, of which the most important, the *Bhagavad-Gita*, is divided into eighteen chapters. The main battle of the *Mahabharata* is itself between eighteen armies and lasts for eighteen days. Of more interest is the number's association with the concept of renunciation. The ancient *Ayyappan* temple complex at *Sabarimala*, which remains an important pilgrimage site to this day, contains eighteen steps (*Pathinettam Padi*) which pilgrims must ascend in order to reach the *sanctum sanctorum* of Lord *Ayyapan*. Although sacred to Hindus, in all likelihood Sabarimala was once an ancient Buddhist temple complex, and that "Lord Ayyappa was once a Buddhist deity" – the Bodhisattva of Compassion, *Avalokitesvara*.[16] The eighteen steps are steep and narrow, and represent eighteen impediments to spiritual liberation which are renounced by devotees as they ascend. The first five represent the senses which imprison us in worldly pursuits. The next eight represent unwholesome qualities of the mind, including sensual delight, anger, greed, and delusion. The next three represent the three gunas; the seventeenth worldly knowledge, and the final step - ignorance.[17]

A Buddhist Reflection: Renunciation

The themes of The Hermit are closely linked to an important practice within Buddhism – "renunciation." Prince distinguishes between three stages of Buddhist "retirement" from the world.[18] The first stage is that of "Outward Renunciation," where someone, moved by the Dharma may decide to leave behind the household life and become a monk or a nun. This is perhaps the most "visible" aspect of Buddhist renunciation, clearly seen in the resolve of many thousands who, every year, shave their heads, exchange their possessions for simple robes and a bowl, and take upon themselves the life of a Buddhist novice. Of course, such outward displays of renunciation are not only limited to Buddhism. A decisive disengagement from society is almost taken as given within Indian spirituality as a whole, given that retreating to a forest (*vanaprastha*) and ascetic renunciation (*samyasa*) are considered the third and fourth stages of life for a committed Hindu. Such outward renunciation within Hinduism is a practice that extends back to the wandering seekers (*shramanas*) of the Buddha's time, and manifests itself today in the four to five million *sadhus* and *sadhvis* who attach themselves to the various shrines, temples, holy cities and ashrams that can be found across India.

The second stage of Buddhist disengagement according to Prince is "True Renunciation," which is really a matter of heart and mind rather than an outward withdrawal from the world. It means living an ethical life, and renouncing "desires"; of freeing the inner world from unwholesome emotions and attachments. The third and final stage is that of "Ultimate Renunciation," which is the renunciation of the "self." This involves the eradication of the "five hindrances" (sensory desire, hatred, sloth, restlessness and doubt) through mindfulness meditation. This in turn leads to the attainment of single-pointed concentration through meditative absorptions (the *jhanas*) – the starting place for "insight" and thus the realization of Nirvana.

Is it possible to attain such spiritual development without the "outward renunciation" of novice life? Although the monastic community provides the freedom and support to pursue the spiritual life away from worldly distractions, there are many examples within the Buddhist texts of lay followers attaining extraordinary spiritual achievements. Yet, the danger of a non-monastic approach is a general toning-down in the meaning and implications of true renunciation. This is already happening in countries like Thailand, where a growing middle-class are abandoning their traditional links with the monasteries, preferring Buddhist "retreats" over the customary Thai practice of temporary novicehood.

In the West, similarly, traditional renunciation has been compromised through spiritual practice accommodating itself to what many clearly perceive to be their self-evident and unalienable "freedoms." This has been particularly the case with the emergence of what David Chapman terms "Consensus Buddhism," which rejects the traditional Buddhist mechanism of "revulsion and renunciation," making the whole idea more palatable to Westerners by pretending that it means "something other" than turning our backs on worldly pleasures and attachments. The true meaning of renunciation he argues has thus become "obscured" in many Westernized forms of Buddhism.[19]

An interesting angle on this whole issue is given by Yeshe. His views are certainly more "palatable" than the option of traditional monasticism, and more positive than Chapman's conclusions. But, whether such renunciation is possible within the context of Western society is a matter which remains to be seen. Yeshe begins by explaining first what renunciation is not. It is not giving up on or avoiding difficult situations. Neither is it running away from the demands and expectations of society. Significantly, he argues, neither is it taking-up Buddhist rituals or spiritual practices such as meditation. Fundamentally, he says, it means that we no longer seek or expect lasting happiness from fleeting sensual pleasures. Renunciation, continues Yeshe, can also be considered in the more positive terms of "definite emergence"; as a concerted effort to break free from our recurring sense of dissatisfaction we experience in everyday life, and begin looking for "other ways" to make our lives fulfilling and significant. Such satisfaction, he concludes, can only be found in the relinquishing of "false refuges" for "inner simplicity."[20]

The Wheel of Fortune (10)

General Overview

The Wheel of Fortune is one of the most symbol-rich cards in the *RWS* deck. Its central image is that of a wheel, surmounted by a sphinx holding a sword over its left shoulder. The wheel's outer rim contains the letters T-A-R-O interspaced with the four Hebrew letters of the *Tetragrammaton* – God's holy name. Upon this rim we find a demonic *Typhon* in the form of a snake descending, and *Hermanubis* as a jackal-headed man ascending. The wheel's inner section contains eight "spokes," upon four of which are written the alchemical symbols for mercury, sulfur, salt and water. At the four corners of the card sit an angel/man, eagle, ox, and a lion, all with open books which they appear to be reading.

Despite such rich symbolism, the card is often interpreted quite simplistically, particularly within a divinatory context. Here, it is usually linked with changes in fortune, luck, or the ending/beginning of a cycle. A less-common interpretation is that it represents deepening knowledge and insight into the nature of the world, life and the self. In short, it is about "revelation" and "learning." This interpretation is conveyed in the four open books. It is also upheld in the card's connection with the Hebrew letter *Kaph* and its associated symbol of the "grasping hand," which as Jayanti says reaches out "understand" and "comprehend."[1] This seems a natural progression from the processes of withdrawal and contemplation initiated in The Hermit.

Although it might not look it at first, the Wheel of Fortune is actually a vehicle – a chariot in fact - making it the second chariot in our journey through the Tarot thus far. But this chariot is very different from the first, which took us out into the realm of worldly experience under the direction of will. This second chariot takes us to the realm within; to reveal hidden truth about the nature of the world and the self. This chariot is in fact the *Merkabah* – the *Chariot of God* or chariot of "descent."

In the Jewish *Tanakh*, the prophet Ezekiel experienced a revelatory vision in which he caught a glimpse of the divine presence above the firmament and its operations below. "As I looked," he says, "a strong wind came out of the north and a great cloud, with brightness round about it, and fire flashing forth continually." From its midst came four creatures with the "form of men," but each with four wings and four faces. Each had "the face of a man in front, a lion on the right side, an ox on the left, and an eagle at the back." As he continued looking, the prophet saw "a wheel upon the earth beside the living creatures, one for each of the four of them." Each wheel was constructed as "a wheel within a wheel." Each had spokes and a rim, which were "full of eyes round about." Wherever the creatures went, "the wheels went beside them," for "the spirit of the living creatures was in the wheels." Above the four *Cherubim* and their "whirling wheels" Ezekiel saw the "likeness of a firmament," and above this was a throne, upon which was seated "a likeness as it were of a human form" – the "appearance of the likeness of the glory of the LORD" (From *Ezek.* 1: 4-28).

In this biblical passage, Ezekiel is offered a glimpse into both the divine presence above the firmament and its operations below, revealed in the whirling elemental forces that turn the world and direct its motion. The prophet's revelatory vision became the basis for a school of early Jewish thought known as *Merkabah* mysticism, focused on the experience of the soul's journey or "descent" into God by way of his holy chariot. Such visionary experiences would be embraced and enhanced by the Kabbalistic schools of the middle ages, which, according to Kauffman Kohler, provided "new life and vigor" to existing Merkabah teachings.[2]

Yet we should recognize that most of Ezekiel's vision was concerned with God's operation within nature itself; that is, "below" the firmament. Insight into the operations of the phenomenal world seems particularly relevant to The Wheel of Fortune's meaning, implied in Waite's inclusion of the four letter word T-A-R-O. Waite's use of this term is undoubtedly based upon Eliphas Levi's anagramatical speculations, which, by his own time, had resulted in the mysterious *ROTA TARO ORAT TORA ATOR*. This is often translated as: "The wheel of Tarot speaks the law of *Hathor* [Ator]." Hathor was an ancient Egyptian earth goddess, symbolizing the phenomenal world in both its beneficent and destructive capacities; as, on the one hand, the *Celestial Nurse*, and on the other, as the devouring lion, *Sekhmet*.

While addressing the topic of deepening insight into the world's operations, the Wheel of Fortune does at the same time deal with the question of self-knowledge. First seen in The Chariot, the sphinx makes its appearance once more, this time atop of the wheel, to again ask its riddle: "What is the creature that walks on four legs in the morning, two legs at noon and three in the evening?" In The Chariot card, as Waite says, the individual can "offer no answer" to the sphinx's riddle, because it is "concerned with a mystery of Nature," while the heroic charioteer is really only concerned with conquests which are "manifest or external and not within himself." Neither, continues Waite, could he "open the scroll call Tora," nor if questioned by the High Priestess, "could he answer."[3] The answer to the sphinx's riddle is not simply "humanity," but the deeper revelation that "humanity" is essentially a process of constant change, and is neither fixed nor static in nature. The physical changes brought about through birth, youth, old age and death are an obvious aspect of this. Yet, the revelation of the card is that despite their physical limitations, humans have the potential for positive inner development and transformation. This revelation is glimpsed in the four alchemical glyphs at the wheel's center, which as Jayanti argues, suggest the ambitious objective of "esoteric alchemy" – the transformation of "ordinary people" or "ordinary elements" into "enlightened beings."[4] Humans may harbor destructive *typhonic* tendencies which can move them away from their potential. Yet, they also hold within themselves the ability to move towards something more positive, symbolized by *Hermanubis*, the rising *psychopomp*. This positive transformation requires patience, reflection, energy and insight, symbolized by the four creatures and their open books – the four elements in transition. These books will remain open until the creatures appear without them, their transformation complete, in The World.

In the Story of the Buddha: Arada and Udraka

King Suddhodana, according to Asvaghosa, learns of his son's departure, and quickly sends his own minister and family priest to the hermitage; but to no avail. The prince crosses the Ganges and "went to Ragagriha with its beautiful palaces." Like his father, the monarch there attempts to dissuade Siddhattha from his path, and instead pursue the "three objects of life" – "religious merit, wealth and pleasure" - in "reverse order." For, says the king, "pleasures belong to the young man, wealth to the middle-aged, and religion to the old."[5]

The prince is again unmoved, and turns towards "the hermitage of the sage Arada," "kinsman of Kalama." (*Alara Kalama* in the *Jataka* text.) Upon their meeting, the sage remarks that the prince looks as one "longing to see who finds a light, – like one wishing to journey, a guide, - or like one wishing to cross, a boat." The prince, eager to learn, implores the sage to "tell me that secret ... whereby thy servant may be delivered from old age, death and disease." The shramana agrees to be his teacher, and to announce "the tenets of his doctrine."[6]

Under his tutelage, the prince gains much insight into "the nature of things." He learns of the roles of desire, ignorance and karma in "the causes of mundane existence," and of the pointlessness of either "sprinkling water upon sacrifices" or reciting "Vedic hymns." He also learns about the existence of the *jhanas* (meditative states) of form and formlessness, which, according to Arada, result in the ultimate realization of "that supreme Brahman ... which the wise who know reality declare to be liberation."[7]

Siddhattha learns and practices Arada's teachings, but at the end of the process is still not satisfied. He comes to the conclusion that this realization cannot be "ultimate," "because it does not teach us how to abandon this soul itself in the various bodies," and the individual is thus "still subject to the condition of birth and has the condition of a seed."[8] He therefore abandons Arada and looks for another teacher.

The prince eventually finds the "hermitage of Udraka" (*Udaka Ramaputta*), and from this second sage learns of other jhanic states, but still "gained no clear understanding from his treatment of the soul." Siddhattha realizes that in the teachings of Udraka, we still have the problem of some form of "self."[9] Udraka, said the Buddha much later in his career, provided a practice which did not lead to either wisdom or Nirvana, but only to the subtle Samsaric state of "neither perception nor yet non-perception."[10]

A Buddhist Reflection: The Wheel of Becoming
The Wheel of Fortune invites some obvious but interesting comparisons with the Buddhist *Wheel of Becoming* (*Bhavachakra*). The Buddhist wheel is a pictorial teaching aid to cyclic existence. "Picture" however is not strictly accurate. It is often conceived of as a mirror which *Yama*, God of impermanence and death, holds aloft to each individual; and, like the sphinx atop The Wheel of Fortune, asks: "Do you know who you are?"

The outer rim of the wheel contains the twelve links of "dependent origination" which condition the constant cycle of rebirth experienced by those living in Samsara. At its center we find the three defilements (greed, hatred and delusion) which perpetuate the wheel's energy and motion. The main area of the wheel shows the *Six Realms of Existence*, within which all Samsaric beings live in relation to their karmic formations.

The most unfortunate realms are the three "lower" ones – the Animal, Hungry Ghost, and Hell realms. Rebirth here is linked respectively to the mental states of ignorance, greed, and anger. The most "fortunate" realms in terms of environment and potential are the "upper" worlds of Humans, Demi-Gods (*Asuras*) and Gods (*Devas*), conditioned by the corresponding mental states of desire, envy and pride. The *Asura* realm is sometimes conflated with the *Deva*, or even viewed as a lower realm, given its negative associations with envy and other unskillful mental qualities. The Human realm is linked with desire and is characterized by the vicissitudes of everyday human existence; but also with the potential for much growth and development. The *Deva* realm is linked with pride, and is reserved for those who have generated enough positive karmic qualities to create a temporary life of divine pleasure and ease. The Deva realm actually consists of six levels of increasing refinement, from the *Devas of the Four Great Kings* to the *Devas wielding Power over the Creations of Others* - the abode of *Mara*, the personification of delusion and desire. The six realms up to Mara's abode constitute the sphere of *kamaloka* – the *Desire Realm*.

Yet, these eleven realms in total do not encapsulate the totality of Samsaric states. The Deva realm can be extended further into the sixteen realms of "form" (*rupaloka*) and the further four realms of "formlessness" (*arupaloka*). These subtle states of existence are reserved for those who have attained extremely advanced levels of meditative awareness, known collectively as the jhanas.

Yet, even these subtle regions are all still part of conditioned Samsaric states, and together with the lower realms comprise what Buddhists term the *Thirty-One Paths of Rebirth*.

As in The Wheel of Fortune, Samsaric beings can move through any of these states in any direction. (Except certain higher states of formlessness after death.) This is symbolized by two illustrations, one on either side of the central hub. The illustration on the right of the hub recalls Smith's depiction of Typhon, and shows humans being dragged down by demons towards the lower realms. The illustration of the left shows beings emerging from Hell on a ladder, and like Hermanubis, ascending upwards. The ascent here is provided by the power of the Buddha, who stands preaching the Dharma; and, like Hermanubis the psychopomp, leads beings towards more favorable conditions of existence. The possibility of alchemical transformation is in fact available in all six desire realms, indicated by a Buddha, who appears in each world to teach its residents the relevant qualities needed to generate spiritual development. The Buddha attached to the Animal realm for example holds a book, indicating the necessity for developing reason and reflection to escape the world of base instincts and ignorance. Yet, of all the realms, it is the Human one which is regarded as the most fortunate to be reborn into; its residents are neither overwhelmed by the tortures and agonies of the lower worlds, nor intoxicated into complacency by the pleasures of the Deva realm.

Some Buddhists understand these realms to be literal places, while others adopt a more psychological interpretation.[11] Many for example view the realms as modes of being, or conditioned patterns of thought and action. Thus, if someone's mindscape is dominated by endless greed and craving, they could be said to be living the life of a Hungry Ghost. Similarly, the realm of the Asuras represents those whose thoughts and deeds are conditioned by habits of envy and competitive striving.

In some depictions of the Bhavachakra, we find a Buddha outside the wheel, pointing to the moon, indicting that escape from Samsaric existence is possible; that enlightenment or Nirvana can be a reality for any that make the required effort. However, this does not mean that Nirvana lies "outside" Samsara. Nirvana, as discussed previously, means removing "wrong perceptions" - the veil of maya that prevents us from perceiving the world as it really is. Howard and Battersby concur, and point out that this is the reason why the *Path of Perfections*– which is revealed extending from Hell to the limits of the Deva realm - is "shown within the Wheel of Life and not outside it."[12]

Justice (11)

General Overview

The central image of the *RWS* Justice card is that of *Titaness Themis*, Greek goddess of Divine Law, social order and custom. Her name is often interpreted as meaning "that which is put in place," derived from *tithemi* – "to put." As with the sphinx in The Wheel of Fortune, Justice here is shown holding a sword aloft, suggesting a continuation and development of the wisdom, insight and understanding begun in the previous card. The sword, as in the sword of *Manjusri* found in Buddhist iconography, or even in the story of King Solomon's judgement over the disputed infant (*I Kings* 3: 16-28), represents penetrative wisdom, cutting away fiction from fact, delusion from truth. Indeed, there are obvious connections between this card and the wisdom theme of The High Priestess, shown by the two pillars that Justice herself sits between, and by the fact that the numerical value of this card can be reduced to that of two (11 = 1+1 = 2).[1]

Waite's switching of Justice from its traditional placement (8) indicates an important insight that he is perhaps not given much credit for; and this is that the spiritual quiescence of the previous two cards demand what Pollack calls an "active response."[2] Within the full spectrum of possibility, the central danger of both The Wheel of Fortune and The Hermit is that of withdrawal and otherworldliness; a Gnostic renunciation of society and the world; one which finds perfect expression in the Christian classic *The Imitation of Christ* by Thomas à Kempis, who said: "Keep thyself as a stranger and a pilgrim upon the earth, to whom the things of the world appertain not ... for here have we no continuing city."[3] The legacy of such dualistic thinking is still evident today, where "spirituality" is often viewed as overextending its remit when it dares to engage with the "real" world of politics, economics and consumerist ethics. As the Brazilian Liberation Theologian Helder Camara was once reported to have remarked: "When I feed the poor, they call me a saint. When I ask why they are poor, they call me a communist."

Unfortunately, much in the Tarot world remains anchored to this dualistic perspective, especially when the interpretation of Justice becomes internalized and psychologized. Many tarot books seem content to simply paraphrase or reiterate Cirlot's contention that Justice is not really concerned with "external justice" but with "inner judgement."[4] Despite its *penchant* for all things "holistic," the Tarot world appears reluctant to move much beyond the individualistic assumptions of New Age "transformation-lite."

There are of course exceptions. Pollack for example points out that Justice assumes the "as above, so below" posture of The Magician, indicating the application of wisdom as action in the material world.[5] Likewise, Jayanti equates the card's "uplifted sword" with the extension of divine justice into the everyday world of inequality and discrimination. This is confirmed says Jayanti with the appearance of the square (matter) on Justice's crown (*Kether*), indicating the manifestation of the divine will within "our everyday world."[6]

It is precisely the summons and challenge of Justice to move beyond a quietist understanding of spirituality; to venture outside our Gnostic bubbles of inner illumination and outer complacency, and rise to the challenge of a much greater vision of transformation. Contrary to à Kempis, a true "imitation of Christ" requires at times engagement and perhaps confrontation with an unjust world; with its "principalities and powers" (*Eph.* 6: 12). As Jesus says: "Do not think I have come to bring peace on earth; I have not come to bring peace, but a sword" (*Matt.* 10: 34). Jesus' allusion to the sword of Justice is of course not a call to armed militancy, but a reiteration of the primary task of the prophet – that of "interference."[7] In relation to this, the *Gospel of Luke* reminds us that immediately following his own hermit-like withdrawal into the wilderness, Jesus returned to his own synagogue, opened the scroll of Isaiah, and declared:

> "The Spirit of the Lord is upon me, because he has anointed me to preach good news to the poor. He has sent me to proclaim release to the captives and recovering of sight to the blind, to set at liberty those who are oppressed, to proclaim the acceptable year of the Lord" (*Lk.* 4: 18-19).

In *Luke's* Gospel, this call to interference appears at the commencement of Jesus' mission, indicating its foundational role. Moreover, it indicates that "justice" is not simply an issue of "fairness," but of liberation from oppression; a demand for freedom, dignity, and the availability of human flourishing. For Jesus, such flourishing, such self-realization, is not only something we should seek to confer on others through engagement and self-sacrifice, but something we ourselves only achieve in the process of doing so. True self-realization is found in the "emptying" (*kenosis*) of the self. In Jesus' enigmatic words: "whoever seeks to gain his life will lose it, but whoever loses his life will preserve it" (*Lk.* 17: 33).

Authentic spirituality, authentic self-realization, requires a balance between contemplation and action, and a greater vision of "transformation." This vision begins with reflection upon the underlying nature of things (The Wheel of Fortune), which leads to the realization that Justice is embedded within the fabric of the world itself. From a truly holistic perspective, injustice is not simply a matter of social inequality, but a rupture in the order of creation, and therefore as Mathew Fox says "a cosmic issue."[8] Authentic spiritually thus moves towards a position of responsibility – not just for one's own personal development – but for *tikkun olam* – the "repairing" of the world, by means of an eventual "Great Return."

In the Buddha's Story: The Rejection of Quietism

Eventually the prince, unconvinced with Udraka's teachings, decides to leave him and strike out on his own. The texts refrain from providing the precise reasons why Siddhattha left the two sages, other than that their teachings still contained a residual element of the self, and thus did not lead to "supreme wisdom" and "Nirvana." As the prince declared to his teachers:

> "How much confusion of thought comes from our interest in self, and from our vanity when thinking 'I am so great,' or 'I have done this wonderful deed?' The thought of thine ego stands between thy rational nature and truth; banish it, and then wilt thou see things as they are. He who thinks correctly

will rid himself of ignorance and acquire wisdom. The ideas 'I am' and 'I shall be' or 'I shall not be' do not occur to a clear thinker ...

"I observe the preservation and transmission of character; I perceive the truth of karma, but see no atman whom your doctrine makes the doer of your deeds. There is rebirth without the transmigration of a self. For this atman, this self, this ego in the 'I say' and in the 'I will' is an illusion."[9]

An interesting angle on this part of the journey is offered by Daisaku Ikeda, who argues that it was really a lack of social engagement within his mentors' teachings which motivated the Buddha's departure. The two teachers, like many other yogic masters of India both past and present, were too intensely caught up in their endeavors to attain liberation from Samsaric existence that they had ignored "the problems of society." It seems quite natural, says Ikeda, that Siddhattha would initially have been attracted to their yogic techniques, but that eventually, the states they made available were below the concerns and aims "of the bodhisattva." For the two sages, jhanic realization had become "an end in itself." The real object of Siddhattha's quest, continues Ikeda, was not personal liberation, but a form of awakening that would "set humanity free" from the sufferings of Samsara. Personal liberation from attachment attained through *jhanic* meditation was only one aspect of emancipation; and thus he parted ways with his teachers, and tried another approach – the way of the ascetic.[10]

A Buddhist Reflection: Global Consumerism and Wisdom as Refusal

In relation to Buddhism it may be tempting to link the theme of Justice to the concept of karma. Indeed, there are no shortages of Tarot books that appear to do just that.[11] Karma is a useful concept. It allows us to reflect upon how our current mindscapes have been conditioned by past thoughts and actions, and how this invariably affects our engagement with the world. Karma also invites us to see how the social structures we create reflect internal perceptions of ourselves and others. Yet, to link the meaning of karma to merely "retributive comeuppance," as many seem to do, is misleading in terms of how Buddhism relates to justice. First, because karma is a natural law that has nothing to do with our subjective notions of "fairness." Second, because it may actually promote injustice – resignation and self-blame on the part of the "victim," and complacency and self-righteousness on the part of the fortunate. A more profitable approach is to examine how Buddhist relates to justice at the level of "interference" – something we have already considered in Buddhism's attitude to the caste-varna system.

Perhaps the greatest contemporary challenge to justice, to the "repairing of the world," is the ideology of global consumerism, with its attendant exploitation and devastation of both natural and human resources. The summons of Justice first invites us to analyze precisely why this ideology, which on the surface seems to promise so much in terms of freedom, flourishing and well-being, actually promotes enslavement and oppression. It then calls us to action that will liberate both ourselves and the world from its pernicious and pervasive grip.

In her insightful paper "How Much is Enough?," Stephanie Kaza highlights three points at which Buddhist wisdom can open our eyes to the spiritual dangers and injustices of consumerism, and how these can be addressed through practical action.[12] In this movement from reflection to action, Kaza's model of Buddhist engagement conforms to what Nelson Foster refers to as the "implicit politics of prajna" – the view that Buddhist wisdom, meditation and reflection will naturally lead to the establishment of ethical and wholesome behaviour in the "politics" of everyday life.[13]

Kaza's first point is that consumerism makes possible the development of a false sense of self. This is an invaluable observation, given that Buddhist compassion is grounded in the elimination of the illusion of ego and an emerging sense of identification with others. The accumulation of material possessions tends to create and reinforce a sense of permanence and individuality. Our possessions are the means by which we create, maintain and delineate our "self" from other "selves" – my car, my house, my music collection. Of course, the realties of impermanence mean that one possession is never enough to satiate our eventual sense of unsatisfactoriness. Thus consumerism generates not only an erroneous sense of self, but one that needs to be constantly propped up with an endless procession of "self-reinforcing possessions." As a corrective to this delusional cycle, Kaza advises the adoption of the Buddhist principle of *santutthi* – contentment and satisfaction with what one has. At a practical level, this may be achieved through practicing simplicity in our lifestyles and restraint in our consumption habits.[14]

The second point is that consumerism "promotes harm to other living beings." The bulk of the goods we acquire are linked with much destruction and loss, whether in the natural world, or through the incapacitating conditions and harmful behaviors experienced by the poor in the factories and sweatshops of the world. As a corrective, Kaza draws our attention to the five basic ethical precepts of Buddhism, and in particular, the prohibition against harming or taking life. At a practical level, this may involve greater mindfulness over the choices we make as consumers, whether it is in adopting a vegetarian or vegan lifestyle, or only acquiring green or fairly-traded goods. At a more committed level of interference, it may mean taking governments and companies to task over their harmful production operations.[15]

Finally, as Kaza argues, consumerism creates desires and attachments, and indeed, cannot exist without them. From a Buddhist point of view, consumer advertising is specifically designed to engage us at the moment it connects with our senses, and generate pleasant sensations which in turn create an endless cycle of craving and grasping. Advertising transforms beings capable of "The Beautiful" into deluded consumers wandering through an ocean of Samsaric dissatisfaction in search of "satiety." As a corrective, Kaza advises that we become more mindful of how consumer advertising manipulates us at the point of sensory contact. At a practical level, ethical responses may include making a conscious effort to reduce the level of advertising we allow ourselves and our families to consume, or making efforts towards the development of alternatives to those wasted hours we spend shopping, whether online or in retail parks.[16]

Kaza's suggestions indicate that "interference" or active wisdom need not entail an all-out war against the "evils of capitalism," but instead, mindful boycotting – a refusal to implicate our lives in systems which reinforce self, attachments, cravings, and harm towards others. This also correlates to what Christian Feldman terms "discriminating wisdom," which recognizes that true wisdom moves beyond mere intellectual insight to embrace a refusal to support or maintain actions that generate "suffering, division, and conflict."[17] Such "discriminating wisdom" appears to engage more fully with the ethical implications of the Justice card than the typical recourse to often distorted concepts of karma, which as Donald Rothberg says, appear in "fatalistic" guises, serving to both "blame the victims" and rationalize arrangements of "power and dominance."[18]

The Hanged Man (12)

General Overview

To set at liberty those who are oppressed; to participate in the repairing of the world. This is the call and the challenge of Justice. But, of course, it is easier said than done. This call demands interference with psychological and social forces that are very resistant to change. Thus, The Hanged Man stands as a pertinent symbol of the cost that may be incurred by those who seek to engage with the "principalities and powers" than reside both within and without.

The Hanged Man shows a man suspended upside down from a Tau cross of living trees. His hands appear to be placed behind his back, perhaps bound, suggesting that he has been positioned here by others. Despite this, his facial expression is without pain, and instead radiates a sense of relaxed focus, further suggested by the beatific corona that surrounds his head. His legs form a figure four, the number of solidity and matter; the same position assumed by the seated Emperor in the *Marseilles* deck, and the inversed form of that assumed by the World Dancer in card 21.

In traditional interpretations, The Hanged Man is associated with a number of related ideas, especially those of abandonment, sacrifice, suffering, punishment and surrender. Alongside these we find more positive themes, such as the gaining of insight and wisdom, and those of rebirth, renewal and regeneration.

The card indicates The Fool's dawning realization that true spiritual progress – the transformation of self and world – cannot be attained through spiritual quietism, but only through a very different route. This route involves direct confrontation with oppositional forces that lie within oneself and within the recognized orders of the world. One message of The Hanged Man is that suffering cannot be beaten by simply attempting to transcend it, but only by immersing oneself in it. And here, the Western image of Christ crucified appears as a potent symbol of immersive *kenosis*, of "self-emptying" in response to the anguish of the world. A further message seems to be a cautionary gesture on behalf of THE ESTABLISHMENT. As in the age-old practice of hanging criminals and traitors at crossroads, this card serves as a clear warning to those who would challenge and transgress the accepted parameters of Urizen's directives – whether psychological, religious or social. "The Traitor" indeed was at one time the actual name for this card; and again, Christ crucified below his criminal *titulus* remains a powerful symbol of such punitive retribution, laid upon those who would dare meddle with the established powers that be. Unfortunately, for Christians beguiled by two-millennia of Fall-Redemption mythology, the crucifixion has come to symbolize and reflect their own paralysis and powerlessness to change either themselves or the world; a knee-bending dependence upon the atoning grace of a wrathful sky-father and his sinless scapegoat. For those with stronger knees – like Oscar Romero, Martin Luther King and Jesus himself - it reminds us of the price that might be paid for wresting the world from the hands of the devil. Such continuous crucifixions are souvenirs of what Fox calls the establishment's "Great Refusal" of "mutuality in relation," the defining feature of Jesus' approach to the world.[1]

Yet, the third message of The Hanged Man is that death and despair do not have the final say. Self-surrender, sacrifice and apparent defeat carry within themselves the seeds of wisdom and regeneration. One is reminded of the myth of Odin, who hung for nine days on the World Tree and received as his boon the wisdom and power of the runes. In Celtic lore we find the myth of the sacrificial king, whose spilled blood will restore the land. Such restoration is integral to the card's symbolism. It is not only implied in the victim's serene expression, or in the living foliage, but by the fact that when this card (12) is placed under The World (21), it forms a complete ankh – the symbol of life. The patriarchal King of Kings, the enthroned Emperor, has started to relinquish his grip on the ankh, and awaits his final transformation as World Dancer.

"By his stripes we are healed" declares Isaiah, in reference to the work of God's *Suffering Servant*. Yet the healing here means more than blood-atonement for transgressing Urizen's *Book of Brass*. It points to a complete re-envisioning of the relationship between God and the world; the healing of a deep wound in our perceptions of the divine. This is brought out with some force by Ruether in her *midrash* on the crucifixion, entitled *The Kenosis of the Father*. Like Blake and Hegel, Ruether sees in Jesus' death the moment of *ultimate kenosis*; the emptying of divinity itself from the Heavens into the hearts of men and women. Through the eyes of Mary Magdalene, Ruether invites us to imagine the scene of the crucifixion, where Jesus calls out to his father, but receives no reply. Perhaps, reflects Mary, there are no heavenly hosts left and God's throne itself is empty. Perhaps this very notion of God as an almighty king has been ended through Jesus' death, and that God himself has now been poured out upon the earth, giving birth to a new vision of the divine within our hearts. This is a vision teaching us to honor the only world we have, and create a new order "without masters and slaves." Yet, with sadness she reflects that although Jesus may have leveled the heavens and emptied God's throne, many of the disciples were "busy trying to fill it again."[2]

In the Story of the Buddha: Surrendering to Asceticism

After leaving Arada and Udraka, Siddhattha fixed a lonely dwelling by the banks of the *Nairanjana* river, whereupon he was visited by five ascetics, "desiring liberation." Led by their example, he began years of intense physical and mental self-mortification, thinking that "this may be the means of abolishing birth and death."[3] He engaged in various practices – including teeth-clenching and breath-suppression – to restrain and compress his mind. In doing so, he felt the "roar of winds" in his ear-holes, as from a smith's bellows.[4] He dwelt in dark and dangerous parts of the forest, and would sleep in charnel sites with bones for a pillow.[5]

At the end of many years he sat there, says Asvaghosa, with "only skin and bone remaining, with his fat, flesh and blood entirely wasted."[6] His body, according to the *Jataka* account, "became emaciated to the last degree ... and became black."[7] According to the Buddha himself, his ribs stuck out like the "crazy rafters" of an old barn, and the skin of his belly was fixed to his backbone.[8] Yet, despite all his efforts, Siddhattha seemed no closer to fulfilling the *bodhisattva* vow he made when he first left the palace – to "save the world of gods and men."

A Buddhist Reflection: The Sacrifice of Thich Quang Duc

During a hot June afternoon in Saigon in 1963, a "peaceful protest" against the Vietnam conflict and the oppressive religious measures of President Ngo Dinh Diem culminated in the self-immolation of the seventy-three-year-old monk Thich Quang Duc. According to sources, Quang Duc sat himself in the lotus position, while a nearby monk poured a five-gallon can of gasoline over him. Quang Duc then opened a book of matches, and set himself alight. During the ten minutes that it took for his burning body to collapse, the monk sat with a serene expression on his face, fixed in a state of meditative contemplation. Even as he burned, says David Halberstam, an American journalist who was present at the scene, he never moved or made a sound, his outward poise "in sharp contrast to the wailing people around him."[9] That this incident was greeted with horrified incomprehension by the Western media is not difficult to understand. From a Western viewpoint, such a violent act seems defeatist, wasteful, and contrary to any notion of a "peaceful protest."

Quang Duc's sacrifice can be related to the view that true social transformation must begin with the conquering of the self and our fear of death. Yet, Quang Duc's actions convey more than an inner victory over the self. His sacrifice was at heart rooted in compassion motivated by identification with the plight of the Vietnamese people. Such compassionate identification has a long history within Buddhism. One of the best loved stories from the *Jataka* accounts of the Buddha's many past lives tells of a prince called *Mahasattva*, who offered up his own body to feed a hungry tigress and her seven starving cubs. More than an act of "pity," which is rooted in the egoic notion of "helping others," this act was a product of identification – Mahasattva was the tigress, and the tigress was Mahasattva.

From a bodhisattva point of view, the aim of such self-sacrifice is the enlightenment of others; or at least, the engine of positive change in others. It is the seed from which personal and social renewal are made possible. As Thich Nhat Hahn says of Quang Duc, his death was a demonstration of his readiness to suffer to enlighten others, and in the process, he stirred a whole population. His sacrifice says Hahn, which in spirit was the same as Jesus' crucifixion, "lit a fire in the hearts of people around the world."[10]

Quang Duc's death helped change public opinion against the American-backed South Vietnamese government and its war against the communist supported Viet Cong. It also contributed to the overthrow of the Diem regime in South Vietnam in November of 1963. Of equal importance, it was responsible for the further spread of "engaged Buddhism," which continues to this day.

Death (13)

General Overview

The *RWS* version of this card shows Death in black armor, riding a white horse. In his left hand he carries a black flag decorated with a white rose. He moves through a field in which we see a dead king, a praying bishop, a despairing woman and a curious child – indicating as Pollack says the essential "democracy of death."[1] In the background, we can see the sun just rising between two pillars. The pillars remind us of those contained in The High Priestess, The Hierophant and Justice, and will appear again, much more closely, in The Moon. Likewise, the sun will appear in many of the subsequent cards, rising further up in the sky, representing revitalization and rebirth. A river also flows through the card, symbolizing perhaps the themes of change and passing time. A vessel, evocative of the funerary boats used for Egyptian Pharaohs, moves eastward, towards the rising sun. The number thirteen has of course a long association with darkness and death, being the number of those at the Last Supper when Jesus was betrayed. Jesus described that night as the "hour of darkness" when he pleaded with his father to "let this cup pass" (*Lk.* 22: 53, 42).

Although inseparable from the themes of sacrifice and rebirth found in the previous card, Death in the Tarot stands as something unique, pivotal, impenetrable; and yet at the same time something mundanely human. In truth, the unavoidable reality of death stands at the heart of all human spirituality, and of course, remains forever the central reference point in issues relating to the meaningfulness of our own lives. In a very real sense, much hinges on how we interpret and respond to this card. The existential dilemma posed by death was eloquently voiced by Tolstoy more than a century ago:

> [A]ll around me I had what is considered complete good fortune. I had a good wife who loved me and whom I loved, good children, and a large estate ... I was respected by my relations and acquaintances more than at any previous time. I was praised by others and without much self-deception could consider that my name was famous ... [Yet] I could give no reasonable meaning to any single action or to my whole life ... Today or tomorrow sickness and death will come (they had come already) to those I love or to me; nothing will remain but stench and worms. Sooner or later my affairs, whatever they may be, will be forgotten, and I shall not exist. Then why go on making any effort? ... How can man fail to see this? And how go on living?[2]

Tolstoy's solution to his existential dilemma was to become a Christian, and his choice of religion does in a sense explain the retrospective pessimism that pervades the passage above. Traditional Christian thought concerning death is generally negative in character. In part, this derives from the influence of Platonism, which considers this world of "stench and worms" to be but a distorted image of a more enduring and perfect order of existence. Yet the negativity is also derived from the view that death is an "error" in God's creation, brought about by the Fall of our first parents, and rectified through Christ's atoning sacrifice and resurrection. Death in traditional Christian thought is the "enemy" that has been "beaten" through the resurrection, and awaits its final vanquishment with the establishment of God's future kingdom, where it will be tossed, alongside Hades, into "the lake of fire" (*Rev.* 20: 14).

A century after Tolstoy, it seems that a few Christians have adopted a more conciliatory attitude towards this oldest of bogeymen. For Don Cupitt and the *Sea of Faith Network*, a Christianity fit for the Twenty-First Century must confine itself to the reality of human finitude. There can be no more vain promises of "jam tomorrow." Indeed, the unproductive belief in an afterlife beyond death robs our present life of its profound meaning and purpose, relegating it to some kind of basic training ordeal completed in preparation for "the real thing." Ironically, an acceptance of finitude and death frees us to act more ethically, more productively, because it makes everything we do intensely significant. The hope of Christianity says Cupitt is not to transcend death, but to transcend the fear of death - the feared demise of the personal ego - and in doing so, enter "glory" and "eternal life." Like Jesus, who compared eternal life to the manner in which flowers and birds live, we too, says Cupitt, must immerse ourselves in the present, in natural harmony with our "pure contingency." In doing so, [d]eath's sting is drawn."[3]

In the Story of the Buddha: At the Point of Death

According to the *Jataka* account, nearing the end of his ascetic endeavors, Gotama was in a meditative trance practicing the "discipline of suppressed breathing." Suddenly, he "was attacked by violent pains, and fell senseless to the ground." A few of the deities who were present travelled to King Suddhodana to inform him that his son was dead, and that he met his end before gaining enlightenment. The king, recalling his son's childhood deeds, simply could not believe the report, insisting that "[d]eath cannot come to my son before he attains to enlightenment." Eventually the Future Buddha regained consciousness, at which point the deities returned once more to the king and informed him that his son was still alive. "I knew that my son could not have died," replied the relieved king.[4]

However, its is clear that Gotama recognized that he was very close to death, and had still not attained the enlightenment he was looking for. In one version of the story, the demon *Mara* approaches the Future Buddha, warning him that a "thousandth part of thee (is the property) of death, (only) one part (belongs to) life." Mara demands that he desist from his endeavors, and live the holy life by doing "good works." In response the Future Buddha declares that he would rather die than give up the quest for enlightenment.[5] Yet, after many years of mortification, Gotama began to realize that it was all "time spend in endeavoring to tie the air in knots," and thus came to a simple and obvious conclusion: "These austerities are not the way to enlightenment."[6]

A Buddhist Reflection: Death as Transformation
In the *Heart Sutra*, the bodhisattva Avalokitesvara makes this particularly enigmatic proclamation: "There is no decay and death, and no end to decay and death." Such a paradoxical assertion derives from a distinction Buddhists make between relative and absolute truth. At the level of relative truth, that is to say, of everyday Samsaric consciousness, suffering and death are inevitable facts of life that exert a profound influence over

us. So much so, that the Buddha named "decay and death" as causal factors in the universal human experience of unsatisfactoriness and suffering (the *First Noble Truth*), and the twelfth link in the chain of dependant origination. In the *Dhammapada*, the Buddha simply observed that "all men fear death."[7] Penetration into the nature of death is therefore of much value within Buddhist practice. In the *Setting Up of Mindfulness Sutta*, "death" is utilized as a meditational tool for the development of insight and wisdom into the human condition. Similarly, the *Path of Purity* invites practitioners to attentively contemplate the various stages of decomposing corpses. Through further study of the various factors surrounding death, including its inevitability and its unpredictability, meditators are granted insights that, as Chand Sirimanne says, lift the shroud of delusions surrounding permanence and our notions of an abiding self; something which may then lead to liberation.[8]

At the absolute level of truth however, "death" begins to lose much of its apparent substance and brute finality. To begin with, if, as Buddhists insist, the ego or self is a delusional construct, a habit of mind rooted in ignorance and craving, then it cannot be said that any "person" actually experiences death. Second, if it is true that there is nothing outside change and impermanence, then death in fact reveals itself to an inherent aspect of that process, rather than something that stands apart in its own right, like some scary bogeyman on a horse. It is therefore more accurate to talk of change and transformation - of phenomena "rolling on" - rather than making a sharp distinction between life and death. In this sense, death reveals itself to be but one instance of change in a constant stream of change. As Thich Nhat Hahn explains in relation to the "death" of a cloud: a cloud will change into rain, and then into grass, and then into cow's milk, and then into an ice-cream. In truth, there is no "birth date" and no "death date" for a cloud; or indeed, anything at all.[9] Our "lives" do not end with the physical destruction of the body. We move on through our children, most obviously. But at a more subtle level, our simple acts of compassion, or even words of kindness, reverberate down through time as our enduring legacy.

Conversely, we could say that "death" is a constant process that occurs every minute, every day. We are in a sense constantly "dying." If we look upon a photograph, or bring forth memories of ourselves from ten or twenty years ago, we can, if we are honest, understand that that person has in many ways "died." But from a Buddhist perspective, the person from a few seconds ago has also "died" in much the same way. We have "rolled on," whether in the many thousands of cells that have decayed and been replaced, or through other subtle changes in mind and body. Such reflections do of course make sense at an intellectual level – but why is it that we do not feel that we have "died," or that we are constantly changing?

This is a question given some consideration by the monk Nagasena in *The Questions of King Milinda*. First of all, Nagasena asks the king if he is the same person as he was when he was a "tender, weakly infant" lying on his back. "No," replies the king. But, continues Nagasena, does that mean that we have new mothers every once in a while, or that a student is not the same as the one who finishes his or her studies, or that someone who commits a crime is not the same as the one being punished? Again the king replies in the negative, and asks Nagasena for a solution to this dilemma. The monk's answer is that we are neither the same from moment to moment, yet neither are we entirely different. Instead there are elements of continuity and coherence within change which generate the impression of permanence. Nagasena uses the example of a candle burning through the night to explain this important insight to the confused king. The candle that burns in the middle of the night is not the same as it was when first lit, but neither is it different. Without the first light, there would be no light in the middle of the night. In the same way, counsels Nagasena,

> the elements of being join one another in serial succession: one element perishes, another arise, succeeding each other as it were instantaneously. Therefore neither as the same nor as a different person do you arrive at your latest aggregation of consciousness.[10]

Why then do we not feel this? Our errors about change arise when we grasp at and cling to elements of continuity – same name, parents, memories – and use them to construct some notion of a permanent fixed identity that seems to stand outside the constant change that pervades it. This, invariably, leads to wrong perceptions concerning the relationship between life and death, and thereon to fear, clinging, unsatisfactoriness, and suffering.

Temperance (14)

General Overview

Temperance is one of the cardinal virtues found in most modern Tarot decks, the other two being Strength (Courage) and Justice. Early Tarot decks contained all four (such as *The Tarocchi of Mantegna*), along with the three revealed virtues of Faith, Hope and Charity. The missing virtue is Prudence, although it has been argued that this virtue remains or is implied in other cards, such as The Hermit.

In the *RWS* deck Temperance is depicted as a winged angelic figure, pouring liquid from one vessel to another, while standing with one foot on the ground and the other over a pool of water. This image is derived in part from classical depictions of the virtue, which show a woman mixing wine with water. Although his/her specific identity is unconfirmed by Waite, some Tarotists have linked the angelic figure with Michael, an angel associated with change and transmutation. According to Katz and Goodwin, Smith may have departed somewhat from Waite's original instructions for this image, and substituted his intended androgynous angel with the Greek goddess *Iris* – a view bolstered with the appearance of yellow iredes on the figure's left. Katz and Goodwin consider this a legitimate interpretation of

Waite's instructions, given that *Iris* is traditionally pictured as a winged goddess, watering the clouds with jugs.[1] In her role as messenger of the gods, *Iris* is associated with the rainbow – the bridge between the world of the gods and the world of mortals. Of interest in this respect is that some Renaissance alchemists described the transmutation of the self in terms of a "rising" and "purification" of human nature from "dust and ashes" to a "spiritual body of rainbow colors."[2]

Temperance is associated with the notions of blending, balancing or "tempering" – one meaning of the Latin *temperantia* from which the word temperance is derived. This tempering theme is so central to the card that some versions of it are called *The Alchemist*, and often employ Renaissance symbols relating to the tempering stages of alchemical processes. The tempering motif is indicated at a simpler and more foundational level within the *RWS* stylization, suggested by the blending of all four of the great elements within the angelic figure herself - earth (left foot), air (wings), fire (triangular symbol on breastplate) and water (right foot).

Although most commentators are aware of the obvious ethical implications of Temperance, there is little in Tarot literature that moves beyond that of advocating a "balanced" approach to the temptations and "enticing indulgences" that life may throw at us.[3] There is also a tendency within Jungian interpretations to internalize the dynamics of this card. Thus Nichols insists that the "ceremony" over which the angel presides is located in a "realm beyond mortal reach." The tempering takes place in "the hero's unconscious."[4]

A more socially-engaged interpretation however may be to approach the symbolism of this card in relation to the practice of *Areatic* or Virtue Ethics – a commitment to the cultivation of "virtue." Virtue Ethics derives from the Aristotelian view that humans can transform and "perfect" themselves through the cultivation of certain moral and intellectual qualities. In this respect, Temperance is the ethical virtue of balance, restraint, moderation or "tempering" with regards to our actions, thoughts and feelings. For Karen Armstrong such "ethical alchemy" constitutes the true heart and aim of religion; its real "perennial wisdom": "If you behave in a certain way, you will be transformed."[5]

Virtue Ethics is grounded in the view that true moral and spiritual development is "agent-centered" – it lies in the personal development of particular but universal human potentials and qualities (the virtues), and in the elimination of others (the vices). The key to the transformation lies in Aristotle's doctrine of *The Golden Mean* where, by the application of practical wisdom, one finds the middle ground between two opposing vices. As Temperance itself relates to the cultivation of balance, it could be said that this virtue occupies the most pivotal position among the cardinal virtues, since the other three depend upon our ability to find the correct mid-point between their respective vices. "Virtue," as an ethical middle ground between extremes, thus appears as the moral-mirror of the alchemists' fabled *coniunctio* - the reconciliation of opposites; the "alchemical wedding."

Aristotle believed that the cultivation of the virtues led to the state of *eudaimonia* – human flourishing – the highest goal of all virtuous reflection and action. There are of course obvious parallels here between Aristotle's views and Jung's concept of individuation, and indeed, Jung's framework has been described as part of the Western tradition of *Eudaimonism*.[6] Aristotle's Virtue Ethics mirrors similar developments in ancient thought, including the Confucian doctrine of "The Unswerving Pivot" (*Zhongyong*), and the Buddhist ideal of the "Middle Way" or Path (*Majjhima pada*) between all ethical and metaphysical extremes.

Although seemingly innocuous, it is precisely the inclusion of Virtue Ethics within Tarot which makes the entire system heretical, subversive, part of the "Secret Tradition." In opposition to traditional Christian thought in which humanity is conceived as a *massa damnata* – intrinsically fallen, corrupt, and incapable of any form of personal or social transformation – the Tarot insists that we are indeed capable of such change, without reliance upon external grace, nor a patient loitering-around until an apocalyptic *End of Days*. Indeed it was on this very issue of transformative potential without reference to the salvific power of Christ that led the Reformation leader Luther to condemn Aristotle as a "damned, conceited, rascally heathen" whom God had sent "as a plague upon us for ours sins."[7] For Christians ironically, it might be refreshing to reflect upon the fact that in the *Beatitudes* Jesus declared that it was only those who had developed particular virtuous potentials – humility, peacefulness, tolerance, forbearance, and a thirst for righteousness and justice – who would "see God" (*Matt.* 5: 8).

Despite its ancient origins, there has been a significant renewal of interest in Virtue Ethics within Christian thought[8] and moral philosophy, rooted in part in what many perceive as the moral bankruptcy left in the wake of the gluttonous excesses of consumer culture.[9] Such renewed interest reflects the observation made by

Gardner's channeled Temperance that we have "lost much" since the giving-up of alchemy.[10]

Behind the angel we can see a path leading to those mountains first indicated in the Death card, which appear below a shining sun-infused crown. This is the revelation that it is through the cultivation of "the middle" – both ethical and metaphysical – that one may find the transmutation of the four great elements long sought after by The Magician, and further indicated in The Wheel of Fortune.

In the Story of the Buddha: The Realization of the Middle Way

After many years of self-mortification, the Future Buddha realized that his ascetic strategy was simply not working. It was "not the way to passionlessness, nor to perfect knowledge, nor to liberation."[11] In one version of the story, he suddenly remembers his experience as a child, sitting under the rose-apple tree, when he attained insight into the suffering of the world from a position of relaxed detachment and equipoise.

In Edwin Arnold's version, found in his epic poem *The Light of Asia*, a number of singing and dancing temple girls, accompanied by musicians, happen to pass the Future Buddha while he sat under a tree. As one sitar player "thumped and twanged," a girl beside him began to sing:

> "Fair goes the dancing when the sitar's tuned;
> Tune us the sitar neither low nor high,
> And we will dance away the hearts of men.
>
> "The string o'erstretched breaks, and the music flies,

The string o'erslack is dumb and music dies.
Tune us the sitar neither low nor high."[12]

From this simple incident, the Future Buddha came to the realization that the only way forward in the spiritual quest is through a position of balance, both physical and psychological. He therefore made the decision to bring to an end his ascetic practices, and he bathed himself in the nearby river. He crawled out, sat under a tree, and a passing cow-girl named *Sujata* offered him her milk rice, believing him to be a powerful tree-spirit. Witnessing this, the five ascetic companions left in disgust, declaring that Siddhattha had abandoned the quest. They then began their journey towards a deer park at *Sarnarth*, near Benares.

The Future Buddha thus strengthened set his mind on the attainment of enlightenment, and walked to the root of an *Asvattha* (Fig) tree in order to meditate. This tree is of much significance in Hindu texts, and is against this background that we should consider the Future Buddha's actions. In the *Bhagavad-Gita*, Krishna describes the Asvattha as the "Tree of Transmigration" - its branches nourished by "the energy of material Nature" and its buds, the "sense pleasures." It roots stretch down into the "the human world" where mortals through selfish actions are held in "karmic bondage" to it. Most people do not see "the real form of this tree." However, the wise do, and holding "the mighty axe of Self-knowledge and detachment," cut this tree's "firm roots," and enter a path that leads to "that Supreme Abode" where "one does not come back to the mortal world again."[13] The Future Buddha's intention however is not to sever this tree of Samsara, but, with an attitude of composed reconciliation towards the world, to sit under it.

Before he gets to tree, the *Jataka* account transforms this scene into one of cosmic grandeur. The Future Buddha stands on the southern side of the tree and faces north, and immediately, "the southern half of the world sank, until it seemed to touch the *Avici* hell, while the northern half rose to the highest of heavens." This tilting process continues, until at last, the Future Buddha comes to the eastern side, and faces West. This, says the text, is the side that "neither tremble nor quakes"; it is the "immovable spot."[14] Thus at last, as Campbell puts it, the Future Buddha arrived at "the supporting point" of the universe, described mythologically, for its real location "is psychological."[15] With his back turned to the tree and facing East, the Future Buddha sits down and makes a mighty vow: "Let my skin, and sinews, and bones become dry ... but never from this seat will I stir, until I have attained the supreme and absolute wisdom!"[16]

It is here, at the verge of penetrating into the true nature of the world and the self, that Mara – the enemy of all spiritual striving – arrives.

A Buddhist Reflection: The Middle Way between all Extremes

At its most practical level, Buddhism could be described as a form of Virtue Ethics following the eightfold path as a golden mean between the ethical extremes of sensory indulgence on the one hand, and asceticism on the other. This at least is how the Buddha presented his insights to the five ascetics in his first ever sermon:

> "There are two extremes that he must avoid who would lead a life governed by his intelligence. Some

> devote themselves to pleasure; their lives are a constant round of dissipations; they seek only to gratify their senses ... Others devote themselves to self-mortification; they deprive themselves of everything; their conduct is gloomy and futile ... From these two extremes, O monks, the Perfect One stands aloof. He has discovered the middle path, the path that opens the eyes and opens the mind, the path that leads to rest, to knowledge, to Nirvana."[17]

This middle ground between indulgence and asceticism is not one of static quiescence, but the energetic center from which the virtuous attitudes and actions of the eightfold path are born – harmlessness, renunciation, right speech, action, and livelihood. "Virtue," says the monk *Silava* in the *Theragatha*, is "the starting point and foundation; the mother at the head of all good qualities." It is "the ultimate weapon." It is the place where "all the Buddhas cross over"; a vehicle that "takes you in all directions."[18] In the *Mahaparinibbana Sutta*, the Buddha makes the following very clear connection between the cultivation of virtuous ethical conduct and the attainment of Nirvana:

> To him who gives shall virtue be increased;
> In him who curbs himself, no anger can arise;
> The righteous man casts off all sinfulness,
> And by the rooting out of lust, and bitterness,
> And all delusion, doth to Nirvana reach!'[19]

However, Buddhism is not just an ethical middle way, but a philosophical one too, as the Buddha denied all extremes, including metaphysical ones. Thus, the Buddha also described his teaching as a middle path between the two extremes of his day regarding the nature of the self and its destiny – the undying *atman* of the eternalists, and the annihilation-at-death proposed by the materialists. "These extremes," as he explains in the *Kaccayanagotta Sutta*, "have been avoided by the *Tathagata*, and it is a middle doctrine he teaches."[20] In this sutta, the Buddha goes on to outline the twelve causal factors in the cycle of dependent origination. As with Nagasena's candle analogy discussed in relation to the Death card, this cycle presents life as a causal process that produces a constant stream of rebirth over countless lifetimes, in which the "self" is neither the same nor different from moment to moment. This "middle" position of *anatta* thus avoids both the eternal *atman* of the *Upanishads*, and the purely materialist views of *shramanas* like Ajita Kesakambali, discussed in the *Bhramajala Sutta*.

In the *Madhyamaka* school of Mahayana Buddhism, the Middle Way refers to the middle ground between the opposing positions that all phenomena either or neither exist or do not exist. As in the analogy of Indra's Net, the *Madhyamaka* position is that all things "exist" in a subtle middle place outside our usual categories of either being or non-being. Life, to use the evocative words of Nichiren Daishonin, is "an elusive reality" that transcends all notions of both existence and non-existence, and yet "exhibits the qualities of both."[21]

The Devil (15)

General Overview

This card shows a claw-footed, goat-legged and horned devil with a reversed pentagram above his head, conforming somewhat to Eliphas Levi's depiction of *Baphomet*, the so-called *Goat of Mendes*. He sits in darkness, perched on a small, black cuboid-shaped pedestal, to which are chained a naked male and female with horns and tails. The sign of Saturn – the God of the Underworld – is indicated by his right hand, while his left, holding a torch, ignites the man's tail. The woman's tail ends in a pomegranate-like shape, suggesting fertility and sexuality. For Waite, both tails indicate "the animal nature."[1] In most interpretations this card is associated with a variety of dark themes, including bondage, materialism, misery, indulgence, addiction, sexual lust, temptation, deception, illusion, and despair.

Waite's Devil, like some depictions of The Emperor, is positioned atop a cube-like block of stone, representing materiality and rational ordering. Yet this is a significantly compacted block, indicating as Pollack suggests a greatly reduced vision of material existence, condensed here to a number of selfish pursuits and desires, especially "monetary, sexual and political."[2] A denial of anything more spiritual to life is also conveyed in the reversed pentagram, indicating allegiance to the material, the sensual, the lustful and the destructive. The dark background to the card also connotes a sense of incompleteness or a lack of knowledge, recognized by Gardner in his channeled Devil, who boasts that he wields his power through our "ignorance" and "blindness."[3]

Like the Magician, The Devil holds one hand up and the other to the ground, signifying that this card also relates to the theme of "will." However, it is not the will of The Devil that confines the two captives to this dark place, but their own. In this respect, as Pollack notes, the Devil with his two captured prisoners stands as a distorted reflection of The Lovers card, which, as we recall, pertains to the issue of "choice."[4] The prisoners, through their own exercise of will have the capacity to leave this place, indicated by the chains which hang but loosely around their necks. Their captivity is rooted in a lack of knowledge and understanding of their innate potential for liberation. The Devil here is that force which, as Gardner's Devil says, denies our "greater possibilities."[5]

The Devil has a long history of development within the Judaeo-Christian tradition. In the Jewish book of *Job* we come across *Ha-Satan – The Accuser*; a member of God's angelic court responsible for tempting and terrorizing the hapless Job away from his piety. By the time of Jesus, and under the influence of Zoroastrianism and Greek culture, this shady angelic lawyer had become *Lucifer* the *Light-bearer* – God's rebellious archangel, fallen from grace through pride, and ruler of Hell. He stands in opposition to God's will and holiness, and his main sphere of activity is that of tempting and leading mortals astray from their spiritual destiny.

The Devil's main role in the Gospels – and one that clearly mirrors Mara's confrontation with the Future Buddha – is to question Jesus' credentials and abilities as God's Son and Messiah, and thus prevent him from embarking on his ministry to the world. Jesus' temptations are described in such a way as to present him as a righteous alternative to God's "unfaithful servant," Israel, who failed its respective temptations during its forty years of sojourn in the desert. Where Israel failed in its prophetic call to be a "light to all nations," Jesus, for the Gospel writers at least, will succeed.

According to *Luke's* account (*Lk.* 4: 1-13), after forty days of fasting in the wilderness, Jesus was approached by the Devil, who, recognizing his weakened state, demands: "If you are the Son of God, command this stone to become bread." Unlike the Israelites, who demanded *manna* from Heaven, Jesus replies with a verse from scripture: "It is written, 'Man shall not live by bread alone.'" In this, Jesus recognizes that there is more to life than material needs and desires, and that the Messiah has come to do more than provide material blessings and equality. A full belly might be a prerequisite for human flourishing, but it is not, as Western civilization clearly shows, its guarantor.

The Devil then proceeds to show Jesus all the kingdoms of the world in a "moment of time." He relates to Jesus that all of their authority and glory have been delivered to him, and that if "you, then, will worship me, it shall all be yours." Again, Jesus responds with a verse from scripture: "It is written, 'You shall worship the Lord your God, and him only shall you serve.'" Unlike Israel, who worshipped a golden calf and demanded a king like all the other nations, Jesus recognizes this for what it is – the idolization of power; the temptation as Messiah to solve the world's problems through political and military authority or might.

In the final temptation, the Devil takes Jesus to the pinnacle of the holy temple in Jerusalem, and getting the hang of things by now, quotes some scripture back at Jesus: "If you are the Son of God, throw yourself down from here; for it is written, 'He will give his angels charge of you, to guard you,' and 'On their hands they will bear you up, lest you strike your foot against a stone.'" Unlike Israel, who constantly demanded "signs" in the desert, Jesus refuses, and answers with another piece of scripture: "It is said, 'You shall not tempt the Lord your God.'" This reply indicates the centrality of faith over proof within the Judaeo-Christian heritage; an attitude of the heart which many now in the West – with some justification – find too difficult to bear. Yet Jesus' final response can be read another way, indicating what ethicist Joseph Fletcher described as the attitude of "positivism" in relation to love or *agape* – the defining principle of Jesus' words and actions.[6] Love's decisions are not made on the basis of evidence, likelihood or calculated success, but in the hope, in the belief and a commitment to the fundamental good nature of the human heart, whether one's own, or others'. The refusal to demand signs is then ultimately a refusal to descend into the paralysis of despair about the human condition; something which is perhaps the greatest challenge and temptation faced by many in the world today.

In the Story of the Buddha: The Confrontation with Mara

Mara, says Asvaghosa, "was afraid." He recognized that should the Future Buddha attain enlightenment, "all this my realm will to-day become empty." He therefore drew close to the Asvattha tree with his "flower-made bow and his five infatuating arrows," along with his three sons –

Confusion, Gaiety, and *Pride* – and his three daughters – *Lust, Delight* and *Thirst.*[7]

Mara begins his temptations through an appeal to dharma – the prince should forget his spiritual quest and "follow thine own duty" to become a mighty ruler of the world, and thereby "gain the higher worlds of Indra." The Future Buddha remains unmoved, and so Mara "discharged his arrow" and set his six sons and daughters before him. Mara is astonished that the Buddha remains unyielding before his daughter *Rati*, the arrow "by which the god *Sambhu* was pierced with love." Enraged, Mara decides that this fool, "destitute of all feeling," deserves "the alarms and rebukes and blows from all the gathered host of the demons." The Future Buddha is assailed from all directions "in grief and anger" by this monstrous horde; but still "the great sage remained unalarmed and untroubled," secure in a resolution that had been acquired "through numberless aeons." The Future Buddha remains steadfast in his quest to become a "great physician" for a world "lying distressed amidst diseases and passions."[8]

Finally, according to the *Jataka* account, *Mara* taunts the Future Buddha with a simple observation – unlike himself, whose achievements and powers are recognized by his mighty army, who can stand witness to the achievements of this mere man? Recalling all his efforts in previous lives, the Future Buddha drew forth his right hand and stretched it towards "the mighty earth" and said to it: "'Are you witness, or are you not ...?' And the mighty earth thundered, 'I bear your witness!' with a hundred, a thousand, a hundred thousand roars, as if to overwhelm the army of *Mara*."[9] This powerful scene, in which the Buddha touches the earth, reminds us that liberation into the "deathless" is not obtained by flight from the phenomenal world, from the incessant flow of birth, death and rebirth experienced in nature; but, through some form of reconciliation with these processes.

Finally, Mara and his army flee "in all directions," and a victory roar is taken up by the gods: "'Mara is defeated! Prince Siddhattha has conquered!'"[10]

A Buddhist Reflection: Mara

Although suggestions have been made for an etymological link between *Mara* and *maya*, the consensus opinion is that Mara derives from the root *mer,* which means "killing" or "death." He also bears a number of ominous epitaphs, including *Popima* ("Evil One"), *Kanha* ("Dark One") and *Namuci* ("Inescapable"). He is also referred to as *Kamadeva* ("God of Pleasure" or "God of Desire") or simply *Kama-Mara* - indicating what Buddhists see as the causal link between sensory attachment and the endless cycle of birth and death within Samsara.

There are at least four different but related ways in which Mara is understood and appreciated within Buddhism. The first is as *Klesa-Mara*, where Mara is viewed as a symbolic embodiment of the three unskillful "poisons" that sit at the center of the Wheel of Becoming; namely, greed, hatred and delusion. As *Mrtya-Mara*, Mara indicates "death" in the sense of the ceaseless process of birth, death and rebirth within Samsara. As *Khandha-Mara*, the demon is viewed as a metaphor for life lived within the five aggregates, especially in the act of grasping or clinging to these components of personality. It is in "the desire of grasping," says the Buddha, that "Mara follows the man." Worldlings are but "creatures of desire ... sticking fast in the realm of death." Conversely, those who give up "greediness for name and form" are no longer subject to "the power of death."[11] Yet it is not just foolish worldlings who need to be on their guard. The Mahayana *Surangama Sutra* further links each aggregate with ten *Mara*s, giving a total of fifty "demons" responsible for generating erroneous meditative insights into the nature of each khandha. Finally, as *Devaputra-Mara*, Mara is recognized as a "son of a god" - a divine being conceived either literally or psychologically; a powerful and malevolent force concerned with keeping all captive to the pleasures and illusions of Samsaric life. In this respect, he mirrors the role of the *Demiurge* within ancient Gnosticism.

Devaputra-Mara is said to be the Lord of the realm of *Devas wielding Power over the Creations of Others* – the highest heavenly abode of the *kama-loka*. One source presents him as being originally a rebellious prince, who usurped control of this realm from another god.[12] Another view is that Mara is not a single being, but a succession of beings. Indeed, the Pali texts seem to suggest it is possible to be reborn as Mara. Whatever the case, Mara is considered to be the one responsible for binding all to the temporal and empty pleasures of Samsara, and the one who confronts any who would dare challenge his authority and rule.

When in human form, Devaputra-Mara is pictured as a kingly ruler riding an elephant. He often appears accompanied by his three daughters – *Tanha* (craving/thirst), *Arati* (aversion) and *Rati* (sexual passion). Later accounts expand his family to include an additional two daughters and three sons – *Confusion*, *Gaiety* and *Pride*. He is also said to command ten legions of demons, each linked to some kind of vice, whether of deficiency or excess. The *Padhana Sutta* from the *Sutta Nipata* describes his army in the following way:

> "Lust thy first army is called, discontent thy second, thy third is called hunger and thirst, thy fourth desire.
>
> "Thy fifth is called sloth and drowsiness, thy sixth cowardice, thy seventh doubt, thy eighth hypocrisy and stupor,
>
> "Gain, fame, honor, and what celebrity has been falsely obtained; and he who exalts himself and despises others.
>
> "This, O Namuki, is thine, the black one's fighting army; none but a hero conquers it, and after conquering it obtains joy."[13]

Within many suttas, Mara's functions are primarily those of temptation and distraction – he tries to prevent the Dharma from being spoken or heard, and distracts or tempts monks and nuns while they meditate. However, his most celebrated role within the scriptures is as the Buddha's spiritual adversary, whether before, during, or after his enlightenment. His persistence derives from his awareness that the Buddha's enlightenment and establishment of the Dharma and Sangha signify the end of his reign over the world.

Many Buddhists understand Devaputra-Mara and his retinue in a symbolic rather than literal sense; as representations of negative psychological forces, impulses, emotions and tendencies, as opposed to metaphysical entities in their own right. Thus, his role is really didactic – a teaching tool to help practicing Buddhists appreciate and conceptualize the inner obstacles and forces they will confront while meditating. As Shaila Catherine says, Mara serves as a "metaphorical image" that allows Buddhists to "depersonalize" the hindrances they may confront during meditation.[14] As such, Mara conforms in some respects to the Jungian notion of the *Shadow* - the darker and perhaps unconscious aspects of one's own nature. Stephen Bachelor describes Mara as the Future Buddha's "devilish twin," revealing a deep-seated conflict within human nature between our capacities for "awakening" and "sanity," and for those of "confusion" and "chaos." Mara is, in reality, the Future Buddha's "own conflicted humanity."[15]

The Tower (16)

General Overview

The *RWS* Tower shows a grey rock-bound stone tower blasted by a thunderbolt, with two figures (usually viewed as male and female) falling from its heights. While one still bears a crown, a larger one appears as if to tumble from the tower top. In earlier renditions of this card, the bolt was surrounded by hailstones or drops of solar fire. In Waite's version, these have been replaced with twenty-two Hebrew *yods*, indicating as Butler says the fire's divine origin.[1]

Traditionally, The Tower has been associated with the depressing themes of misfortune, destruction, disaster, ruin and sudden calamity. The 19th-Century occultist Papus for example linked it with the story of the Fall of Adam and Eve and their entrance into the material world.[2] This is also suggested by a 17th-Century *Minchiate* version of the card, which shows Adam and Eve being driven forth from the Gates of Eden.[3] Other negative interpretations have linked this card with the biblical story of the *Tower of Babel*, when humanity in its foolish pride attempts to penetrate the divine mysteries, and is chastised by God for doing so. In this interpretation the two falling figures may, as Katz and Goodwin suggest, represent "Nebuchadnezzar and his vizier."[4]

Within the spectrum of possibility however, the card connotes themes of a much more positive nature. Indeed Waite himself rejected the view of it being either the "chastisement of pride" or "the fall of Adam," and was drawn to Papus' alternative explanation – "the materialization of the spiritual world"; the two figures indicating the end to a "false interpretation" of reality. Overall, the card for Waite indicates the "rending of a ... House of Falsehood."[5] A similarly positive interpretation may be deduced from this card's probable links with medieval artistic depictions of the *Harrowing of Hell*, where Christ is shown knocking the gates of Hell asunder, and freeing those trapped inside. This definition is bolstered with The Tower's links with an earlier version of the card known as *The Castle of Plutus* – *Plutus* being the Greek God of wealth, corresponding in many ways to the Semitic *Mammon*, the New Testament demon of greed and materialism. In this case, the two figures perhaps represent the chained figures of the previous card, set free at last. For both Pollack and Banzhaf, the card represents a psychological breakthrough into a new realm of consciousness and self-understanding, in which our erroneous perceptions of the world are destroyed in a "single blinding flash."[6]

In the Story of the Buddha: The Three-Fold Knowledge

After his defeat of Mara, the Buddha remained meditating under the Bodhi tree and under a full moon, where it is said that he gained three subsequent realizations into the deathless state, known collectively as the *Three-Fold Knowledge*. In the "first watch of the night" he gained the knowledge of his previous existences. In the *Bhayabherava Sutta*, the Buddha recounts that when he had purified his mind, he directed it towards the recollection of past lives. He remembered various births and deaths, including names, appearances and places of origin, until at last he "reappeared here."[7]

In his post "The First Watch of the Night," Mark Knickelbine puts forward a "naturalistic" explanation of this realization, based upon his reflections on *metta* ("loving-kindness"). In metta meditation, as we explored in The Lovers card, Buddhists attempt to extend thoughts and feelings of love towards others, even those we do not "like." Knickelbine admits that this can be a challenging undertaking, but points out that it can be achieved through the recognition that we all share fundamental things in common. Perhaps the meaning of the first watch experience then is that enlightenment awakens us to an experience of "our common humanity." At whatever time and however we are born, we all share in the basic existential conditions of Samsaric life; and, at the same time, the same "potential to wake up."[8]

Knickelbine's reflections can also be applied to some extent to the Buddha's realization in the "second watch of the night," known as the attainment of *The Divine Eye* or sometimes *Omniscience*. This is perhaps not omniscience in the sense of knowing all things in the universe, whether past, present and future, but an awareness of how beings come into and out of existence, according to their karmic qualities. In the *Bhayabherava Sutta* the Buddha recounts that with the *Divine Eye* he saw all manner of beings pass away and reappear, and understood how they move from one life to another "according to their actions."[9]

In the "third watch," as the first morning star was appearing in the sky, the Buddha's mind fathomed

Dependent Origination – the twelve causal factors that keep beings bound to the cycle of Samsara. At this moment, according to the *Jataka* narrative - in words that recall both Jesus' mission statement in *Luke's* Gospel, and our two prisoners from the Death card - "[t]he blind from birth received their sight; the deaf from birth their hearing; the cripples from birth the use of their limbs; and the bonds and fetters of captives broke and fell off."[10]

A Buddhist Reflection: The Vajra of Enlightenment
When reading interpretations of the Buddha's life, the victory over Mara is often considered as a prelude to the Future Buddha's enlightenment. Thus Keown et al. argue that his "deep meditations" and subsequent realizations were all made possible because he was set free from the "spiritual hindrances represented by Mara."[11] Yet, it could be read that it was precisely in his victory over *Khandha-Mara*, over his clinging to the aggregates of self – symbolized in The Tower as a tumbling crown - that the Future Buddha severed his ties to the realm of death, and achieved enlightenment. In the "leaving of desire," says the Buddha, "Nibbana is said to be." Through severing all attachments to the aggregates, one has "destroyed the view of oneself (as really existing), so one may overcome death; the king of death will not see him who thus regards the world."[12] With a metaphor that is particularly appropriate to our image of the blasted Tower, the Buddha compares his victory over Mara to a house being torn down, its architect both recognized and understood:

> "Many births have I traversed seeking the builder; in vain! Weary is the round of births. Now art thou seen, O Builder. Nevermore shalt thou build the house! All thy beams are broken; cast down is thy

cornerstone. My mind is set upon Nirvana; it has attained the extinction of desire."[13]

From this perspective, the subsequent realizations experienced by the Buddha constitute deepening insights into this new state of freedom that he discovered in his liberation from Khandha-Mara.

Like color to a blind person, this new state lies outside the parameters of conceptual communication. It has to be experienced to be understood. Nevertheless, Buddhism offers a number of evocative metaphors to help grasp this elusive state of being. It is a "cooling" or "blowing out" of a raging fire (Nirvana). It is the extinction of desire and craving (*Tanhakkhaya*). In the *Samyutta Nikaya*, the Buddha offers a comprehensive list of synonyms, including "the truth," "the deathless," "freedom," and "the refuge."[14]

One of the most evocative Buddhist symbols for enlightenment is the Sanskrit term *Vajra*, translated as both "diamond" and "thunderbolt," clearly seen in The Tower card, and suggesting both the indestructible and instantaneous or sudden nature of awakening. This "thunderbolt" mirrors the *satori* experience of Zen Buddhism, where the mind, grappling with the impossible logic of the *koan*, suddenly breaks through into an intuitive grasp of reality.

The Thunderbolt as symbol of power has its origins in the *Rig-Veda*, where it is described as the weapon of the Rain-God *Indra*, who uses it to chastise the wicked. According to tradition, the Buddha is said to have taken this weapon of destruction, and bent its prongs to form the shape of a sceptre – the *dorje* of Tibetan or Vajrayana Buddhism.[15]

As a ritual tool, the dorje usually takes the form of a scepter with a spherical central section, with ribbed-shaped prongs at the ends. The dorje can be single-sided, but most are double-sided, and a few are quadruple-sided. The central section is said to represent Sunyata – the primordial nature of the universe and the mind – while the double-ends represent Samsara and Nirvana. In ritual practice, the dorje is often used in conjunction with a bell (*ghanta*). These two objects symbolize a variety of things for the practitioner – in particular, the union of the masculine forces of skillful means or compassion (*dorje*) with the feminine force of wisdom (*ghanta*).

The Vajra is associated with a number of yidam deities, in particular, *Vajrasattva* – the *Thunderbolt Being* invoked during purification rituals, and depicted as holding a dorje to his heart. In relation to our card, it is an interesting coincidence that Vajrasattva was said to reside within a dark iron tower or stupa located in Southern India, and that the Buddhist philosopher Nagarjuna – the founder of the Middle Way school – journeyed there to receive Tantric teachings from the deity within. There are many Vajrasattva *stupas* which remain in central Java to this day.

The Return:
From The Star to The World

Introduction

One of the sustained criticisms of Jungian-inspired psycho-spirituality is its apparent lack of social perspective, critique and engagement; its devout focus upon *The Self*. The world of nature and others is ignored; or worse, utilized as a solipsistic mirror to gauge one's own progress towards individuation. As Maurice Friedman pointed out in the 1970s, there is a danger in Jung's conception of individuation that the world and the people outside become either "an obstacle to or a function of the inner"; the means towards "the becoming of one's self."[1] A typical example of such inner focus is Nichols, who restricts considerations of the social relevance of the Hero's Journey to one paragraph within her review of The World card.[2] As such, much contemporary Tarot practice and interpretation appears to conform to what Carl Raschke recognized as the link between cultural disintegration and the rise of *Gnosticism* – the periodic emergence of private symbol-systems indicating attempts by a disinherited aristocracy (and now middle-class) to hold onto some semblance of control or meaning through a turn to the world within.[3]

However, while there is certainly a "danger" of the world disappearing with Jungian-inspired approaches, this does not negate the view that "inner alchemy" may serve as a necessary prequel to transformative engagement with the world. Indeed, what both Jung and Buddhism share at heart is the recognition that the social structures we create are really reflections of the minds that built them. "All that we are" said the Buddha (including the world we create), "is the result of what we have thought: it is founded on our thoughts, it is made up of our thoughts."[4] Indeed, the grotesqueries of the last century are apt reminders that radical shifts to either Right or Left solve little when they are driven by those with darkened mindscapes.

Moreover, the view that individuation takes us away from the world is in fact a misinterpretation of Jung's ideas. It is clear that Jung saw self-realization as a process which carried within itself certain social and moral implications. It was Jung's opinion, according to an interview he gave with the BBC in 1946, that individuation necessitated "ethical responsibility," and that the "maintenance and further development" of society depended upon the influence of individuated "moral leaders."[5] This rise to "ethical responsibility" relates to Jung's understanding of individuation itself, which contrary to often individualistic interpretations, demands the expansion of the self into wider fields of identification. The individuated self says Jung is no longer incarcerated in the trivial, touchy and private world of the ego, but participates in a wider sphere of interest, bringing the individual into a "binding, and indissoluble communion with the world at large."[6]

This movement into "the world at large" was also recognized by Campbell in his understanding of *The Return* element within the Hero's Journey. For Campbell, a return to society is a natural and archetypal aspect of the individuation process. It represents a deep human longing to share and teach what one has discovered, in order to be of benefit to the community or the world at large. The "norm of the monomyth" says Campbell requires that the hero return from his or her seclusion, and with the new wisdom that has been attained, begin a process that will renew "the nation, the planet, or the ten thousand worlds."[7]

Unfortunately, one of the most glaring omissions in Tarot literature has been any form of development on this third and final aspect of the journey – the "return" to renew "the nation, the planet." Most of this comes down to world-ignoring presentations of individuation, and dualistic interpretations of "spirituality." In this final section, I will endeavor to present a more expansive and engaged vision of *The Return*; one that that accords more with both Campbell's and Jung's ethically and socially-relevant understanding of individuation. The Buddha's story, as we shall see, is one which appears in harmony which such a widened vision of transformation. In exploring the Buddha's return to society, we will begin with his initial refusal to teach, leading to the eventual setting-up of the Sangha. We will then move on to consider the nature of the Buddha's teaching and its effects, and end with some reflections of the Buddha's *Parinirvana* – his *Great Extinction*.

The Star (17)

General Overview

The *RWS* version of The Star shows a naked kneeling woman, pouring liquid from two pitchers; one into a pool of water, and the other onto land. Her right foots rests on top of the water, while the left is on the ground. Above her in the sky are eight eight-pointed stars. Seven of these are white, while the eighth and largest central star is yellow. In the background and to the right of the woman, a small bird sits perched on a tree.

The Star is often associated with the idea of "hope"; of truth, light and life overcoming darkness and despair. In this card we find, as Papus says, a "mysterious voice" which "whispers courage."[1] Jayanti agrees, and equates the central star with the "Star of Bethlehem" and the birth of Jesus, who "brought hope" to a distressed and fearful world.[2] Similarly for Waite the card represents "Sirius, also called fantastically the Star of the Magi."[3] This theme of hope is expressed in the nativity narratives themselves, declaring that "a day shall dawn upon us from on high" when an infant shall be born who will "give light to those who sit in darkness and in the shadow of death" (*Lk.* 1: 78-9).

Another associated theme is that of renewal or regeneration. Although Waite offers little in the way of explanation as to why he chose these stars, the number eight is traditionally associated with revitalization and rebirth. We are reminded for example that God saved eight individuals in the ark in order to initiate a new covenant between Himself and creation. Or, that male Jewish infants are brought into the covenant eight days after birth. Or, that the baptismal font, symbolizing new life in Christ, is traditionally octagonal in shape. Moreover, there are also eight beatitudes - eight elements of ethical alchemy that generate human flourishing and the right to be called a "son/daughter of God." Overall it seems, The Star card's numerical value (17 = 1+7 = 8) is not purely coincidental.

The biblical texts themselves look forward to a day when God will establish a *New Covenant* between himself and the world; a universal covenant based upon inner trust and a conscious awareness of the divine: "I will put my law within them, and I will write it upon their hearts" (*Jer.* 31: 33). This is a time, according to the prophet Joel, when God shall "pour out ... [his] spirit on all flesh; your sons and your daughters shall prophesy, your old men shall dream dreams, and your young men shall see visions" (*Joel* 2: 28). This of course was the ancient prophetic passage utilized by Peter at Pentecost, when Jesus' followers were filled with the power of the Spirit. He told the crowds gathered that day that Jesus, whom "you crucified and killed by the hands of lawless men" had been raised up, "having loosed the pangs of death." His resurrection meant that the humanity was no longer "abandoned to Hades," and that the "ways of life" had now been revealed to any who would listen. "[B]e baptised," he urged, and "you shall receive the gift of the Holy Spirit" (*Acts* 2: 14-8, 27-8, 38). For the New Testament writer Paul, this new order is one in which there is "neither Jew nor Greek, there is neither slave nor free, there is neither male nor female" (*Gal.* 3: 28). It is a new order based upon "the law of the Spirit of life" which frees us from "the law of sin and death." It is a new order towards which "the whole creation has been groaning in travail" (*Rom.* 8: 2, 22).

Peter's and Paul's ecstatic insights into the nature of the New Covenant conform in some respects to Joachim of Fiore's vision of the *Age of Spirit*, which replaces both the *Age of the Father* and the *Age of the Son*; or, in astrological lore, the *Age of Aquarius* which succeeds both those of *Aries* and *Pisces*. Traditional depictions of *Aquarius the Water-Bearer* - usually shown amidst the stars, pouring water from a pitcher - do of course bear more than a passing resemblance to the woman from The Star card. Within the more serious elements of the New Age Movement[4] the figure of Aquarius is associated with a distinct set of humanistic and environmental ideals, including democracy, feminism, equality, holism, simplicity, conservation, and new forms of spirituality based upon a growing sense of global connectedness.

An integral part of this Aquarian hope is the birth of a renewed and revitalized civilization, grounded in wisdom and a fresh understanding of our connection with nature and the earth. This movement toward a new unity of wisdom and "earthiness" is reflected in Pollack's interpretation of The Star, which considers the water-bearer as embracing both the "inner sensitivity" of the High Priestess and the "passion" of the Empress.[5] This new unity is also suggested in the card's obvious relationship with the ancient Mesopotamian Goddess *Inanna* (*Lady of the Heavens*), often depicted with an eight-pointed star, perhaps representing Venus' eight-year synodic cycle. Inanna is associated with sexuality, fertility, creation, and strength; but also with resurrection from death in the underworld, and the wresting of power (the *mes*) from *Enki*, the god of Wisdom, which she uses to establish civilization. A renewed connection with creation and the world is also suggested in the card's seven minor stars, which, as we discussed with The Empress, may represent the "seven mothers" of the Pleiades – the nurturing and consuming forces of life within the phenomenal world. Alternatively, the eight stars as a collective may represent the Egyptian *Ogdoad* – the eight primal deities responsible for bringing creation out of chaos. It is interesting to note that the eight stars generate forty-eight points in total – a number that can be reduced to 12 (The Hanged Man) and further to 3 (The Empress). Perhaps this indicates new perspectives on the "Great Mother" gained through the sacrificial act of our hanged king of kings.

Another important theme of the card is that of "communication." For Waite, the act of pouring represents the Great Mother "communicating to those below in the measure that they can receive her understanding."[6] Likewise, Pollack argues that the Goddess pouring her pitchers onto both water and land points to the liberated energy of The Tower moving simultaneously between "inner transformation" and "the physical world."[7] This theme is reinforced with the appearance of the small bird usually considered to be an *Ibis* – a symbol of *Thoth*, the Egyptian God of communication, language and writing. (Incidentally, Thoth was viewed as the one who impelled and led the Ogdoad in the act of creating the cosmos.) For Papus similarly, this card, which he connects with the Hebrew letter *Peh*, indicates "the sign of speech" and thus the "Word in action in nature."[8]

In the Story of the Buddha: The Decision to Teach

According to tradition, the morning star appeared in the sky as the Buddha's mind fathomed the cycle of dependent origination. The Buddha then remained under or near the Bodhi tree for seven week after this, contemplating what to do. At one point Mara returns along with his daughters, applauding him for his achievement, and urging him that he should now take up his full responsibilities as a mighty ruler according to his caste dharma; or alternatively, die in the full knowledge of Nirvana: "'O holy one, be pleased to enter Nirvana, thy desires are accomplished.'" The Buddha refuses, declaring that he will "'first establish in perfect wisdom worlds as numerous as the sand, and then I will enter Nirvana.'" With a shriek, Mara "went to his home." During the sixth week of his enlightenment, the Buddha meditated at the foot of a *Mucalinda* tree. It began to rain heavily, and so, the giant king cobra, *Naga Mucalinda*, offered to shelter the Buddha from the elements, raising his hood above his head. The King of the Nagas "protected the Buddha, who is himself the source of all protection, from the rain, wind, and darkness, covering his body with his own hood."[9] According to Campbell, the serpent represents the power and energy of nature. This scene thus reveals a perhaps overlooked aspect of the Buddha's experience of awakening, namely: "reconciliation with the force of nature that supports the world."[10]

However, according to the *Ariyapariyesana Sutta* the Buddha remained "inclined to inaction"; a "refusal" as Campbell would say, grounded in his awareness that his discovery might be too difficult to comprehend by those living in "lust and hate." The creator god *Brahma*

Sahamapati, perceiving the Buddha's thoughts, appears before him and urges him to teach for the sake of those with "little dust in their eyes"; those who will understand what he has to say.[11]

As he listens to Brahma's entreaty, and filled with compassion for the lost, the Buddha looked across the world, and saw many with keen understanding who would respond to his teachings. Thus, for the sake of those who had ears to hear, the Buddha decided to open the "door to the Deathless." But to whom should he teach? Through his visionary powers the Buddha discerned that his first two teachers had died. His mind then turned to his five ascetic companions who looked after him during his austerities. Perceiving they were now living near Benares in the Deer Park at *Isipatana*, he set out to meet them.[12]

A Buddhist Reflection: "To Save the World of Gods and Men"

What exactly is a Buddha? The answer seems obvious – it is someone who has experienced enlightenment; someone who is "awake." Yet, different Buddhist traditions differentiate between different types of awakened beings. The Theravadin tradition for example makes a clear distinction between a Buddha and an *Arhat* or *Worthy One*. Here, *Buddha* refers to one who has figured out and attained enlightenment through their own insights and resources. The Arhat by contrast is one who has awakened through the benefits of received teachings (Dharma) and the fellowship of other practitioners (Sangha). Buddhism also makes a distinction between a *Samyaksambuddha* (a *Fully Pure* Buddha who teaches others) and a *Pratekyabuddha* (*Private Buddha*) – the latter being someone who becomes awake through their own resources, but does not teach the Dharma.

To remain a "Private Buddha" was the first temptation faced by Gotama after his enlightenment under the Asvattha tree, based it seems on his assumption that no one would be able to understand what he had discovered. Like Jesus, tempted to be borne away by angels, the Buddha felt that his insights could not be communicated to a society engulfed in its own darkness. So, we must ask - what motivated the Buddha to engage with the world, and formulate his insights in such a way that would make them intellectually accessible? Fundamentally it was based on a sense of compassion for those lost in Samsara. Such compassion is rooted in a sense of identification; the realization that the suffering of one is at the same time the suffering of all. "Compassion," as Jack Kornfield rightly says, is founded upon a "sense of our shared suffering."[13] Conversely, the awakening of one holds in itself the potential for the awakening of all. This perhaps explains the enigmatic saying which the Zen tradition attributes to the Buddha at the moment of his enlightenment: "Seeing this morning star, all things and I awaken together." The Buddha's subsequent establishment of a casteless Sangha, open to both men and woman, and his vision of a life based in moral virtue, wisdom and meditation, represent his pragmatic efforts to establish a culture of universal awakening; his attempt to "save the world of gods and men."

However, it is fair to say that as Buddhism has carried itself forwards through the ages, much of this energy and potency has been lost or forgotten. Despite its grand vision of transformation, the central achievement of traditional Buddhism, as Gary Snyder has argued, has been helping a few "dedicated individuals" with their "cultural conditioning." As a whole, Buddhism has been noticeably accepting of "the inequalities and tyrannies" of the political systems it has been obliged to co-exist with.[14]

The traditional Buddhist vision of transformation has also encountered a number of problems in its dialogue with Western culture. The first has been its rather clumsy-looking and at-odds stance with what Michael Welton has described as the West's "narrative of progress." Teachers from traditional Buddhist countries have had the onerous task of relating the Dharma to complex societies of wealth and abundance, with extensive traditions of "human rights, liberal democracy and collective welfare." Within this narrative, "religion" has for the most part been removed from its pre-Enlightenment position of power, to become a mostly personal and private concern.[15]

Another problem has been consumer culture's ability to assimilate and repackage all things as harmless commodity. At the bookstore, whether actual or virtual, we enter a latté-drenched maya-world, where Buddhism competes with Buddish self-help or the latest *Ramtha* for our spiritual and financial affections. Mara's demons have been hard at work, turning Samatha meditation into Corporate Mindfulness Training,[16] and Tantra into Neo-tantra. The transformative vision of Buddhism has become a personal lifestyle option, a productivity tool; another exotic nugget in my unique book-collection of "me." In response to the "conjuror's trickwork" of the West, "Buddhism," as Sulak Sivaraksa plainly puts it, "does not know what to do."[17] As discussed in relation to the Justice card, Buddhism does potentially have much to offer in terms of a wise and discriminating response to the dominant consumerist ideology of our times. Yet, many may doubt that we are about to witness a society-wide transformation of values on the basis of this fact. In the West, as it was in the days of the original casteless Sangha, converts to Buddhism are drawn principally from the intellectual classes. The rest, as Michel Clasquin-Johnson puts it, "did as they were told."[18]

But all is not doom and gloom. First, what Buddhism really does have in its favor is our misery. The spiritual malaise that helped foster the growth of Buddhism long ago seems much like our own. Like those ancients who experienced the unfixing of the pole star, and life as a frog at the bottom of a dried-up well, we too have had our "losses," perhaps more so:

> loss of meaning, feelings of alienation and powerlessness, unhappiness in the midst of the glut of material possessions, despair over deepening discrepancies between rich and poor, social fragmentation, moral confusion and pervasive personality disorders and addictions, plus an ever degrading eco-structure.[19]

It is obvious that many in the West are hungry for something more meaningful than that which consumer culture can supply; for healthier ways to relate to themselves, others, and to the planet. Second, there is hope in the human potential for change and transformation. Contrary to mainstream Christian pessimism, there is, as Snyder says, nothing in what we now know about human nature or social organisation which fundamentally necessitates that any society should be repressive, or fashion only "violent frustrated personalities."[20] Third, as Dominique Side points out, there are a number of features within Buddhism which make it particularly attractive to a growing number of discerning Westerners – its elevation of reason over faith, it's ongoing dialogue with science, its lack of hierarchical authority, and its emphasis upon personal insight and self-development.[21]

Finally, and perhaps most importantly, "Buddhism" as universal compassion is neither defined by nor confined to issues of doctrinal allegiance. It is rooted primarily in the belief that we all in some measure possess *the bodhisattva world*; that we all have the innate potential to cultivate *The Beautiful*, transforming ourselves, society and the world in the process. Moreover, this potential can be cultivated in myriad ways, the traditional path of the received teachings of the Buddha being but one of them. The West has a number of its own significant spiritual resources which reflect or can be utilized to reflect a Buddhist understanding of the spiritual life, whether we call it "Buddhist" or not. "The presence of Buddhism in society," says Sivaraksa, does not mean having card-carrying Buddhists in charge of every institution, but that these institutions be permeated by those who live by "humanism, love, tolerance, and enlightenment."[22]

For some, this definition of Buddhism as *dharma-farers in spirit* might be too amorphous to be of any real meaning or value. Yet, we are reminded that the Dalai Lama himself defines his "simple religion" as "kindness,"[23] indicating what he considers to be Buddhism's primary allegiance to practice over doctrine, which only functions as an external support to compassionate action in the first place. As the Buddha himself says in the *Dhammapada*:

> If a man is a great preacher of the sacred text, but slothful and no doer of it, he is a hireling shepherd, who has no part in the flock.

If a man preaches but a little of the text and practices the teaching, putting away lust and hatred and infatuation; if he is truly wise and detached and seeks nothing here or hereafter, his lot is with the holy ones.[24]

The Moon (18)

General Overview

The *RWS* Moon closely follows the *Marseilles* version of the card, showing a moon above two towers, under which two dogs (in Waite's version, a dog and a wolf) appear to be howling. A serene face is set within the surface of the moon, which also shows the waning, waxing and full aspects of its cycle. Thirty-two rays of light are shown around the moon's perimeter, perhaps suggesting that the moon is eclipsing the sun, blocking out most of its illumination. In the lower section of the card a lobster or crayfish is shown emerging from a pool of water. At the card's center a path is shown, winding between the lobster and the dogs, leading through the two towers to the mountains beyond. The towers appear to be those first seen distantly in Death, indicating that our Hero is coming to the end of his or her sojourn in the *Land of Trials*, and is about to emerge into the light of the everyday, back into society.

Despite what we might expect, this Return card is usually interpreted quite negatively within Tarot literature, associated with such themes as fear, fantasy, lunacy, deceit and distortion. According to Waite, the card represents the "life of the imagination apart from life of the spirit." The moon's reflected light only illuminates "our animal nature," represented by the dog and the wolf. The lobster represents something even more primitive –

"that which comes up out of the deeps, the nameless and hideous tendency which is lower than the savage beast"; a primeval horror within humanity which seeks to "attain manifestation."[1] For Papus, similarly, this card indicates that the soul has left the world of spirit and fallen completely into the lower world of matter, from which "it can descend no lower." The three animals represent "servile spirits," "savage souls" and "crawling creatures" which all seek the individual's destruction.[2] Comparable negative appraisals attend Jungian interpretations of the card. For Nichols, the card represents the Hero's "bleakest" point in his travels, in which he has lost his human identity and sunk to the level of an animal and the "watery unconscious" of the "prehistoric crawfish." If he can find no conquest here, his devouring unconscious will overwhelm him, "resulting in psychosis."[3]

Within the spectrum of possibility the card has more positive connotations, including intuition, powerful dreams, "the female element ... [or] women in general,"[4] and guidance through "potentially unfriendly territory."[5] The Neopagan and Wiccan movements – as Pollack herself recognizes[6] – would also be inclined to offer a more positive appraisal of this card, reflecting the "triumph" as opposed to the "trials" of The Moon. Within feminist Wicca in particular, the moon has come to symbolize a recovery and reaffirmation of the "shadow" that patriarchal culture and spirituality has denied or devalued – sensuality, sexuality, mystery, nature, darkness, the feminine, and indeed, women. This reaffirmation of the lost or devalued is recognized by Gardner's channeled Moon, who declares that the way forward lies in a "remembering of what you have forgotten."[7] In *Dianic Wicca* especially, the Moon has come to represent the immanent presence of *Diana*, the

Great Goddess of nature and childbirth, whose power and energy can be "drawn down" during full moon rituals.

In Roman mythology, Diana (*Bright Sky*) is the virgin goddess of the hunt, the moon, nature, childbirth and women. She supplants the earlier *Titan* moon goddess *Luna*, but retains her name as an epitaph. In statuettes and reliefs she is shown carrying a bow, accompanied by a deer or hunting dogs - a likely origin of the two canines in The Moon card. Indeed, many early Tarot decks make The Moon's link with Diana much more explicit than the *Marseilles'* stylization. For example, The Moon from the 15th-Century *Tarocchi of Mantegna* is entitled *Luna*, and depicts a goddess in a sky-chariot holding a crescent moon.[8] For Kaplan, the 17th-Century *Tarocchini of Mitelli* simply shows "Diana beneath the moon."[9] The link between The Moon and Diana is also made obvious in many modern decks, including Place's *Alchemical Tarot* and Waldherr's *Goddess Tarot*.

In regards to our poor lobster, I am tempted to ignore explanations related to the astrological sign of Cancer or to the chthonic monstrosities of the unconscious, and settle instead for the simple fact that lobsters and similar crustaceans are affected by lunar forces, the biggest catches often being made just before a full moon. Our Renaissance counterparts may not have known about depth psychology, but they did recognize the pull of the moon on the contents of their lobster pots.

The "pull of the moon" is certainly something which brings out Wiccans to celebrate the power of the Goddess, as revealed in her celestial presence, in the cycles and rhythms of nature, and in what Starhawk perceives as the "pulsating power" that works in harmony with menstrual processes. In addition, continues Starhawk, the Goddess is "the liberator." She is venerated at the full moon because she connects humans with their deepest drives and emotions; aspects of ourselves which threaten those systems "designed to contain them." She liberates her worshippers from "fixed perceptions," "blind beliefs," and "fear."[10]

This understanding of Diana as "liberator" may derive in part from her ancient association with the succession of the *rex Nemorenis* – the High Priest of Diana who could be challenged to mortal combat by a slave at any time, the victor then resuming the priestly office. But perhaps the greatest influence on our understanding of Goddess as liberator comes from a small book published in 1899 by the folklorist Charles Leland, entitled *Aradia or The Gospel of the Witches*. The book, which was very influential in the development of modern Wicca, purports to be a translation of a manuscript which Leland claims he received from an Italian hereditary witch by the name of *Maddalena*. The first section is in the form of a *Gospel*, recording the words spoken by the Goddess Diana to her daughter *Aradia*, who is to be reborn as a woman in order to teach and spread witchcraft. Aradia in turn gives counsel concerning the revolutionary task which lies ahead:

> And when the priests or the nobility
> Shall say to you that you should put your faith
> In the Father, Son, and Mary, then reply:
> "Your God, the Father, and Maria are
> Three devils ...
>
> "For the true God the Father is not yours;
> For I have come to sweep away the bad,

The men of evil, all will I destroy!

Ye who are poor suffer with hunger keen,
And toil in wretchedness, and suffer too
Full oft imprisonment; yet with it all
Ye have a soul, and for your sufferings
Ye shall be happy in the other world,
But ill the fate of all who do ye wrong!"

The work of "all witchcraft," declares Aradia, is "to destroy the evil race (of oppressors)."[11]

Another goddess associated with the moon is the triple-aspected *Hekate*, viewed by modern Wiccans as representing both the three phases of the moon and the three important phases of a woman's life – maiden, mother and crone. The figure of Hekate can also be found in The Moon cards from a significant number of Tarot decks, including Dugan's *Witches Tarot*, Zadok's *Mansions of the Moon Tarot*, and Greene's *Mythic Tarot*. Diana and Hekate share a number of similar features; indeed Diana is sometimes viewed as one aspect of Hekate. Like Diana, she is a goddess of childbirth, and is also usually depicted surrounded by dogs. In addition, Hekate carries the epitaphs of light-bearer (*phosphoros*) and key-bearer to all mysteries (*kleidophoros*). Of relevance to Smith's depiction of The Moon is Hekate's association with "liminal" or "threshold" places, such as gateways - the entrances and exits to which were often guarded by *Stygian* dogs, such as *Cerberus*. This conforms to Smith's depiction of the two canine-defended towers (or *Hekataea*), which together form a gateway to the everyday world, towards which our Hero must now venture forth.

A neglected aspect of The Moon's symbolism within most Tarot interpretation is its association with what could be termed "transformative community." Aradia for example commands her followers to assemble together "[o]nce in the month, and when the moon is full" to adore the "potent spirit of your queen," the "great Diana." Together as community, her worshippers will be taught "all things as yet unknown," and "ye shall all be freed from slavery."[12] Similarly, in Rabbinical and Kabbalistic symbolism, the moon is associated not only with of sephirah of *Malkuth* (the world), and God's *Shekinah* or feminine presence, but, as Eliezer Segal says, with the people of Israel "in exile." The Moon, according to Segal points towards both the future redemption of the people of Israel, and to "a remedying of alienation within God him/herself."[13] A similar *Luna-Ecclesia* connection existed within early Christianity – a point recognized by Jung.[14] The moon became identified with both Mary and the Church community; the "bride" which bears social witness to the light of the "Son," and awaits union with her bridegroom and lover.

In the Story of the Buddha: Turning the Wheel of the Dharma

The Buddha set out to wander by stages to Benares, and to the five ascetics, now residing at the Deer Park at *Isipatana*. When the five first saw him, they agreed among themselves that they would only address him as "friend," and not pay him any respect for having abandoned the spiritual quest for a life of luxury. The Buddha rebukes them, and tells them that "friend" is not an appropriate term for one who has attained the status of a *Tathagata* - a fully enlightened one. The Buddha approached, and set forth his intentions: "I shall teach you the Dhamma."[15] Under a full moon, on that "lunar day sacred to Vishnu,"[16] the Buddha thus set in motion the "Wheel of the Dharma," instructing the five ascetics on the core aspects of his teachings. The Buddha eventually won them all over, and they attained liberation from "bondage."[17] The five, now transformed in their hearts and minds, requested to embark on the Buddha's vision of the religious life. Touching their heads, the Buddha thus brought them into his new "mendicant order."[18]

A Buddhist Reflection: The Sangha – Community of the Moon

In Buddhism the moon is revered as a highly auspicious symbol, indicting both the luminosity and "coolness" of awakened consciousness. In the Tibetan tradition, the moon is often shown as a crescent under a solar disc, indicating the view of enlightenment as a union of compassion (moon) and wisdom (sun). In the Wheel of Becoming, the Buddha is often depicted pointing at both, indicating the human potential for liberation from Mara's realm of death.

According to tradition, the most important events in the Buddha's life were said to have taken place under a full moon, including his birth, renunciation, enlightenment, first sermon, and death. Interestingly, an epitaph for the Future Buddha of the world – *Maitreya* – is *Prince Moonlight*. Of particular note in reference to Smith's rendition are the thirty-two rays of light surrounding the moon – the marks of a Mahapurusha, suggesting the appearance of a Buddha in the world.

In Theravadin countries even today, Buddhist practice is organized around the phases of the moon. The full moon and new moon in particular are regarded at times of significant spiritual reflection and training, and during these days lay Buddhists will often extend their normal practice of the "five precepts" to eight of the "ten precepts" followed by novices. The new moon and full moon days are especially important to ordained monks (*bhikkhus*) and nuns (*bhikkhunis*), when they will come together as a community and recite the *Pattimokkha* precepts. These are the standards of ethical conduct expected of those who are ordained; the principles that regulate and maintain the harmony of the monastic community – The Sangha.

The Sangha is one of the three refuges and jewels of Buddhism, indicating what Buddhists hold to be the foundational role of supportive fellowship in the quest for spiritual development. According to the Buddha in the *Upaddha Sutta*, the companionship, friendship and support offered by the Sangha represents not just "half," but the "whole" of the spiritual life.

The Sangha really began when the Buddha "set in motion" the teaching of the Dharma through his first sermon under a full moon to the five ascetics at the Deer Park near Sarnath. Here, we are told, the ascetic Kondanna gained insight and awakening. "'Kondanna has indeed understood!'" exclaimed the Buddha.[19] Initially, admittance to the Sangha was a very simple affair; but as it became increasingly organized, more complex procedures and regulations for admittance and community cohesion were developed. Today, *Sangha Day* remembers not the five ascetics from the Deer Park, but the Buddha's first recitation of the Pattimokkha precepts to 1250 arhats – again under a full moon - at *Veluvana Vihara*.

The Sangha was a truly revolutionary community for its time. Moving against the norms of Brahminical culture, the Buddha opened the doors of his new movement to the lowest castes, and redefined Brahmin status in terms of ethical conduct. Although hesitant at first, he also opened the doors of his new movement to women, liberating them from a society which severely curtailed their social and spiritual opportunities. This sense of liberation and emancipation from crushing domesticity is given full expression in a poem by *Sumangala's mother*, found in the *Therigatha* collection:

> O woman well set free! how free am I,
> How throughly free from kitchen drudgery!
> Me stained and squalid 'mong my cooking-pots
> My brutal husband ranked as even less
> Than the sunshades he sits and weaves alway.
>
> Purged now of all my former lust and hate,
> I dwell, musing at ease beneath the shade
> Of spreading boughs–O, but 'tis well with me![20]

The Sangha has a variety of functions, the primary one being to provide the best environmental conditions for individual and communal spiritual development. Yet, it is also there to provide an example of enlightened living to the lay community. From its inception, the Buddha made it quite clear that the Sangha should not develop in isolation from society as a whole, and towards this end, forbade its members from owning property or growing and preparing their own food. The Sangha was made to be dependant on the larger community for its survival and sustenance. As a reciprocal gesture, the monks and nuns were obliged to provide the laity with spiritual example, teaching and guidance. The Buddhist monk or nun as Ling says has not rejected society to chase private illumination, which would be in direct opposition to Buddhism's "repudiation of individualism." In contrast with traditional practices of the time, which insisted that spiritual development meant "a life of solitude," the Sangha represented "life in the community."[21] The third role of the Sangha appears more revolutionary – to stand together as one community, and from this position of strength and solidarity, communicate the Buddha's message of liberation to the whole world:

> "Therefore, stand ye together, assist one another, and strengthen one another's efforts. Be like unto brothers; one in love, one in holiness, and one in your zeal for the truth. Spread the truth and preach the doctrine in all quarters of the world, so that in the end all living creatures will be citizens of the kingdom of righteousness. This is the holy brotherhood; this is the church, the congregation of the saints of the Buddha; this is the Sangha that establishes a communion among all those who have taken their refuge in the Buddha."[22]

The Sun (19)

General Overview

The *RWS* version of this card shows a naked smiling child, riding bare-back on a white horse. In his left hand he bears a red banner on a pole. Behind the child we see a wall, with four sunflowers clearly visible. Above the child, the sun shines in its full glory.

There can be little doubt that the figure of The Sun card is that of the Greek solar deity *Apollo*, God of intelligence, reason, medicine and light. In art, just like our child in the card, Apollo is often depicted as a nude youth, conforming to Greek aesthetics of male perfection. Apollo is also associated with horses, particularly in the Celtic lands influenced by his cult, where he went by the title of *Apollo Atepomarus – The Great Horseman*. The wall in the card reminds us that the name *Apollo* is derived from the Doric term *apella*, meaning wall or enclosure, reflecting the god's link with animal husbandry. The sunflowers behind the wall recall the story of his lover *Leucothea* and her sister *Clytia*, whom he turned into a sunflower for betraying his trust. His banner and pole, like that of St George's, celebrate his victory over some chthonic horror, in this case, *Python*. The child's flower crown is also suggestive of Apollo's crown of bay laurel. A number of Tarot decks make the card's connection with Apollo more explicit, from Giovanni Vacchetta's 1893 design, to that found in the more recent *Mythic Tarot*.

Apollo became the poster boy for the European Enlightenment; a pertinent symbol for the forces of light and reason, science and technology, which would drive away all traces of irrationality and superstition. Yet the danger of Apollo's sun, as with The Emperor, is in its denial of the dark, the intuitive, the emotional and the irrational, and the lopsided elevation of detached intellectualism and reliance upon technological innovation. The peril of Apollo's "brightness" as James Hillman says, is that it presents of vision of life severed from "feminine ways," and is thus psychologically destructive.[1] The technological and otherworldly trajectory of such lopsided thinking perhaps finds its most apt expression in the memorable image of the 1969 "Apollo" landing-team, plunging their flag of scientific transcendence into the *pythonic omphalos* of the actual moon.

Apollo's Enlightenment Project, which sought to build a new society based on reason married to the narrative of progress, has failed. It has failed because it unsuccessfully addressed the question of the inner creative life of humanity, and our need to maintain what Jung terms the "psychic balance." "Progress" we have certainly made, but this has been achieved through further secondary narratives of regulation and control, based on the view that our "fallen" and irrational nature needs constant subjugation, surveillance, or denial, if civilization is to "endure." The Enlightenment project has mirrored Freud's view that civilization sits atop a broiling cauldron of selfish, violent and pleasure-seeking impulses, and therefore can only continue through a certain measure of "coercion."[2] We have to this extent been left in an oppressive world "bereft of the gods," and yet ironically, for an elite at least, one that has divinized the seven deadly sins.

There is a dawning apprehension that this state of affairs cannot continue indefinitely. The nightmarish and explosive emergence of religious fundamentalism – from the Middle-East to the Mid-West - can no longer be glibly passed over as mere medievalism to be pacified with the baubles of conglomerate franchising; but indications of a bursting forth of repressed psychological forces that must be attended to.[3] What we need in effect is a new "religion," whether we call it this or not. Our hope, as many now realize, lies in the establishment of a religious form of life that can bring together the worlds the reason and sentiment, of rationality and emotion, and marry them together in a new *mysterium coniunctionis* fit for the Twenty-First Century.

As a united pair, the Tarot cards of Sun and Moon suggest such a new synthesis. This is recognized by Gardner's channeled Sun, who declares that although we have served him with "increasing efficiency" over the centuries, by himself in us, we "become too bright." We have allowed him "no queen upon which to shine." He urges us to worship "my queen, your imaginations" as we worship him. In the same way, his channeled Moon declares that neither a "womb centered" nor "head centered" civilization is now enough - "[y]ou need both to perform miracles."[4] Such a union reflects what Owen Barfield's developmental model of human consciousness describes as the era of *Final Participation*, in which humanity moves once more towards a position of reconciliation with nature, psyche and the body; grounded in a new holistic synthesis of reason, imagination, and creativity.[5] The religious form of this emerging era is that of a re-enchanted "everyday life"; a numinous materialism blending the worlds of mystery and technology, emotion and reason, liberation and social cohesion. This is a marriage which heals the trauma bequeathed to us in the cultural and spiritual transition from the matrifocal Empress to the patriarchal Emperor and his theological extension, The Hierophant. It is a union which seeks the best of both worlds and at the same time provides an alternative to the rule of all transcendent patriarchs. In the ecstatic, visionary, and certainly prophetic theology of Sophocles: "'Lord Helios [Sun], Lord of the Sacred Flame, You who are the weapon of Hekate of the Roads, which she bears when she leads in Olympus ...'"[6]

A hint of this new synthesis is actually contained within The Sun card itself. We are reminded that Apollo is not merely the God of reason and light, but also that of prophecy, poetry and music, often depicted with a lyre in his hand. He has close ties too with the world of nature, being the defender of herds and flocks. Ethically, he is associated with the Golden Mean, the middle way of virtue and moderation, his oracular shrine at Delphi bearing the words *meden agan* – "nothing in excess." In mythology he is also depicted as a skilled archer, working in harmony with his twin sister *Artemis*, the hunter goddess of the moon, often conflated with Diana. This important partnership with his sister is perhaps vaguely recalled in some older renditions of The Sun card, which show naked twins laughing and celebrating together. The image from the *Wirth* deck in particular stands out as being very suggestive of this divine pair. Of note too is the fact that one of Apollo's epithets is *Hekatos* – the masculine form of Hekate, often translated as *far-reaching one* or *shooter from afar*.

The bringing together of the natural and spiritual, the rational and the imaginative, in a new meaningful unity, is a striking feature of Neopaganism and other earth-based spiritualities. Why? – because when divinity is viewed as something within rather than above nature, then science can be seen as the means of investigating the sacred reality of which we are all part. In pantheistic spiritualities, as Harold Wood says, "knowing God" is "ecology in its broadest sense." By means of scientific investigation, the pantheist attains a closer relationship with what he or she conceives as "the divine."[7] For Starhawk, similarly, a Goddess religion of the future should be "firmly grounded in science." Worship in Goddess religion can move from meditations on ancient Goddess images to reflections on "the structure of the atom." An earth-centered spirituality can take the insights from the various sciences and combine them with ritual and myth, to inspire us with "wonder at the richness of life."[8] Yet it is not just in its conversation with science that Neopaganism shimmers with the spirit of Apollo. As Howard Eilberg-Schwartz has recognized, Wicca and other contemporary earth-based spiritualities are "Enlightenment Religions" because they share a number of important ideals and attitudes with their humanistic forbears. These include antagonism towards organized religion; the location of authority within the self and community – not text or tradition; and a pragmatic, eclectic and experimental approach to belief and truth.[9]

The Sun's vision of a possible future spirituality also reaches out to embrace a renewed sense of wonder, play and creativity. This is particularly apparent in the symbol of the naked child, riding his horse with natural and playful abandon, without stirrups, reins or saddle to support him. Nichols concurs, and views the card as indicating a sense of "play" and "delight"; a return to that neglected part within which remains "experimental, primitive and whole."[10]

In this respect it is notable that Matthew Fox and others link the growth of creation-centered Christianity with a renewed appreciation of human creativity. Indeed, one of the sustained criticisms of mainstream Christianity has been its separation of spirituality from creativity and imagination. Nicolas Berdyaev for example considers the rupture between church and world, salvation and creativity, to be the most "tormenting" problem of our age. He traces this problem to a religious heritage that teaches that creativity is of little value in relation to the fate of the individual's soul after death. It is difficult to be creative when "one is threatened with damnation." He suggests that the Church move away from this "degenerate" form of Christianity towards one that embraces the ancient concern with *theosis* - the transfiguration of the world and humanity, not "personal salvation."[11]

For Fox, creativity is an integral part of what it means to be made "in the image of God." We are reminded too, he says, that Jesus was not a priest nor an intellectual, but a poet and storyteller who told his followers to "do likewise."[12] In the creation-centered tradition, God's creative powers are viewed as ongoing, not chained to the *Genesis* creation narrative. Fox shares the views of medieval mystics like Meister Eckhart, who declares that the essence of God is "birthing" and that God from his "divine maternity bed" has extended to us the same power to "eternally give birth."[13] We are called, says Fox, to be "co-creators" with the divine.

In the Story of the Buddha: The Spread of a Reasonable Dharma

After the establishment of the Sangha, the Buddha spend the remaining forty-five years of his life teaching the Dharma to any who would listen, and debating with those who were antagonistic towards his new philosophy of awakening. His empirical and logical outlook, as G. S. P. Misra reports, heralded "a new trend in the realm of thinking" which was to have a profound impact on Indian religiosity.[14] A substantial part of this new approach was an unflinching critique of the practices of the Brahmins, especially the efficacy of their rituals, which seemed to deny the empirically and ethically obvious. He opposed the Brahminical view that by washing in a sacred river one could purify oneself from breaches of caste duty or ethical misconduct. In the *Vatthupama Sutta*, the Brahmin *Sundarika Bharadvaja* inquires of the Buddha why he did not bathe in the nearby *Bahuka* river, which brought liberation, merit, and washed away "evil actions." In reply the Buddha stated the obvious – no amount of washing can purify someone committed to "cruel and brutal deeds." To be pure, one must be "pure in heart."[15] In the *Therigatha*, the Bhikkhuni *Punnika* added to the Buddha's critique, pointing out that the logic of such rituals would lead us to the conclusion that frogs and turtles, water snakes and crocodiles, all "straight to heaven will go." Moreover, if these streams carried away our evil, they would also "bear away thy merit too, leaving thee stripped and bare."[16] The Buddha, as previously mentioned, was also critical of blood sacrifices, which he saw as wasteful, cruel and ethically of little use. A better "sacrifice" would be that of deeds filled with compassion and generosity. Overall, the Buddha saw an unreflective reliance upon ritual as one of the "ten fetters" which prevented humanity's ethical development and spiritual awakening.

By contrast, the Buddha invited people to follow the Dharma by first putting it to the test in their own lives. In the *Kalama Sutta*, as mentioned previously, he told his followers to abandon the ten traditional sources of belief, and trust their own judgement and reasoning. When people recognize within themselves that his teachings lead to well-being and "happiness," then they should adopt and practice them.[17]

Another feature of his message was a pragmatic and agnostic approach to issues of a supernatural or metaphysical nature. In the *Kevatta Sutta*, the householder *Kevaddha* informs the Buddha that there are many potential converts in the nearby settlement of *Nalanda*. He suggests that if a monk were to perform a miracle, then he would gain many new adherents. While not denying the reality of supernormal powers, the Buddha replies that there is only one real miracle – the "miracle" of instruction; the "miracle" of the Dharma. On another occasion, the Buddha met an ascetic by the bank of a river who had practiced austerities for twenty-five years. The Buddha asked him what he had gained from all those years of self-mortification. With some pride, the ascetic replied that he could now walk on water. Here, the Buddha pointed out that his miraculous achievement was worth a penny, since he could cross the river on the nearby ferry for that price. It would have been better for him to have used his time to develop insight into suffering and attachment, and liberation from them.[18] Such pragmatism is also found the Buddha's attitudes to the great "indeterminates" – for example, what happens to an enlightened person after death, or whether the world is eternal or not. In the *Culamalunkya Sutta* the Buddha compared a person absorbed in such questions to a man shot with a poisoned arrow, refusing to have it removed until he discovered the caste of the person who shot him, or what kind of wood the arrow was made from. That person would surely die, with no answers. In the same way, counsels the Buddha, if we want to live we must put vain speculations aside, and stick to that which is really important: the realities of birth, ageing, death, grief and despair – the remedy for which "I prescribe here and now."[19]

Although notable for its empirical pragmatism, the Buddha's approach was also marked with a sense of creative innovation. He re-visioned the concept of "Brahmin" membership in terms of ethical conduct as opposed to natural birthright. In this way, he provided a rationale for establishing a spiritual community which cut across all caste divisions, and eventually, gender divisions. His insistence that the Sangha members should never own property nor prepare their own food meant that spiritual development could never be an individualistic pursuit, practiced away from society at large. Another creative move was to insist that his message did not eradicate but coexist with and absorb the religious, superstitious, and aesthetic norms of the communities it encountered. With the exception of the Brahmin priesthood and the sacrificial system, the Buddha, as Ling says, assumed a by-and-large "tolerant attitude" towards the religious customs of his day. In relation to folk beliefs and practices, he demonstrated a creative appreciation of the function that mythology and ritual occupied "in the lives of unsophisticated people."[20] This skillful approach resulted in the slow transformation of Buddhism's outward appearance in some places, but one which nevertheless retained the integrity of its core teachings. This is a process that can clearly be seen in Buddhism's interaction with Tibet's original *Bon* tradition. Such innovations reveal creativity to be one of the hallmarks of an awakened mind. A mind without defilements, without unwholesome preoccupations, is at the same time one which uncovers the potential for natural and unconstrained creativity.

A Buddhist Reflection: Buddhism and Science

Buddhism, especially in its Mahayana/Vajrayana forms, is truly Apollonian in character, bringing together the worlds of reason and empirical pragmatism with those of emotion, mystery, and artistic creativity. This affective and artistic dimension is clearly found in various elements of the Tibetan tradition, whether sacred dance, chanted mantras, *thankha* painting, *mandala* construction, or the ecstatic prophecies of the *Nechung* oracle. In Zen Buddhism, similarly, meditation works in collaboration with a vast array of artistic pursuits, including poetry, calligraphy, the martial arts, gardening, and even tea-making.

Yet perhaps the main attraction of Buddhism for many in the West has been its apparent compatibility with science, or at least, a scientific sensibility. This attitude was clearly shown in a discussion between the renowned astrophysicist Carl Sagan and the Dalai Lama. Sagan asked him a question which he presented to most religious leaders he engaged with – what would he do if science disproved one the central tenets of his faith, for example, rebirth? The Dalai Lama's response was hardly expected: "Tibetan Buddhism," he replied, "would have to change."[21] More explicitly, the Dalai Lama has written that if scientific investigation were to decisively show certain claims in Buddhism to be false, then Buddhism must "accept the findings of science and abandon those claims." Spirituality, he says, must be in accord with the "insights and discoveries of science."[22] Such words reveal what is for many an attractive aspect of the Buddhist mentality – of putting reason and empirical evidence before speculation, dogma, or tradition. This pragmatic approach has set the baseline for others to go even further in their visions of a "religionless" or at least "agnostic" Buddhist culture of awakening, divested of harmful archaic accretions that have fastened themselves to the Buddha's original vision of liberation. As Batchelor argues, blind allegiance to unverifiable beliefs, such as the six realms of existence or retributive karma, directs us away from "the Buddha's agnostic and pragmatic perspective." The Buddha did clearly accept karma, but in contrast with the understanding of many "religious Buddhists," he focused on its "psychological" as opposed to "cosmological" repercussions.[23]

However, one of the most thought-provoking areas within the Buddhist-Science dialogue concerns an apparent convergence between various Buddhist concepts (especially emptiness and interdependence) and scientific theories relating to the nature of reality. In relation to Physics for example, there seems to be some resonance in the Mahayana distinction between relative and absolute levels of truth (discussed in The Fool and The High Priestess) and the distinction physicists make between Newtonian and Quantum descriptions of reality. This is a distinction between a diverse world of things, events, identities and causes, and one as the Dalai Lama says in which there are no "discrete, independent realities."[24] The Buddhist view of the interconnected nature of reality also coincides with observations of protons and their apparently simultaneous interaction at distance, which points towards a "nonseparable" understanding of the world.[25] Again, Heisenberg's Uncertainty Principle, which for many physicists suggests the inseparable role of the observer in the reality being observed, seems congruent with certain philosophical strands within Buddhism; from the extreme idealism of *Yogacara*, which saw the world as an extension of mind, to the Middle Way of the *Prasankiga* school, which views the world as having only relative existence, reliant upon our shared language and concepts.[26]

Another area of fruitful dialogue has been in the area of consciousness research. Western models of consciousness have tended towards understanding it solely in terms of behavior or physical processes within the brain. Such models have tended to overlook its subjective dimension, focusing instead upon that which can be observed and measured. For the Dalai Lama, a comprehensive model of consciousness requires the integration of such third-party reductionism with "the subjective experience of the individual."[27] Buddhism, with its long history of rigorous investigation into this subjective dimension, may contribute towards a fuller picture of the mind. One way in which such collaboration has already been seen is in the area of "neuroplasticity" – the brain's capacity for transformation and adaptation. Experiments involving the brain-monitoring of experienced Buddhist meditators have confirmed that mind-training (*bhavana*) leads to observable changes in the brain, and with this, alterations in psychological traits that were previously assumed to be fixed.

Judgement (20)

General Overview

This card illustrates a popular subject amongst artists of the Renaissance – The Last Judgement. This is the "end-time" when, according to the *Book of Revelation*, "the seventh angel blew his Trumpet" and it was time "for the dead to be judged." (*Rev.* 11: 15, 18). The card shows the angel Gabriel, blowing the "Last Trumpet," and the dead rising from their tombs. The Trumpet itself is depicted with a cross-emblazoned banner hanging from it, perhaps representing the idea of resurrection. In a departure from traditional Tarot renditions of this theme, Waite has shown six rather than three figures rising from their graves – three in the immediate foreground, and three on the other side of some watery expanse. Another modification is that both sets of figures depict a man and a woman with a child between them. In previous decks - for example, the *Visconti-Sforza* or *Marseilles* - the naked couple is usually depicted with an old man.

At the darker side of the spectrum of possibility, this card carries within itself the apocalyptic themes of judgement and cleansing destruction. The card is after all that of the Last Judgement, and Gabriel, as Cirlot reminds us, is the "angel of the apocalypse"; the one who "sounds the last Trump" in the "valley of Jehoshaphat."[1] The apocalypse is the "unveiling" of the end of the world. For the Abrahamic faiths in particular, this describes the final battle between the forces of good and evil, the resurrection of the dead, and God's judgement upon the righteous and the damned. As Gabriel revealed to the prophet Daniel: "And many of those who are asleep in the dust of the earth shall awake, some to everlasting life, and some to shame and everlasting contempt" (*Dan.* 12: 2). From this perspective, the three figures on the far shore perhaps represent those doomed to perdition, cut off from the righteous – as in Michelangelo's rendition of this scene - by the river *Styx*.

A second theme in this card, and one that is linked to the first, is that of "transition." The card as Fairfield says evokes a sense of "passing from one phase of life into another."[2] Pollack sees not only transition but decision-making, suggesting that the cross on the flag indicates a crossroads in thinking.[3] We can sum all this up in Greer's proposal, which is that the card is the harbinger of a *paradigm shift* – the unexpected appearance of a "new perspective"; or, more negatively, "resisting transformation."[4] In this interpretation, the three on the far shore may represent the actualized potentialities of those figures nearest to us, while the river suggests the difficult waters of transition.

The much-used if not over-used concept of the *paradigm shift* ultimately derives from Thomas Kuhn's *The Structure of Scientific Revolutions*. In his book Kuhn set out to challenge the tacitly assumed view that scientific knowledge and understanding increases incrementally over time. Instead, Kuhn argued that many advances are made during short periods of dramatic shifts in thinking; they are "revolutions" in understanding. Kuhn compared such revolutions of the mind to a gestalt-like change in perception.[5] Although Kuhn's study was limited to the scientific disciplines, his concept of the *Paradigm Shift* has become a general colloquialism for dramatic transitions in general, particularly cultural ones. It has for example occupied a central place within New Age thinking from the 1980s onwards. What is particularly apparent, and of much relevance to The Judgement card, is that opposition to new cultural paradigms is often cloaked within the language of the apocalypse. In her number one best-seller *The Hidden Dangers of the Rainbow*, the evangelical writer Constance Cumbey described the then-emerging New Age in terms of a Satanic Conspiracy for world domination. Many in the evangelical right would still be happy with Cumbey's initial assessment that the rise of feminism, gay rights, eastern mysticism, environmentalism, anti-war protests and Neopaganism are "definite signs of the end times."[6] Yet such apocalyptic fervor in the face of cultural change is certainly not confined to Christianity's kooky corner. In a 2013 sermon to his congregation at the Kazan Cathedral in Moscow's Red Square, the head of the Russian Orthodox Church, Patriarch Kirril, declared that the legal recognition of gay marriage was a "very dangerous sign of the apocalypse"; a step on the "path of self-destruction."[7]

Yet the sword of the apocalypse cuts both ways. For the old guard, the emerging new paradigm of the "Ecological Age"[8] looks like the end of the world – a leftist, pagan, godless, unnatural and perverted realm of the anti-Christ which will usher in God's cleansing judgement. For the proponents of this new paradigm, it is precisely an impending apocalypse towards which the old ways are steering us which must be avoided – the apocalypse of patriarchal fragmentation, blind consumerism, capitalistic greed, global militarization and ecological catastrophe. As Ruether puts it, exponential population growth, diminishing resources, pollution, and state violence have now become "the four horsemen of the new global apocalypse."⁹ It appears that the words "Interesting Times" fall well-short of the sense of crisis, dread, and dislocation for all those living within a period of immense cultural and environmental shift – a perceived destabilization of reality itself, for which the only reasonable recourse seems to be to the tortured rhetoric of *The Eschatos*.

Yet a third interpretation of this card focuses upon the themes of awakening and rebirth; themes which cannot be neatly separated from the first two. Our sense of impending disaster and dislocation says Jung is simultaneously the end-point of a pregnancy which "heralds the throes of birth."¹⁰ This sense of rebirth is something recognized by Place in his *Alchemical Tarot* deck, in which the Judgement card depicts young stalks of corn emerging from the *Place of the Skull* (*Golgotha*) - the site of the crucifixion, which in legend was also the hill under which the first Adam was buried. The awakened in Christ are a "new race"; children of a "new Adam." As Paul says: "if any one is in Christ, he is a new creation; the old has passed away, behold the new has come" (*2 Cor.* 5: 17). In this reading, the watery expanse in the *RWS* card represents the waters of baptism and new life.

According to Gardner's channeled Judgement, the "old self" will be "born again"; changed into a "new and vibrant being." Such transformation becomes possible when we listen more carefully "to the Moon and the Sun."¹¹ Gardner's alignment of Moon, Sun and transformation brings to mind the *Great Work* of the Renaissance alchemists. Indeed, it is notable that Smith's rendition of the card suggests a fusion of elements from the *Chymical Wedding* found in various alchemical woodcuts, as in those of 16th-Century *Rosarium Philosophorum*.[12] These illustrations show the *hieros gamos* (sacred marriage) of *Sol* and *Luna*, their sexual union, putrefaction in the grave, and the emergence of some new form of life – the *Philosopher's Stone* or *Divine Child*. The Divine Child, which in our card stands with his back to us between his naked parents, is often viewed as a symbol of spiritual rebirth and transformation. For Cirlot, the child represents the "future," "inner simplicity," and identification with the "god within us."[13] For Jung, the divine child or *puer aeternus* is viewed as symbolic of an emerging potential towards the Self, brought about by the union of all opposites within the psyche – Sol and Luna, male and female, good and evil, dark and light, the conscious and the unconscious.[14] A simpler interpretation might be that the child represents a new form of consciousness arising in the world; the shape of its full disclosure not yet revealed, suggested by his or her concealed identity. Pollack agrees, and argues the presence of six rather than three figures indicates that this transformation is not merely about the individual, but about the progress of humanity as a whole.[15]

In the Story of the Buddha: Conflict and New Life

The Buddha's teachings may have signified the birth of a new culture of awakening, but this does not mean that they were not without opponents, whether from within or without. The Brahmins obviously had much to lose in the Buddha's vision of a rational, casteless, non-theistic and ritual-free society. Their loathing for this new egalitarian order is clearly expressed in the *Aganna Sutta*, where the Buddha questioned *Vasettha*, a recent Brahmin convert to his teachings, on the how his former colleagues viewed his apostasy:

"The brahmins, lord, say thus: Only a brahmin is of the best social grade; other grades are low. Only a brahmin is of a clear complexion; other complexions are swarthy. Only brahmins are of pure breed; not they that are not of the brahmins. Only brahmins are genuine children of Brahma, born of his mouth, offspring of Brahma, created by Brahma, heirs of Brahma. As for you, you have renounced the best rank, and have gone over to that low class—to shaven recluses, to the vulgar rich, to them of swarthy skins, to the footborn descendants. Such a course is not good, such a course is not proper, even this, that you, having forsaken that upper class, should associate with an inferior class, to wit, with shaveling friar-folk, menials, swarthy of skin, the offscouring of Our kinsman's heels. In these terms, lord, do the brahmins blame and revile us with characteristic abuse, copious, not at all stinted."[16]

This vitriol intensifies in later Hindu apocalyptic, as in the *Bhavishya Purana*, which casts the Buddha as the ninth avatar of Vishnu, incarnated to lead many astray with his false *nastika* dharma. In the *Kalki-Purana*, Vishnu descends as the apocalyptic avatar *Kalki*, whose mission among other things is to annihilate Buddhists, outcastes, men controlled by women, and re-establish the caste-varna and sacrificial systems. According to the *Bhagavata Purana,* Kalki, riding his white horse *Devadatta*, will "kill by the millions" those who have "dared dress as kings."[17] Kalki's horse *Devadatta* ("God Given") does of course have other links with apocalyptic conflict, being the name of Arjuna's conch which, according to the *Bhagavad-Gita*, he blew before his all-out battle with his cousins the *Kauravas*. This conch was blown in the name of "duty and fame," lest he "incur sin." Surprisingly enough, Devadatta was also the name of the Buddha's rather nefarious cousin, who attempted to split the Sangha, and even kill the Buddha himself.

Yet the Buddha recognized that another apocalyptic battle was one that took place within. In his conflict with Mara and his many demons, we see the archetypal template for the inner struggle that accompanies spiritual transformation. It is therefore of little surprise that many of the Buddha's teachings were communicated through the metaphors of battle and conflict. "If one were to conquer a thousand thousand in the battle—he who conquers self is the greatest warrior,"[18] he declared in the *Dhammapada*.

As the same time, the Buddha's teachings offered his followers a new sense of freedom; a "rebirth" characterized by ethical integrity, bliss, simplicity, harmlessness, and fellowship with nature. The transformative power of the Dharma is recorded in both the *Thera-* and *Therigatha* - the poetry of the early monks and nuns. "My name is 'Harmless,' though I used to be harmful" declares one former bandit called *Angulimala*, describing his new-found status. Although evil in the past, with much "blood on my hands," now "I don't harm anyone." This bandit, who was once "swept away in a great flood," went "to Buddha as a refuge." Now "free of debt," he sits in the wilderness, "at the foot of a tree," "out of *Mara*'s reach."[19] For another monk, the Buddha's message brought with it a sense of spiritual union with the forces of nature. "The water is clear and the gorges are wide, monkeys and deer are all around; festooned with dewy moss, these rocky crags delight me!"[20] From such communion springs a sense of kinship and compassion for all living things: "Just as a mother would be good to her beloved and only son; so, to creatures all and everywhere, let one be good."[21]

Another component of this rebirth is an acceptance of and coming to terms with inevitable grief and loss. The poetry of *Vasitthi* for example records the story of a young woman lost in grief after the death of her child. In her confused and forsaken state, she was "[n]aked, unheeding, streaming hair unkempt," living in the "scourings of the streets, and where the dead lay still." Then at the city of *Mithila*, she met the "Great Tamer of untamèd hearts"; the one who "[gave] back my heart to me." Putting his teachings into practice, she received "great good fortune" with "all sorrows ... hewn down," and understood "the base on which my miseries were built."[22] A corollary to this is an acceptance of one's own morality, and the freedom that this brings. In death "there is no fear" recounts one monk, recognizing that life in this world is "like grass and wood," and there is nothing "to be [called] mine."[23] For the awakened, says another monk, there is no longer any craving "to dwell in this world or the next." The awakened mind knows "the arising and passing of the world," without "clinging to anything."[24]

For women, life within the Sangha brought freedom from the drudgery of social expectations; from life restricted to that of a dutiful wife. As *Mutta*, wife of a poor Brahmin family married off to a hunchback, but later released to the Sangha, explains: "O free, indeed! O gloriously free am I in freedom from three crooked things: from quern, from mortar, from my crookback'd lord!"[25] This rebirth also freed women from sexualizing forces, whether from within or without. "How was I once puff'd up, incens'd with the bloom of my beauty," recounts *Vimala*, daughter of a prostitute, "I at the door of the harlot stood, like a crafty hunter, weaving his snares, ever watchful." But now, with "shaven head, wrapt in my robe," she goes "forth on my daily round for food" and sits "'neath the spreading boughs of forest tree." In her new life, Vimala has broken all those "evil bonds that fetter gods and men."[26] For some nuns, like *Soma*, the destruction of "Mara's language" extended to that of gender differentiation itself – a point we will explore in our final card – The World.

A Buddhist Reflection: Buddhism at the Apocalypse

For those with sympathies towards an emerging Ecological paradigm, Buddhism is viewed as one solution to the perceived destructive inclinations of the old. Kurt Spellmeyer for example contrasts the "timeless" world-affirming philosophy of Zen Buddhism with the apocalyptic "mental architecture" of Western spirituality, which remains *contemptu mundi* at heart.[27] Unlike the Abrahamic religious traditions, which consistently view the future in terms of a linear shift from this world to the "world to come," Buddhism is neither particularly eschatological nor apocalyptic in outlook. Many Buddhists share the Hindu view that the present is simply one moment in a grander cyclic process of continuous destruction and renewal. Others argue that death and rebirth are constants, and that enlightenment means to awaken to this fact, and begin to live life fully in the present. However, Buddhism does have its apocalyptic moments, and it is to two of these that we now turn.

One of the earliest examples of Buddhist apocalyptic is the *Sermon of the Seven Suns*, found in the *Anguttara Nikaya*. Here, the Buddha describes a time of cataclysmic destruction, in which seven different suns appear in the sky, each causing growing devastation until the earth itself is consumed in a vast conflagration. The main aim of the text however seems not to be that of prophetic speculation, but to impress upon the reader the all-pervasive nature of impermanence, and humanity's inability to deal with this fact – a weariness that culminates in an intense longing for worldwide annihilation.

Yet, the apocalyptic vision that has generated the most curiosity and interest from around the world in recent times is that of the *Kalachakra* or "Wheel of Time" *Tantra*. The *Kalachakra Tantra* revolves around a theory of the cycles of time, from the cosmic to the personal. These Tantric teachings, which utilize deity yoga and mandala construction, enable the practitioner to move from a state of Samsaric ignorance to awakening, thence to compassionate activity in the world. The teachings have gained much publicity since the Dalai Lama's decision to conduct *Kalachakra* initiations all over the world. Since 1954, the Dalai Lama has presided over more than thirty such initiations or "empowerments," motivated by what he sees as the *Kalachakra*'s links to future world peace.

The text of the abridged *Kalachakra Tanta* is divided into five sections. The first, which we will discuss here, concerns the "external" cycle of time – the cyclic process of disintegration and renewal within the cosmos, the world, and society. One controversial[28] section in particular concerns the story of the first *Kalki* king of Shambhala – King Manjushri-yashas. The name *Kalki* indicates the probable Hindu origins of this story in the myth of Kalki the final avatar of Vishnu, who will destroy evil in an apocalyptic battle at the end of the Kali-Yuga. In the *Kalachakra* account, Manjushri-yashas becomes aware of an impending invasion by barbaric forces (*mlecchas*), and so, prepares his people for battle. In contrast with the Hindu Kalki, who prepares for war by restoring the purity of the Hindu dharma and the caste varnas, our Buddhist king decides to unite all varnas into a single family of *vajra* brothers and sisters. He does so by gathering all within his *Kalachakra* mandala palace in Shambhala, where he explains to those gathered that each religion at heart teaches the same moral principles. The population can become "vajra" brothers and sisters while still being faithful to the "pure teachings" of their own religions. United, the people will withstand the invasion. This ecumenical perspective is still adopted in present-day *Kalachakra* empowerments, where observers are asked to "unite in brotherhood and sisterhood" by the act of remaining faithful to the ethical ideals of their respective religious traditions.[29]

For Berzin, the story indicates that the Buddhist solution to contemporary struggles against terrorism, warfare and violence is for humanity to "face them with ethical solidarity." Moreover, the graphic scenes of warfare and violence that pervade the text may actually point towards a psychological battle against "barbaric" emotions led by ignorance and confusion. For Berzin, the *Kalachakra* apocalypse is at heart an apocalypse of the mind.[30] This is a view shared by John Newman, who argues that this Tantric path is really concerned with overcoming the "inner barbarism" that creates evil in the world. The apocalyptic triumph of the vajra community is really a "victory of gnosis over spiritual nescience."[31]

In the *Kalachakra* ceremony, this psycho-apocalyptic drama along with the attendant belief in the impermanence of all things is expressed through the creation and destruction of the *Kalachakra* sand mandala.

Giuseppe Tucci observes that most sand mandalas – like the one constructed at the *Kalachakra* ceremony - depict an inner palace (symbolic of the enlightened mind) with four T-shaped gates, guarded by four terrifying deities. These gates, as Tucci observes, open out onto all that lies outside conscious control, including destructive desires and emotions. These "impediments" (*vighna*) appear in mandala art as a confused and indistinct mass of demons. Whirling about in the darkness like Mara's army, they approach the open gates of the palace and threaten to enter. They represent those barbaric forces within our own minds which at times "burst forth" and possess us. The deities who guard the gates have both defensive and offensive roles; preventing dangerous and disintegrating forces from entering the palace, but also transforming the impediments, leading them towards "the realms of light."[32]

The *Kalachakra* narrative ends with the defeat of the barbaric forces, and the appearance of a new Golden Age. Yet the cycles of time as Berzin notes will eventually move beyond this age too, culminating in another Kali-Yuga, and beyond this into yet another cosmic cycle of creation and dissolution.[33] At the climax of the *Kalachakra* ceremony itself, the sands of the dismantled mandala are gathered together and scattered into a stream or river – in the hope that the peace of the enlightened mind may eventually encompass the world.

Against the prophets of doom, the *Kalachakra* points to the emergence of an (albeit temporary) "Golden Age" of peace within the world and within the ever-turning cycles of time. Yet, as the world itself is "led by mind and fashioned by mind," this emerging culture necessitates an "inner apocalypse" – the will to do battle with our mental barbarians, and bring to birth a new vision of the self and its relations.

The World

General Overview

In the *RWS* deck, The World depicts a naked woman partially covered with a sash, holding a wand in each hand, and positioned within a *mandorla* wreath. She appears to be dancing, with her left leg in front of the right – the reverse of that shown in both The Hanged Man and The Emperor (*Marseilles* deck). In each corner we find one of the four creatures first shown in The Wheel of Fortune – an eagle, bull, lion and man/angel. The card contains echoes of medieval depictions of *The Coronation of Mary*, depicting Mary as *Queen of Heaven*, crowned by the Trinity, and surrounded by the four evangelists. In most traditional interpretations this card signifies a sense of victory, completion and fulfillment. Some interpretations go further, equating it with a more definite sense of finality or perfection – the attainment of the *Summum Bonum*. It represents, says Waite, "the perfection and end of the Cosmos," and "the state of the soul in the consciousness of Divine Vision."[1] In Jungian interpretations the meaning of this card is often internalized, reflecting a diminished view of individuation. Thus Banzhaf writes that it signifies that our "hero has become whole," uniting all oppositions within himself: "masculine and feminine ... conscious and unconscious."[2]

It is however possible to forward a more naturalistic, humanistic and expansive interpretation of The World. The most glaringly-obvious but passed-over aspect of this card is its clear environmental message. A spirituality of "the world" is one that fully embraces the world, and our deep and indissoluble connections to it. For Jung, humanity's malaise derives in part from our disengagement from nature,[3] and thus meaningful Jungian individuation, as Jeremy Yunt has argued, must relate to the extent to which we rekindle a sense of connection and participation with the "vitality, richness and depth of the natural world."[4]

A spirituality in and of the world would identify with two ideas in particular. The first, as Don Cupitt suggests, is that we now recognize ourselves fully as "naturalized citizens," giving up the ghost of "dual citizenship." To embrace this world we must learn to celebrate our transience and our mortality within it, giving up our denial and fear of death (the "trial" of the Death card), and the belief that our life here is no more than a test in preparation for some more enduring realm of "unchanging perfection." The spirituality to be embraced will be "ecohumanist" in outlook, finding "eternal life" and "glory" in our finitude and within the constant flux of life.[5] The World Dancer of this card, like *Shiva* within his own wreath of flame, calls us to celebrate and dance to the natural rhythms of life and death, creation and dissolution. Life, as Starhawk says, is not an "untempered absolute," but something entwined in "a dance with death." It is only this dance with dissolution which maintains "the possibility of new life."[6] Ironically, an acceptance of finitude and death frees us to act more ethically because it makes everything we do intensely significant and transparent. Here, ethical action proceeds from a center of genuine virtue and kindness without expectation – karmic, post-mortem or otherwise.

Second, a spirituality of "the world" would also require an expansion of the self into wider fields of identification. On this point Pollack directs our attention to the sashes at both top and bottom of the mandorla wreath which are tied as open-ended infinity loops, signifying a new sense of openness within the self towards the world and the universe.[7] Yet this expanded self is not the "soluble self"; the pure and passive relationality of the patriarchal feminine.[8] In her nimble dance with wands, we encounter in the World Dancer a relational-self working in harmony with directed will; a dance which supplants the tired immobility of the enthroned Emperor and his tightly held ankh. Nevertheless, there remains a sense of completion and accomplishment within this card. The four elements of inner alchemy – which we previously encountered in various forms in The Magician, The Wheel of Fortune, and Temperance – are now fully manifested, indicating a new sense of ethical balance and creative refinement.

In some versions of this card the World Dancer appears in androgynous form, suggesting, not simply the integration of masculine and feminine qualities, but a new fluidity of being and consciousness that moves beyond this binary dualism. It is interesting to note in this respect a growing gender-fluidity within many of today's young "millennials," who recognize gender as a "social construct," and perceive traditional gender binary norms as both "limiting, and unnecessary."[9] Yet, in terms of our changing perceptions of the self, the world and divine, Pamela Coleman Smith's depiction of a female dancer is equally appropriate. Jung would agree, recognizing the Assumption of Mary in 1950 as an event which confirmed both the sovereignty of archetypal imagery over tradition, and our contemporary psychological and social demands for gender parity, "metaphysically anchored in the figure of a 'divine' woman."[10] Yet, Smith's World Dancer points to more than sexual equality or a return to "feminine" values. It is women, not because of some intrinsic "feminine" nature, but because of their deliberate exclusion from public life, that have as Mary Grey argues been left at home to cultivate and maintain the despised, rejected and projected values of patriarchal culture. It is by way of their projection onto women that the "relational strengths" needed for our survival and flourishing have been preserved and maintained. Women says Grey have quietly kept alive the "relational process" that lies at the heart of humanity and the world itself. It is therefore women - the enforced bearers of the *anima mundi* - who hold the key to a new "redemptive spirituality."[11]

In the story of the Buddha – The Death of the Buddha

As we said, a spirituality of the world, a spirituality that truly embraces the world, is at the same time one that recognizes and even celebrates our finite and impermanent place within it. This is perhaps conveyed in the Shiva-like dance of the World dancer, but also, it may be contended, in the creatures found at each of the four corners. Together, these represent not only the four elements and virtues, but as Gottfried de Purucker has argued, the four turning seasons of the world, and the four passing stages of human life.[12] With this in mind, we turn now to the final episode in the Buddha's journey – his death.

The story of the Buddha's final months are recorded in the *Mahaparinibbana* (*Great Extinction*) *Sutta*.

Approaching 80, and while on retreat, the Buddha suddenly became extremely ill. His attendant, Ananda, became alarmed, and expressed concern that the Buddha had not left clear instructions as to how the Sangha should proceed in the event of his death. The Buddha replied that after his death the monks and nuns should take themselves as their own lamp, as their own refuge. The Buddha recovered somewhat, and continued on his journey. Ananda however, was still in a state of grief; and so the Buddha reminded him of a central aspect of his teachings – the all-pervasive nature of impermanence:

> "But now, Ananda, have I not formerly declared to you that it is in the very nature of all things, near and dear unto us, that we must divide ourselves from them, leave them, sever ourselves from them? How then, Ananda, can this be possible - whereas anything whatever born, brought into being, and organized, contains within itself the inherent necessity of dissolution - how then can this be possible that such a being should not be dissolved?"[13]

The Buddha we are told then went to *Pava*, and a Mango Grove belonging to *Cunda* the Blacksmith. Cunda invited the Buddha and his followers to a specially prepared meal, which according to the tradition, contained spoiled food. After eating this deadly meal, the Buddha travelled onwards to the Salla Grove of the *Mallas*, where he informed Ananda that he was weary, and asked his attendant to spread a robe on the ground for him. Ananda, wrapped up in his own grief concerning the Buddha, and in regret concerning his own lack of spiritual development, disappeared from sight. The Buddha asked a monk to fetch him back, and he explained to Ananda once more the impermanent nature of the world; but also, that if he persisted in his practice, he too would gain liberation.

Word was sent to the nearby town of *Kusinara* that the Buddha was about to die, and so many came to witness this event, and listen to his final words. The Buddha asked his followers if there was anything in the teaching that they had not understood, and then, in his last words, reminded them once more about the fundamental nature of life: "'Decay is inherent in all component things! Work out your salvation with diligence!'"[14] The Buddha, it is said, then entered the jhanic states of consciousness, and moving into the fourth state of mental absorption, he died. At this moment, the God of Creation, *Brahma*, uttered these words:

> "They all, all beings that have life, shall lay
> Aside their complex form - that aggregation
> Of mental and material qualities,
> That gives them, or in heaven or on earth,
> Their fleeting individuality!
> E'en as the teacher - being such a one,
> Unequalled among all the men that are,
> Successor of the prophets of old time,
> Mighty by wisdom, and in insight clear –
> Hath died!"[15]

And so, our *Play in Full*, our *play of The Fool*, comes to a close. Except, as the Buddha himself said: "One who sees the Dharma, sees me."

A Buddhist Reflection: Buddhism, Gender, and the Environment

Susan Murcott describes the Buddha's establishment of the female Sangha as a "radical experiment for its time."[16] This may be so, yet if we take the Pali texts at face value, then it appears that its institution was perhaps more complex and problematic than we might at first be led to suppose. According to the *Cullavagga*, the Buddha was initially very reluctant to allow women into the Sangha and it was only after number of promptings from his attendant and close friend, Ananda, that he eventually relented, adding that he saw in this move the eventual demise of the Sangha. In addition he required that all Bhikkhunis submit to the "eight heavy rules" (*garudhammas*) which meant that they were forced to show deference to the Bhikkhus at all times.

The modern feminist response to this narrative has been quite predictable in a sense, taking the view that the eight rules especially are textual interpolations, created by later monks determined to assert their "legitimate" authority over the nuns.[17] Such modern critiques do of course prompt a very obvious question – are they motivated by a desire to reveal what the Buddha actually said, or to confirm a deeply-held opinion about what an "enlightened being" simply could not or ought not have said? The Sangha aside, the Pali Canon contains a number of other "troublesome" passages and views for those with emotional investments in an idealized vision of the Buddha's attitude to women. For example, although the Buddha states in the *Cullavagga* that women are just as able as men to attain enlightenment, in the *Bahudhatuka Sutta* he mentions limitations on many other forms of spiritual attainment. Women it seems cannot become Mara, Brahma, or more importantly, a Buddha. In the

Anguttara Nikaya he differentiates between seven types of wives – only those who act as "mothers," "sisters," and "handmaids" to their husbands will "go to heaven." The rest will go to hell.[18] Or what are we to make of the Buddha's view that if a woman happens to be "ugly, of a bad figure, and horrible to look at, and indignant, poor, needy, and low in the social scale," then it is due to a "spiteful, angry, enraged, and sulky" disposition from a previous life?[19] Today, it is hoped that we would search for more reasonable and "enlightened" explanations; in issues relating to genetics, diet, economic disadvantage and patriarchal aesthetics perhaps. On the issue of "ugly women," the Dalai Lama in an interview with Michaela Doepke recounted the story of a previous interview with a French journalist, in which he was asked if there could ever be a female Dalai Lama. He replied in the affirmative, but added "half-jokingly" that she would have to be beautiful, given that an "ugly woman" would not be particularly "effective."[20] *Très drôle.*

Putting the Dalai Lama's *faux pas* aside, the answer to such textual problems is not simply to brush them under the carpet, nor to erase them in the name of an idealized vision of what an enlightened being ought to have said, but to focus instead on what Buddhism is and what it is not. It is not a "religion" defined by or confined to the indisputable authority of ancient texts. It is though an insightful diagnosis of the human condition, in which all texts and practices serve as a provisional and pragmatic raft towards healing and wholeness. This raft is best maintained through what we might call *The Rule of Kalama – If it accords with reason, and is conducive to the good, for the one and the many, adopt it and practice it.* This rule would advocate a skillful approach to the original teachings, selecting those which are concordant with reasoned and reasonable Twenty-First Century insights and understanding, and discarding the rest as unworkable chaff. I'm sure the Buddha would agree. As such, a "reasonable" response to the issue of women's partial and subservient role within the Sangha – as is still the case in Thailand and other places – would demand that we do not approach it in relation to notions of traditional values or scriptural authority, but as Karma Tsomo argues, to questions concerning basic human rights.[21]

Returning to scripture, there are a number of insights from the Pali texts which can be skillfully employed in the service of gender parity, of which I wish to highlight anatta – the view that there is no real self behind the constantly changing and impermanent khandhas. One of the most discerning lines of enquiry in the Pali suttas is that although belief in such a self signifies attachment to the five khandhas, this attachment extends further to the issue of gender differentiation. Our attachment to form is at the same time an attachment to gender-form. In the *Soma Sutta*, the Bhikkhuni *Soma* recognizes this deep-seated attachment when she is assailed by Mara, who taunts her with the words:

> "That vantage-ground the [male] sages may attain is hard to reach. With her two-finger consciousness that is no woman competent to gain!"

In response Soma states that gender makes no difference to those whose "'hearts are firmly set, who ever move with growing knowledge onward in the Path.'" She continues however with these profound words: "'To one for whom the question doth arise: Am I a woman in these matters, or am I a man, or what not am I, then? To such a one is Mara fit to talk!'" Mara leaves, dejected, realizing that "'Bhikkhuni Soma knows me.'"[22] This inquiry into ignorance as attachment to gender-identity is pursued more rigorously by the Buddha himself in the aptly named *Bondage (Sannoga) Sutta*. A "woman" he says is one who ""attends inwardly" to feminine faculties, gestures, poise, and desires, and outwardly to the respective masculine qualities in others (heterosexually speaking of course). He repeats this same analysis in reference to a "man." By attending to these internal and external qualities, humans grasp at and become bound to a particular perception of their own masculinity or femininity, and to the external show of certain gender qualities in others. It is only in refusing to attend to such inner and outer qualities that both women and men "transcend" their femininity and masculinity and escape "bondage."[23] "Self-grasping," as Rita Gross has argued, is not just grasping at ego, but an ego that has been acutely hardened by its occupancy within a male or female body. In our quest for freedom and enlightenment, attachment to gender qualities may well be the hardest and last element within our conditioned ego "to lose its grip on us."[24]

The World card reveals to us a need to cultivate a meaningful practice of "letting go," which must extend itself to the masculine-feminine polarity. It suggests a movement beyond our psychological obsessions with and attachments to binary gender differentiation, where we may attain, at least in some measure, that fluidity to which the World Dancer points.

The World card is not only concerned with a new consciousness regarding the gender polarity, but with the self's relations with the world as a whole. In his still much–debated essay from 1967, Lynn White Jr. set out to describe what he regarded as "The Historical Roots of Our Ecologic Crisis." He argued that our environmental problems derive from the Judaeo-Christian narrative concerning human nature. The Bible, he said, has taught us that humans are a special creation apart from the world and its creatures, and that we have been granted "dominion" over our God-given estate. White then argued that despite the claim that we live in a post-religious or post-Christian era, this religious narrative continues to condition our beliefs and attitudes about ourselves and the rest of the world, which retains only instrumental value insofar as it serves our purposes. White concluded that since the problem was essentially religious in nature, it necessitated a religious solution; a new narrative about human nature and its relations with the world. He went on to name Buddhism as a possible candidate in this respect, being "very nearly the mirror image of the Christian view."[25]

However, as with the issue of gender, the Buddhist "story" is not as clear-cut as White thought. As discussed in relation to The Empress, the early Buddhist attitude to nature appears very ambivalent at times, focusing as Schmithausen says on it more destructive side, and its symbolic relationship with sensual attachment and the endless cycle of Samsara. It is also notable, as Stephen Kellert has pointed out, that Buddhist-inspired countries such as Japan and China are well-known for their extremely poor conservation record.[26] Yet as with gender, it is possible to adopt a skillful attitude to Buddhist teachings; to uncover aspects that accord with reason, and are conducive to the universal good. Buddhism espouses a number of ethical qualities that may contribute towards a strong environmental ethic, including contentment (*santutthi*), non-violence (*ahimsa*) and compassion (*karuna*). However, I wish to focus our discussion here to the underlying metaphysical framework within which such virtues might be encouraged to develop and flourish. This framework would embrace the concepts of rebirth (*punabbhava*), emptiness (*sunyata*) and no-self (*anatta*).

The principle of rebirth conceives our current lives to be a very small episode from a potentially unending continuum of phenomena in flux. With this continuum, we have taken on the form and consciousness of myriad life-forms – from bacteria to plants to chimpanzees. (Indeed, the *Kusanjali Jataka* recounts the Future Buddha's life as a clump of grass.) If we take this picture of our "life" to heart, then it may allow us to develop a sense of kinship with and compassion for the countless life-forms to which we are connected. This sense of kinship is explored by the Buddha in the *Mata* (*Mother*) *Sutta*, where he states that from "'a beginning [that] cannot be pointed out'" beings have been "'enveloped in ignorance and bound by craving, running from one existence to another.'" In terms of our links with others within this process, "'you could not find a being who was not your mother [father, sister, brother] in the past, in this long train of existences.'"[27] A deeper awareness of such universal "kinship in suffering" – whether it be reflected upon in meditation or simply discussed in a Biology class – may provide the foundations for a greater degree of empathy and restraint in our dealings with the other living organisms of this planet.

As previously discussed in relation to The Fool and The High Priestess, the principle of emptiness within Buddhism does not mean that things do not exist, but that ultimately, all things lack "own-being" and are intrinsically related to and dependant upon all other things. When integrated with the principle of anatta, this understanding may provide the basis for expanding our usually limited notions of self into wider fields of identification; to take on, as Shantideva says, "all beings as my self." This is something pursued by Buddhist activist Joanna Macy, who believes that such principles may provide a model for the development of an "ecological self." For Macy, along with other Ecofeminists and Deep Ecologists, the environmental problems which threaten our planet originate within a "pathological notion of the self." She names Buddhism as one of a number of non-dualistic spiritualities which may contribute towards the "dismantling of the ego-self" and the creation and establishment of an "eco-self." She notes the important role that Buddhist wisdom, meditation and morality may play in the development of a deeper sense of interconnection with the environment, and the establishing of a more perceptive understanding of "social engagement."[28] We are now summoned, as Macy says, to shake off an issue of "mistaken identity" - the erroneous belief that we are little more than separate beings in competition with one another. It is now time to realize our true nature; as beings "co-extensive with all life on this planet."[29]

The metaphysics of no-self, emptiness and interconnection, along with the ethics of contentment, harmlessness and compassion, may combine to form a new vision of the Sangha, the "Community of the Moon." While traditional models of the Sangha have sometimes been criticized for providing an individualistic and quietist approach to enlightenment, we must not forget that this was not the Buddha's original intention, which was concerned primarily with centering the Sangha's activities within the wider community. The ethics and metaphysics of interdependence would suggest that we now envisage "community" in much wider terms of identification and engagement, fulfilling in a very real sense the Buddha's vision of the Sangha as the "whole of the spiritual life." Such as expanded view of the Sangha was first voiced by Bill Devall in 1990, when he proposed the development of bio-regionally based "eco-sanghas," where practitioners would ground their spiritual development and sense of communality in a commitment to conserving and protecting local natural habitats.[30] The concept of the *Eco-Sangha* has now gained widespread and international appeal, with many – like the one in Forres, Scotland - pledged to finding ways to make the metaphysics of interconnection and the ethics of compassion a "foundation for our practice." The aim of such communities is to "respond to the ecological challenges ...with wisdom, ethics and mindfulness."[31] With the emergence of this new understanding of Buddhist community, the West has not only completely side-stepped the issue of women's ordination – a still-divisive issue within traditional Buddhism - but has, as Jim Deitrick suggests, raised the game entirely, by moving the notion of Sangha membership beyond further distinctions between lay and monastic, and even human and non-human. This, he concludes, promises to have repercussions far beyond issues connected to the relative position and standing of men and women within Buddhism.[32]

Conclusion

In this book I have endeavored to highlight some remarkable connections between Tarot and the Buddha's journey towards enlightenment and his return to the world. While some might regard a few of the links I have made as being tenuous at best, and my interpretations of certain cards a little unorthodox, I still believe that overall, there is a remarkable degree of congruity between the Buddha's journey and the narrative sequence of the Major Arcana. However, in no way am I attempting to provide here yet another *de Gébelin*-inspired Manifesto describing "What the Tarot is Really About." These are my personal views, which hopefully, may challenge the reader to consider some fresh perspectives on the cards. The cards are after all "doctrinally foundationless," their interpretation as Bill Butler says "largely a matter of individual choice."[33] Indeed I agree with Bradford Hatcher that the history of Tarot interpretation is largely one of "men and women making stuff up, and then trying to find acceptance for the stuff they made up." There never was a "Golden Age" of Tarot in the past says Hatcher, nor an original key to its "real" interpretation. Tarot is an on-going "open source project"; an evolving process in which we are constantly stoking "an artificial entity that is seemingly intelligent and moves through time gaining wisdom as it goes."[34] In this respect, it is hoped that the ideas discussed here will contribute at least something to the evolving venture that is Tarot.

Notes

General Introduction

1. E. J. Thomas, trans., *Buddhist Scriptures* (London: John Murray, 1913), accessed October 21 2016, http://www.sacred-texts.com/bud/busc/busc09.htm#page_43.
2. From the *Visuddhi Magga* in Henry Clarke Warren, trans., *Buddhism in Translations* (New York: Atheneum, 1987/1896), p. 248.
3. See for example Stephen Batchelor, *Buddhism Without Beliefs* (London: Bloomsbury Publishing, 1998/1997).
4. Bradford Hatcher, *Tarot as a Counseling Language: Core Meanings of the Cards*, Correspondences Section (n. p.), accessed October 18 2016, http://www.hermetica.info/Tarot.htm.
5. Sangharakshita's views are discussed in Vishvapani, *Introducing the Friends of the Western Buddhist Order* (Birmingham: Windhorse Publications, 2001), p. 43.
6. Bradford Hatcher, op. cit, Introduction Section (n. p.), accessed October 18 2016, http://www.hermetica.info/Tarot.htm.
7. Robert M. Place, *The Buddha Tarot Companion: A Mandala of Cards* (Minnesota: Llewellyn Publications, 2004), p. 3.
8. *ibid*.
9. Cynthia Giles for example differentiates between four possible interpretations of Tarot divination – the rational, the psychological, the psychical and the metaphysical. A rational interpretation would consider Tarot divination as a brand of charlatanry, whereby "predictions" are based on the reader's perceptive observations of client details, statistical probabilities and stereotypes. This is "divination" *á la* Sherlock Holmes. A psychological interpretation may focus on the therapeutic setting of Tarot reading itself, the mild trance-like states this may provoke, and the subsequent psychological effects – such as heightened awareness, increased connectivity with unconscious material, sharpened intuition, and a growing correspondence between reader and client perspectives. A psychical interpretation may consider divination in relation to supposed latent abilities of the mind, such as telepathy, clairvoyance and precognition. A metaphysical interpretation may introduce more speculative models of "acausal" insight; for example, Jung's theory of Synchronicity, or Bohm's theory of Implicate Enfoldment. See Cynthia Giles, *The Tarot: History, Mystery and Lore* (New York: Simon & Schuster, 1994/1992), *Chapter Seven: Tarot as a Way of Knowing*, pp. 126-42.

10. Benebell Wen, Holistic Tarot: *An Integrative Approach to Using Tarot for Personal Growth* (Berkeley, California: North Atlantic Books, 2015), pp. 4-5, 15.
11. Thomas Saunders, *The Authentic Tarot: Discovering Your Inner Self* (London: Watkins Publishing, 2007), p. xxv.
12. Thich Nhat Hahn, *Freedom Wherever We Go: A Buddhist Monastic Code for the Twenty-First Century* (California: Parallax Press, 2004), p. 58.
13. See for example Arthur Rosengarten, *Tarot and Psychology: Spectrums of Possibility* (Minnesota: Paragon House, 2000).
14. This reflects what Mary Greer describes as the *Magical* style of Tarot practice. This involves focusing upon the highest potential suggested in any given card, and employing techniques to begin change towards those potentials. The cards themselves function primarily as meditational aids in the process, and provide the means of a "breakthrough" towards realizing a "desired possibility." See Mary K. Greer, *Tarot Mirrors: Reflections of Personal Meaning* (California: Newcastle Publishing, 1988), p. 38.
15. Rosengarten, *op. cit.*, p. 65.
16. C. G. Jung, *Collected Works, Vol.9i: The Archetypes and the Collective Unconscious*, Herbert Read and Michael Fordham and Gerald Adler, eds., R. F. C. Hull, trans. (London: Routledge & Kegan Paul, 1959), para. 89.
17. Joseph Campbell and Richard Roberts, *Tarot Revelations*, third edition (San Anselmo, CA: Vernal Equinox Press, 1987/1979), p. 43.
18. C. G. Jung, *Collected Works, Vol. 10: Civilization in Transition*, Herbert Read and Michael Fordham and Gerald Adler, eds., R. F. C. Hull, trans. (London: Routledge & Kegan Paul, 1964), para. 431.
19. *ibid.*, para. 512.
20. C. G. Jung, *Modern Man in Search of a Soul*, (London: Routledge & Kegan Paul, 1962/1933), p. 235.
21. C. G. Jung, *Collected Works, Vol. 5: Symbols of Transformation*, Herbert Read and Michael Fordham and Gerald Adler, eds., R. F. C. Hull, trans. (London: Routledge & Kegan Paul, 1956), para. 336.
22. Anthony Storr, *Jung* (London: Fontana Press, 1986/1973), p. 89.
23. This of course is not to suggest that there are no other ways to read a Tarot card. Many practitioners adopt "psychic," "intuitive," "gestalt" and other approaches to the cards, relying upon personal insights and feelings over Jungian interpretations.
24. Joseph Campbell, *The Hero with a Thousand Faces*, commemorative edition (Princeton: Princeton University Press, 2004/1949), p. 28.

25. *ibid.*, p. 32.
26. Joseph Campbell, *The Masks of God: Oriental Mythology* (Middlesex: Penguin, 1985/1962), pp. 253ff.
27. Joseph Goldstein, "The Example of the Buddha," accessed October 23 2016, http://tricycle.org/magazine/the-example-of-the-buddha/.
28. Eden Gray, *A Complete Guide to the Tarot* (New York: Bantam, 1972/1970), p. 228.
29. Rachel Pollack, *Seventy-Eight Degrees of Wisdom – A book of Tarot* (London: Element, 1997/ 1980), pp. 22-3.
30. F. Max Muller, trans., Max Fausboll, trans., *Sacred Books of the East, Vol. 10: The Dhammapada and Sutta Nipata* (Oxford: Clarendon Press, 1881), accessed October 21 2016, http://www.sacred-texts.com/bud/sbe10/sbe1014.htm.
31. Dzogchen Ponlop, *Rebel Buddha: A Guide to a Revolution of Mind* (Massachusetts: Shambhala Publications, 2010), p. 39.
32. Adrian Chan-Wyles, "Carl Jung and Buddhism," accessed October 22 2016, https://thesanghakommune.org/2013/04/18/carl-jung-buddhism/. For a more negative appraisal of the Jung-Buddhism relationship, relating specifically to a perceived Jungian misappropriation of Buddhist doctrines and concepts, see Donald S. Lopez, *Prisoners of Shangri-La: Tibetan Buddhism and the West* (Chicago: University of Chicago Press, 1999/1998).
33. Rosengarten, *op. cit.*, p. 160.
34. Joan Bunning, *Learning the Tarot* (San Francisco: Weiser Books, 1998), p. 10.

The Fool (0)
1. Campbell and Roberts, *Tarot Revelations*, p. 68.
2. See for example Pollack, *Seventy-Eight Degrees*, p. 27, and Amber Jayanti, *Living the Tarot* (Minnesota: Llewellyn Publications, 1993), p. 21.
3. Place, *Mandala of Cards*, p. 135.
4. Lama Thubten Yeshe, *Introduction to Tantra: A Vision of Totality* (Boston: Wisdom Publications, 1989/1987), p. 116.
5. Gene Reeves, trans., *The Lotus Sutra* (Boston: Wisdom Publications, 2008), p. 296.
6. Batchelor, *Buddhism Without Beliefs*, p. 100.
7. Yeshe, *op. cit.*, pp. 15-6.
8. Gene Reeves, *The Stories of the Lotus Sutra* (Massachusetts: Wisdom Publications, 2010), p. 207.
9. Pollack, op. cit., p. 26.

10. Deepak Chopra, *Buddha: A Story of Enlightenment*, (New York: HarperCollins, 2007), p. 27.
11. Muller, *The Dhammapada*, accessed October 18 2016, http://www.sacred-texts.com/bud/sbe10/sbe1007.htm
12. J. E. Cirlot, *A Dictionary of Symbols*, second edition (London: Routledge & Kegan Paul, 1971/1962), p. 112.
13. Mary K. Greer, *21 Ways to Read a Tarot Card* (Minnesota: Llewellyn Worldwide, 2014/2006), p. 1.
14. Thick Nhat Hahn, Melvin McLeod, ed. *The Pocket Thich Nhat Hahn* (Colorado: Shambhala Publications, 2012), p. 94.
15. Richard Gardner, *The Tarot Speaks* (London: Tandem, 1974/1971), p. 136. For the most part, Gardner's work comes across as the genuine article, lunging violently in stream-of-consciousness style between the millennial, the incomprehensible, and the deeply libidinous. Yet hidden within the clutter are a number of gems of penetrating insight, some of which will be revealed as our inquiry progresses.
16. Shen Hui, *Sermon on Sudden Awakening*, in E. A. Burtt, ed. *The Teachings of the Compassionate Buddha* (New York: Mentor, 1982/1955), pp. 234-5.
17. Huang-Po's Sermon from "Treatise on the Essentials of the Transmission of Mind" in Daisetz Teitaro Suzuki, trans., *Manual of Zen Buddhism* (1934), accessed October 18 2016, http://www.sacred-texts.com/bud/mzb/mzb04.htm.
18. Marcus Katz & Tali Goodwin, *Secrets of the Waite-Smith Tarot* (Minnesota: Llewellyn Publications, 2015), p. 118.
19. See Gene Reeves' commentary on this parable, *The Stories of the Lotus Sutra*, p. 108.

The Way of The World: From The Magician to The Chariot

Introduction

1. Pollack, *Seventy-Eight Degrees*, pp. 22, 43.
2. Rosemary Radford Ruether, *New Woman/New Earth: Sexist Ideologies and Human Liberation* (New York: Seabury Press, 1975), p. 204.
3. Rosemary Radford Ruether, *Sexism and God-Talk* (Boston: Beacon Press, 1993), p. 22.
4. Beth, "Fool's Journey: What Makes a 'Feminist' Tarot?" accessed October 18 2016, http://www.autostraddle.com/fools-journey-what-makes-a-feminist-tarot-350230/.

The Magician (1)

1. From the *Jataka Introduction* in Henry Clarke Warren, trans., *Buddhism in Translations* (New York: Atheneum, 1987/1896), p. 5.
2. *ibid.*, p. 15.
3. From the *Majjhima Nikaya*, quoted in Mircea Eliade, "Time and Eternity in Indian Thought," in Ralph Manheim, trans., *Man and Time: Papers from the Eranos Yearbooks* (London: Routledge and Kegan Paul, 1958), pp. 173-200 (p. 188).
4. For more on the links between the *lokapalas* and the four elements see Benjamin Preciado-Solis, *The Krsna Cycle in the Puranas: Themes and Motifs in a Heroic Saga* (Delhi: Motilal Banarsidass, 1984), pp. 63-4; see also the correspondence table in "Shitenno = Four Heavenly Kings," accessed October 24 2016, www.onmarkproductions.com.
5. From a Chinese translation of the *Mahapadana Sutta*, discussed in Miriam Levering, "The Precocious Child in Chinese Buddhism" in Vanessa Sasson, ed., *Little Buddhas: Children and Childhoods in Buddhist Text and Traditions* (Oxford: Oxford Press, 2012), pp. 124-56 (p. 133).
6. Yeshe, *Introduction to Tantra*, p. 140.
7. From the *Samyutta Nikaya*, discussed in Walpola Rahula, *What the Buddha Taught*, revised edition (London: Gordon Fraser, 1985/1959), p. 25. Before we accuse the Buddha of being a mere materialist here, we must remember that Buddhism denies the absolute nature of any khandha. Ultimately all things – including form – neither exist nor do not exist; this is the teaching of the middle path.
8. Muller, *The Dhammapada*, accessed October 24 2016, http://www.sacred-texts.com/bud/sbe10/sbe1003.htm.

The High Priestess (2)

1. I have utilized Rosengarten's notion of the "Spectrum of Possibility" when approaching a number of the cards. This is the view that interpretations should take account of both the wide range of meanings that can be associated with the cards, including their oppositional qualities. I feel that this idea is of particular relevance to a Buddhist point of view, given that Buddhism is not only concerned with enlightenment, but also the processes which prevent us from attaining it. For Buddhists, the wisdom of Nirvana cannot be separated from ignorance of Samsara. See Rosengarten, *Tarot and Psychology*, p. 129.

2. Quoted in Martin McNamara, *Targum and Testament Revisited: Aramaic Paraphrases of the Hebrew Bible*, second edition (Cambridge: Wm. B. Eerdmans Publishing, 2010), pp. 148-9.

3. From *The First Revelation of James* in Marvin Meyer, ed., *The Nag Hammadi Scriptures: the International Edition* (New York: HarperCollins, 2007), pp. 324-30 (p. 328).

4. From the *Jataka Introduction* in Warren, *Buddhism in Translations*, p. 49.

5. Asvaghosa, E. B. Cowell, trans., *Buddhacarita: Acts of the Buddha* (USA: Createspace, 2015), 1: 54.

6. Warren, *op. cit.*, p. 50.

7. Asvaghosa, *op. cit.*, 1: 74, 77.

8. Alexander Berzin, "The 32 Major Marks of a Buddha's Physical Body," accessed November 15 2016, http://studybuddhism.com/en/advanced-studies/lam-rim/refuge/the-32-major-marks-of-a-buddha-s-physical-body.

9. From Shantideva's *Bodhisattvacaryavatara*, in L. D. Barnett, *The Path of Light* (New York: E. P. Dutton and Company, 1909), accessed October 24 2016, http://www.sacred-texts.com/bud/tpol/tpol11.htm.

10. Ayya Khema, *Being Nobody Going Nowhere: Meditations on the Buddhist Path* (Boston: Wisdom Publications, 1987), p. 70.

11. See Buddhini, "Thich Nhat Hanh: Nirvana as the Cessation of Wrong Views, Wrong Perceptions and Suffering," accessed October 24 2016, http://spiritualnotreligious.blogspot.co.uk/2011/10/.

12. Rahula, *What the Buddha Taught*, p. 49.

13. Khema, *op. cit.*, p. 22.

14. Quoted in Tom Lowenstein, *The Vision of the Buddha* (London: Duncan Baird Publishers, 1996), p. 65.

15. Edward Conze, trans., *Buddhist Wisdom: The Diamond Sutra and The Heart Sutra* (New York: Vintage Books, 2001/1958), p. 97.

16. From the *Diamond-Cutter Sutra*, in E. B. Cowell, F. Max Muller and J. Takakusu, trans., *Buddhist Mahayana Texts: Sacred Books of the East, Vol 49* (Oxford: Clarendon Press, 1894), accessed October 24 2016, http://www.sacred-texts.com/bud/sbe49/sbe4929.htm.

17. Conze, *Buddhist Wisdom*, p. 21.

18. Quoted in Daisaku Ikeda, *Unlocking the Mysteries of Birth and Death ... and Everything In Between* (Santa Monica: Middleway Press, 2003), p. 123.

19. From Shantideva's *Bodhisattvacaryavatara*, in L. D. Barnett, *op. cit.*

Notes

The Empress (3)
1. Sallie Nichols, *Jung and Tarot: An Archetypal Journey* (San Francisco: Weiser Books, 1984/1980), p. 103.
2. See Owen Barfield, *Saving the Appearances: A Study in Idolatry*, second edition, (Middletown, Connecticut: Wesleyan Press, 1988/1957).
3. Pollack, *Seventy-Eight Degrees*, p. 45.
4. Starhawk, *Dreaming the Dark: Magic, Sex & Politics*, second edition (London: Unwin, 1990/1982), p. 10.
5. Hajo Banzhaf, *Tarot and the Journey of the Hero* (Maine: Samuel Weiser, 2000), p. 42.
6. Campbell, *The Masks of God: Oriental Mythology*, pp. 62, 17.
7. Simone de Beauvoir, H. M. Parshley, trans., *The Second Sex* (London: Picador, 1988/1949), esp. pp. 160, 108.
8. Hans Jonas, *The Gnostic Religion: The Message of the Alien God and the Beginnings of Christianity*, second edition (Boston: Beacon Press, 1963/1958), pp. 110, 147.
9. Rosemary Radford Ruether, "Motherearth and the Megamachine: A Theology of Liberation in a Feminine, Somatic and Ecological Perspective" in Carol P. Christ and Judith Plaskow, eds., *Womanspirit Rising: A Feminist Reader in Religion* (San Francisco: Harper & Row, 1979), pp. 43-52 (p. 47).
10. For popular feminist readings of matrifocal culture, see Marija Gimbutus, "Women and Culture in Goddess-Oriented Old Europe" in Charlene Spretnak, ed., *The Politics of Women's Spirituality* (New York: Doubleday, 1982), pp. 22-31; and Riane Eisler, "The Gaia Tradition and the Partnership Future: An Ecofeminist Manifesto" in Irene Diamond and Gloria Orenstein, eds., *Reweaving the World: the Emergence of Ecofeminism* (San Francisco: Sierra Club, 1990), pp. 23-34. For feminist views on a matrifocal /patriarchal transition, see Starhawk, *The Spiral Dance: A Rebirth of the Ancient Religion of the Great Goddess*, 20th Anniversary Edition (San Francisco: Harper, 1999/1979); and Monica Sjoo and Barbara Mor, second edition, *The Great Cosmic Mother: Rediscovering the Religion of the Earth* (San Francisco: Harper, 1991/1987). For critiques of this hypothesis, relating especially to the issue of historical veracity, see especially Mary Jo Weaver, "Who is the Goddess and Where Does She Get Us?" in *Journal of Feminist Studies in Religion*, Spring 1989, 5:1, pp. 49-64. However, despite such criticisms, many feminists point out that the matrifocal hypothesis would in no way be compromised if there were definite proof that few matriarchies ever existed. Weaver is right when she argues that the hypothesis functions primarily as "utopian

poetics" – a creative and imaginative reconstruction of the past that generates motivation for change and transformation in the present.
11. Asvaghosa, *Buddhacarita*, 1: 17, 20.
12. Warren, *Buddhism in Translations*, p. 46.
13. Asvaghosa, *op. cit.*, 1: 25.
14. From *The Diamond-Cutter Sutra*, in Cowell et al., *SBE: Buddhist Mahayana Texts*, accessed October 24 2016, http://www.sacred-texts.com/bud/sbe49/sbe4929.htm.
15. See R. C. Zaehner, *Hinduism* (Oxford: Oxford University Press, 1985/1962), p. 76.
16. Recounted in Campbell, *Hero with a Thousand Faces*, p. 106.
17. Lambert Schmithausen, "The Early Buddhist Tradition and Ecological Ethics" in Richard K. Payne, ed., *How Much is Enough? Buddhism, Consumerism and the Human Environment* (MA: Wisdom Publications, 2010), pp. 171-222 (p 197).
18. Starhawk, *The Spiral Dance*, p. 51. For a more recent example see John Halstead's 2012 article "Why I Don't Dig the Buddha" at www.patheos.com.
19. Robert A. F. Thurman, "Nagarjuna's Guidelines" in Fred Eppsteiner, ed., *The Path of Compassion: Writings on Socially Engaged Buddhism*, second edition (California: Parallax Press, 1988/1985), pp. 120-44 (p. 127).
20. Ken Wilbur, *Up From Eden: A Transpersonal View of Human Evolution* (Boston: Shambhala, 1986/1981), esp. pp. 7, 111, 133, 146, 147, 260.
21. See John Myrdhin Reynolds, "Kurrukulla: The Dakini of Magic and Enchantments," accessed November 1 2016, http://vajranatha.com/teaching/Kurukulla.htmwww.vajranattha.com.
22. Thubten Chodron, *How to Free Your Mind: The Practice of Tara the Liberator* (Boston: Snow Lion, 2005), pp. 78, 142.

The Emperor (4)
1. Nichols, *Jung and Tarot*, p. 106.
2. See C. G. Jung, *Collected Works, Vol.9i: The Archetypes and the Collective Unconscious*, Herbert Read and Michael Fordham and Gerald Adler, eds., R. F. C. Hull, trans. (London: Routledge & Kegan Paul, 1959), para. 178.
3. Ecofeminism is so-called because it holds there are conceptual links between the oppression of women and the oppression of nature, and that the liberation of one is bound up with the liberation of the other. For Ecofeminists, patriarchy is understood primarily in terms of a "conceptual framework" - a particular way of organizing

our experience of the world that has been linked with male oppression, but does not necessarily indicate how all men think, nor exclude the possibility that some women may be as equally "patriarchal" in their views. For Ecofeminists, the patriarchal mindset is one characterized by value-hierarchical dualisms - the splitting-up of reality into a series of binary opposites, in which one side is perceived as being of more value and worth than the other, providing a rationale for its domination. Moreover, through the process of cultural reinforcement, each side is also linked with a particular gender and a cluster of qualities, values and characteristics. Thus "masculine" becomes attached to men, reason, rationality, action, light, and spirit; and "feminine" to women, emotion, the irrational, passivity, darkness, matter, and by extension, nature. See Karen J. Warren, "Feminism and Ecology: Making Connections" in *Environmental Ethics*, Spring 1987, Vol. 9, pp. 3-20.

4. Jung, *CW9i*, para. 178; and C. G. Jung, *Collected Works, Vol.5: Symbols of Transformation*, Herbert Read and Michael Fordham and Gerald Adler, eds., R. F. C. Hull, trans. (London: Routledge & Kegan Paul, 1956), para. 540.

5. William Blake, *The Book of Urizen*, accessed November 13 2016, http://www.public-domain-poetry.com/william-blake/book-of-urizen-excerpts-9209.

6. For Ecofeminists, the male self of patriarchal culture is the "seperative self." This is a falsely-constructed model of the self as a constant and abiding entity that intentionally and hygienically severs itself from its surroundings. It is also one half of a dyad; the other being the "soluble self" or the model of selfhood proffered to women. This is a self that is no-self, consisting of pure sentiment and relationality. As a functioning pair, the male embodies self without connection, and the female, its opposite. See Catherine Keller, *From a Broken Web: Separation, Sexism and Self* (Boston: Beacon Press, 1986), esp. pp. 205, 7, 206.

7. Edward C. Whitmont, *Return of the Goddess* (London: Arkana, 1987/1983) pp. 80, 144.

8. Warren, *Buddhism in Translations,* p. 53.

9. ibid.

10. Campbell, *Masks of God: Oriental Mythology*, p. 254.

11. Asvaghosa, *Buddhacarita*, 1: 10.

12. ibid., 1:13.

13. From the *Cakkavatti Sihanada Sutta* in Trevor Ling, ed., *The Buddha's Philosophy of Man* (London: Everyman, 1993/1981), pp. 112-25 (pp. 115, 119).

14. Norm Phelps, *The Longest Struggle: Animal Advocacy from Pythagoras to PETA* (New York: Lantern Books, 2007), p. 22.
15. Annie Kelly, "Gross National Happiness in Bhutan: the big idea from a tiny state that could change the world" in *The Guardian*, accessed November 1 2016, https://www.theguardian.com/world/2012/dec/01/bhutan-wealth-happiness-counts.
16. From a statement by the *Gross National Happiness Commission*, 2015, quoted in Michael Givel, "Mahayana Buddhism and Gross National Happiness in Bhutan," *International Journal of Wellbeing*, 5.2 (2015), pp. 14-27 (p. 23).

The Hierophant (5)
1. A. E. Waite, *The Pictorial Key to the Tarot* (New York: Parragon edition, 1978/1910), p. 91.
2. *ibid*, pp. 88, 91.
3. Pollack, *Seventy-Eight Degrees*, p. 56; Banzhaf, *Tarot and the Journey of the Hero*, p. 49.
4. From Waite's *The Key to the Tarot* reproduced in *The Rider Waite Tarot Cards Instructions* booklet (London: Rider Books, 1993), p. 5.
5. Paul Fenton-Smith, *The Tarot Revealed* (Australia: Simon & Schuster, 1995), p. 176.
6. Blake, *Urizen*, accessed November 13 2016, http://www.public-domain-poetry.com/william-blake/book-of-urizen-chapter-ii-9264.
7. A term used by thealogian Mary Daly in her book *Gyn/Ecology: The Metaethics of Radical Feminism* (Boston: Beacon Press, 1999/1978).
8. Gardner, *The Tarot Speaks*, pp. 71-2.
9. Pollack, *op. cit.*, pp. 55, 56.
10. Asvaghosa, *Buddhacarita*, 2: 24, 28.
11. From the short story *The First Meditation*, accessed November 5 2016, http://www.bodhitales.org/the-first-meditation.php.
12. From the *Sigala Sutta* in Bhikkhu Bodhi, ed., *In the Buddha's Words: An Anthology of Discourses from the Pali Canon* (Massachusetts: Wisdom Publications, 2005), pp. 117, 118.
13. Alan Watts, *The Way of Zen* (New York; Vintage 1985/1957), p. 163.
14. John Powers, *Introducing Tibetan Buddhism* (New York: Snow Lion Publications, 1995), p. 271.
15. Yeshe, *Introduction to Tantra*, p. 105.

16. From the Dhammapada in W.D.C Wagiswara and K.J. Saunders, trans., *The Buddha's Way of Virtue* (London: John Murray, 1920), accessed November 13 2016, http://www.sacred-texts.com/bud/wov/wov16.htm.
17. From the *Mahaparinibbana Sutta* in Paul Carus, *Buddha: The Gospel* (Chicago: The Open Court Publishing Company, 1894), accessed November 3 2016, http://www.sacred-texts.com/bud/btg/index.htm.
18. Ling, *The Buddha*, esp. chapters 4 and 5.
19. From the *Maitri (Maitreya) Upanishad* in K. Narayanasvami Aiyar, trans., *Thirty Minor Upanishads (*Madras: 1914*)*, accessed November 3 2016, http://www.sacred-texts.com/hin/tmu/index.htm.
20. From the *Anguttara Nikaya* in Bhikkhu Bodhi, *In the Buddha's Words*, p. 88.
21. From the *Kutadanta Sutta* in T. W. Rhys Davids, trans, *Dialogues of the Buddha: The Digha-Nikaya: The Sacred Books of the Buddhists, Vol. II* (London: Oxford University Press, 1899), accessed November 3 2016, http://www.sacred-texts.com/bud/dob/index.htm.
22. From the *Rig Veda* in Ralph T.H. Griffith, trans., *The Rig Veda* (1896), accessed November 3 2016, http://www.sacred-texts.com/hin/rigveda/rv10090.htm.
23. The *Bhagavad-Gita* (18: 44). The social stratification embodied in the doctrine of the three gunas is still found today in the presentation of a three-stranded thread to only those Hindu boys of the "twice-born" varnas at the moment of their coming of age.
24. From *The Bhagavad-Gita* (2: 31-33) in Kashinath Trimbak Telang, trans., *The Bhagavadgita: Sacred Books of the East, Vol. 8* (1882) accessed November 3 2016, http://www.sacred-texts.com/hin/sbe08/index.htm.
25. Muller, *The Dhammapada*, accessed November 3 2016, http://www.sacred-texts.com/bud/sbe10/sbe1028.htm.
26. From the vows quoted in Himansu Charan Sadangi, *Dalit: The Downtrodden of India* (Delhi: Isha Books, 2008), p. 104.

The Lovers (6)
1. See Sallie Nichols, *Jung and Tarot: An Archetypal Journey* (San Francisco: Weiser Books, 1984/1980), p. 132. Nichol's interpretation highlights one criticism that feminists have made of the Jungian "Hero's Journey"; namely that it might be exactly what it says – descriptive of the male experience. It raises the obvious question of whether women actually have a journey, or if they simply sit at home

until their questing men-folk recover their "lost feminine." There are a few exceptions. Mary Greer for example does make an attempt to sketch out a possible "Heroine's Journey" in appendix D of her work on *Tarot Reversals*; but the very fact that she does so underscores its general absence elsewhere. With some pathos she recognizes that the heroine's journey may not even go noticed, never mind celebrated. See Mary K. Greer, *The Complete Book of Tarot Reversals* (Minnesota: Llewellyn Publications, 2012), p. 255. My own position on this matter is that the general themes of the cards address every person, regardless of gender. An awareness of the limitations and the conflicts of life, the inner reflections these prompt, and the desire for a more actualized and fulfilled existence, are universally human - not the proclivities of one gender.

2. Nichols, *op. cit.*, p. 134.
3. From the Preface to Irenaeus' *Against Heresies: Book V*, in A. Cleveland Coxe, Alexander Roberts, James Donaldson, eds., *Ante-Nicene Fathers: The Writings of the Fathers down to A.D. 325. Volume 1: The Apostolic Fathers, Justine Martyr, Irenaeus* (New York: Christian Literature Publishing Co., 1885), p. 526.
4. Nichols, *op. cit.*, p. 137.
5. Although Smith's rendition only shows four fruits, the Case B.O.T.A. deck makes the link with sensuality clearer by depicting five.
6. Warren, *Buddhism in Translations*, p. 55.
7. Asvaghosa, *Buddhacarita*, 2: 31-2.
8. John Stevens, *Lust for Enlightenment: Buddhism and Sex* (Boston and London: Shambhala, 1990), pp. 7-8.
9. Asvaghosa, *op. cit.*, 2: 26.
10. Stevens, *op. cit.*, p. 6.
11. From Yeshe Gyaltsen's version of the life of the Buddha in Robert A. F. Thurman, *Essential Tibetan Buddhism* (NJ: Castle Books, 1995), p. 69.
12. From the *Sigala Sutta* in Bhikkhu Bodhi, *In the Buddha's Words*, p. 117.
13. From the *Mahadukkhakhandha Sutta* in Bhikkhu Bodhi, *op. cit.*, p. 197.
14. From the story of *Subha of Jivaka's Mango-grove* (Canto XVI), in Mrs. Rhys Davies, trans., *Psalms of the Early Buddhists: Psalms of the Sisters* (London: Pali Test Society, 1909), accessed November 5 2016, http://www.sacred-texts.com/bud/pos/pos19.htm.
15. From the *Hevajra Tantra*, quoted in Powers, *Introducing Tibetan Buddhism*, p. 226.
16. *ibid.*, p. 251.
17. *ibid.*, p. 252.

18. Georg Feuerstein, *Tantra: The Path of Ecstasy* (Colorado: Shambhala Press 1998), p. 271.
19. The Skeptic Tantrika, "Kundalina Danger – The Real Dangers of Tantra," accessed November 5 2016, http://tantrasoul.blogspot.co.uk/2013/04/kundalini-danger-real-dangers-of-tantra.html.
20. Paramananda, *Change Your Mind: A Practical Guide to Buddhist Meditation*, (Birmingham: Windhorse Publications, 2002/1996), pp. 47-70.
21. Thubten Chodron, *How to Free Your Mind: the Practice of Tara the Liberator* (Boston & London: Snow Lion, 2013), pp. 32, 33.

The Chariot (7)
1. Waite, *The Pictorial Key*, p. 96.
2. Nichols, *Jung and Tarot*, p. 139.
3. Irreverent Feminist, "The Chariot," accessed November 6 2016, https://irreverentfeminist.wordpress.com/2010/12/16/.
4. Nichols, *op. cit.*, p. 145.
5. Warren, *Buddhism in Translations*, p. 56.
6. Asvaghosa, *Buddhacarita*, 3: 36, 46, 61.
7. Robert A. F. Thurman, "Nagarjuna's Guidelines" in Fred Eppsteiner, ed., *The Path of Compassion: Writings on Socially Engaged Buddhism* (Berkeley: Parallax Press, 1988/1985) pp. 120-144, (pp. 130-1).
8. Warren, *op. cit.*, p. 57.
9. *ibid.*, pp. 60, 61.
10. Pollack, *Seventy-Eight Degrees*, p. 44.
11. Gardner, *The Tarot Speaks,* p. 82.
12. Pollack, *op. cit.*, p. 68.
13. From the *Milindapanha* in Warren, *Buddhism in Translations*, p. 134.
14. Dominique Side, *Buddhism: World Religions* (Oxfordshire: Phillip Allan, 2005), pp. 92-3.

Departure and Trials: From Strength to The Tower

Introduction
1. A term from the story of *Subha* in Mrs. Rhys Davies, *Psalms of the Early Buddhists: Psalms of the Sisters*, accessed November 6 2016, http://www.sacred-texts.com/bud/pos/pos19.htm.

2. George Gordon Noël Byron, *Manfred*, Act 2 Scene 2, in *The Complete Works of Lord Byron, Vol. 4* (Paris: Baudry, 1825), p. 25.
3. Pollack, *Seventy-Eight Degrees*, pp. 22-3.
4. Banzhaf, *Tarot and the Journey of the Hero*, p. 22.
5. Pollack, *op. cit.*, p. 23.

Strength (8)
1. Fenton-Smith, *The Tarot Revealed*, p. 184.
2. Jayanti, *Living the Tarot*, p. 127.
3. See images in Kaplan, *The Encyclopedia of Tarot*, pp. 36, 40.
4. Waite, *The Pictorial Key*, pp. 100, 103.
5. Nichols, *Jung and Tarot*, p. 102.
6. Banzhaf, *Tarot and the Journey of the Hero*, p. 98.
7. Waite, *op. cit.*, p. 100.
8. Pollack, *op. cit.*, p. 74.
9. Banzhaf, *op. cit.*, pp. 97-8.
10. Warren, *Buddhism in Translations*, p. 61.
11. Asvaghosa, *Buddhacarita*, 5: 61, 63, 64.
12. Warren, *op. cit.*, p. 62.
13. Definition of Kanthaka in marathi.indiandictionaries.com, accessed November 7 2016.
14. Warren, *op. cit.*, p. 62.
15. *ibid.*
16. Barnett, *The Path of Light*, accessed November 7 2016, http://www.sacred-texts.com/bud/tpol/tpol10.htm.
17. *ibid.*, http://www.sacred-texts.com/bud/tpol/tpol04.htm.
18. From the *The Collection of Pure Dharma Sutra*, discussed in Geshe Namgyal Wangchen, *Awakening the Mind of Enlightenment* (London: Wisdom Publication, 1987), p. 123.
19. Geshe Kelsang Gyatso, *The Bodhisattva Vow: The Essential Practices of Mahayana Buddhism* (London: Tharpa Publications, 1995/1991), p. 11.

The Hermit (9)
1. Lady Lorelei, *Tarot Life Planner* (London: Bounty Books, 2014/2004), p. 36.
2. Jayanti, *Living the Tarot*, p. 142.
3. Gardner, *The Tarot Speaks*, p. 88.
4. Saunders, *The Authentic Tarot*, p. 25.
5. Waite, *The Pictorial Key*, p. 104.
6. Pollack, *Seventy-Eight Degrees*, pp. 77-9; Wen, *Holistic Tarot*, pp. 91-2.
7. Banzhaf, *Tarot and the Journey of the Hero*, p. 79.

8. Nichols, *Jung and Tarot*, p. 168.
9. Warren, *Buddhism in Translations*, p. 63.
10. Asvaghosa, *Buddhacarita*, 5: 80-1, 78.
11. Warren, *op. cit.*, p. 64.
12. Asvaghosa, *op. cit.*, 5: 84.
13. Warren, *op. cit.*, pp. 65, 66.
14. *ibid.*, p. 67.
15. Asvaghosa, *op. cit.*, 6: 1; 7: 1.
16. See Rajeev Srinivasan, "The Buddhist Connection: Sabarimala, and the Tibetans," accessed November 9 2016, http://www.rediff.com/news/dec/31rajeev.htm.
17. See Pretoria Bhajanai Mandram, "Holy 18 Steps," accessed November 9 2016, http://www.ayyappaa.org.za/ayyappanworship/holy-18-steps/.
18. T. Prince, "Renunciation" in *Collected Bodhi Leaves: Volume II*, (Kandy: Buddhist Publication Society, 2010), pp. 65-80.
19. David Chapman, "Renunciation is the engine for most of Buddhism," accessed November 8 2016, https://vividness.live/2013/11/22/renunciation-in-buddhism/.
20. Lama Yeshe, *Introduction to Tantra*, pp. 83, 54.

The Wheel of Fortune (10)
1. Jayanti, *Living the Tarot*, p. 155.
2. From Kauffman Kohler's article on *Merkabah* in the *online Jewish Encyclopedia*, accessed November 9 2106, http://www.jewishencyclopedia.com/articles/10698-merkabah.
3. Waite, *The Pictorial Key*, pp. 96, 99.
4. Jayanti, *op. cit.*, p. 153.
5. Asvaghosa, *Buddhacarita*, 10: 1, 28, 34.
6. *ibid.*, 12: 1-2, 13-4, 15.
7. *ibid.*, 12:18, 23, 30, 65.
8. *ibid.*, 12: 69-70.
9. *ibid.*, 12: 82.
10. From the *Majjhima Nikaya* in Warren, *Buddhism in Translations*, p. 338.
11. See for example David Nichtern, *Awakening from the Daydream: Reimagining the Buddha's Wheel of Life* (Somerville, MA: Wisdom Publications, 2016).
12. Peter Wren Howard and Christine Battersby, notes on the "Tibetan Wheel of Life," found on the reverse of a Tibetan Wheel of Life poster, which was reproduced by permission of the Director of Samye-Ling Tibetan Centre (published by Peter Wren Howard, England, 1990).

Justice (11)
1. Pollack, *Seventy-Eight Degrees*, p. 92.
2. ibid., p. 91.
3. Thomas à Kempis, William Benham, trans., *The Imitation of Christ* (London: C. J. Nimmo, 1886), accessed November 10 2016, http://www.sacred-texts.com/chr/ioc/ioc024.htm.
4. Cirlot, *A Dictionary of Symbols*, pp. 166-67.
5. Pollack, op. cit, p. 92.
6. Jayanti, *Living the Tarot*, pp. 167, 168.
7. Matthew Fox, *Original Blessing: A Primer in Creation Spirituality* (New Mexico: Bear & Co., 1983), p. 260.
8. ibid., p. 70.
9. Paul Carus, *Buddha: The Gospel* (Chicago: The Open Court Publishing Company, 1894), accessed December 3 2016, http://www.sacred-texts.com/bud/btg/btg10.htm.
10. Daisaku Ikeda, *The Living Buddha: an Interpretive Biography*, (Santa Monica, CA: Middleway Press, 2008/1973), pp. 42, 43, 43-4, 44.
11. See for example Jayanti, *op. cit.*, pp. 169, 179; Greer, *Tarot for Your Self*, p. 240; Place, *The Buddha Tarot Companion*, p. 168.
12. Stephanie Kaza, "How Much is Enough? Buddhist Perspectives on Consumerism" in Richard K. Payne, ed., *How Much is Enough? Buddhism, Consumerism and the Human Environment* (MA: Wisdom Publications, 2010), pp. 39-61.
13. Nelson Foster, "To Enter the Marketplace" in Fred Eppsteiner, ed., *The Path of Compassion*, pp. 47-64.
14. Kaza, *op. cit.*, pp. 49, 47, 58.
15. ibid., pp. 49, 47, 54.
16. ibid., pp. 48, 55, 58.
17. Christian Feldman, "Nurturing Compassion" in Eppsteiner, *op. cit.*, pp. 19-23 (pp. 21, 22).
18. Donald Rothberg, *The Engaged Spiritual Life: A Buddhist Approach to Transforming Ourselves and the World* (Boston: Beacon Press, 2006), p. 61.

The Hanged Man (12)
1. Fox, *Original Blessing*, p. 395.
2. Ruether, *Sexism and God-Talk*, pp. 11-2.
3. Asvaghosa, *Buddhacarita*, 12: 89, 91.
4. From the *Maha-Saccaka Sutta*, translated by Thanissaro Bhikkhu, accessed November 13 2016, http://www.accesstoinsight.org/tipitaka/mn/mn.036.than.html.

5. From the *Maha-sihanada Sutta*, translated by Nanamoli Thera and Bhikkhu Bodhi, accessed November 13 2016, http://www.accesstoinsight.org/tipitaka/mn/mn.012.ntbb.html.
6. Asvaghosa, *op. cit.*, 12: 96.
7. Warren, *Buddhism in Translations*, p. 70.
8. From the *Maha-sihanada Sutta*, *op. cit.*
9. David Halberstam, *The Making of a Quagmire: America and Vietnam during the Kennedy Era* (London: Rowman & Littlefield Publishers, 2007), p. 128.
10. Thich Nhat Hahn, *Love in Action: Writings on Nonviolent Social Change* (Berkeley, California: Parallax Press, 1993), p. 43.

Death (13)
1. Pollack, *Seventy-Eight Degrees*, p. 101.
2. Leo Tolstoy, Maudes translation, "A Confession," accessed November 13 2016, https://en.wikisource.org/wiki/A_Confession_(Maudes_translation)/IV.
3. Don Cupitt, "Learning to Live With One Foot in the Grave," accessed November 14 2016, http://www.sofn.org.uk/press/ofigrave.html.
4. Warren, *Buddhism in Translations*, p. 70.
5. From the *Padhana Sutta* in V. Fausboll, *The Sutta Nipata* (Simplicissimus Book Farm edition, n.d.), p. 119.
6. Warren, *op. cit.*, pp. 70-1.
7. Muller, *The Dhammapada,* accessed November 14 2016, http://www.sacred-texts.com/bud/sbe10/sbe1012.htm.
8. Chand R. Sirimanne, "Symbols in Theravada Buddhist Meditation (Bhavana)," accessed October 23 2016, http://www.buddhismandaustralia.com.
9. Thich Nhat Hahn, *No Death, No Fear: Comforting Wisdom for Life* (New York; Riverhead Books, 2002), pp 25-6.
10. From the *Milindapanha* in Warren, *Buddhism in Translations*, p. 149.

Temperance (14)
1. Katz and Goodwin, *Secrets of the Waite-Smith Tarot,* p. 171.
2. From a German alchemist's prayer in Manly Hall, *The Secret Teachings of all Ages: An Encyclopedic Outline of Masonic, Hermetic, Qabbalistic, and Rosicrucian Symbolical Philosophy* (New York, Dover Publications, 2010/1928), p. 451.
3. Bunning, *Learning the Tarot,* p. 141.
4. Nichols *Jung and Tarot,* p. 250.

5. Karen Armstrong, *The Spiral Staircase* (New York: Anchor Books, 2005/2004), p. 270.
6. See David L. Norton, *Personal Destinies: A Philosophy of Ethical Individualism* (N.J., Princeton University Press, 1976).
7. Martin Luther, "An Open Letter to The Christian Nobility of the German Nation Concerning the Reform of the Christian Estate, 1520" in James Atkinson, ed., *Luther's Works Vol 44: The Christian in Society I* (Philadephia: Fortress, 1966), pp. 115-217 (p. 115).
8. See Joseph Kotva, *The Christian Case for Virtue Ethics* (Washington D. C.: Georgetown University Press, 1997).
9. See for example Peter Smith, "Virtue Ethics: An Ancient Solution to a Modern Problem," accessed November 15 2016, https://scientiasalon.wordpress.com/2014/09/25/virtue-ethics-an-ancient-solution-to-a-modern-problem/
10. Gardner, *The Tarot Speaks*, p. 103.
11. Asvaghosa, *Buddhacarita*, 12: 98.
12. Edwin Arnold, *The Light of Asia* (London: Trubner and Co., 1879), p. 145. I have searched in vain for the original scriptural version of this sitar episode. The *Lalitavistara Sutra* mentions ten village girls who provide the Future Buddha with alms, and various daughters of the "Naga king" who played music for him as he approached the "Seat of Enlightenment"; but there is no mention of a sitar. However, the *Sona Sutta* has the Buddha offering advice to young monk called *Sona* on the best way to meditate, and uses the example of a correctly-tensioned *vina* (lute) to do so. Perhaps Arnold combined these to create an imaginative re-telling of the Future Buddha's discovery of the Middle Way.
13. Swami Swarupananda, trans., *Srimad-Bhagavad-Gita* (Mayavati: Advaita Ashrama, 1909), accessed November 16 2016, http://www.sacred-texts.com/hin/sbg/sbg20.htm.
14. Warren, *Buddhism in Translations*, pp. 75, 76.
15. Campbell, *Oriental Mythology*, p. 17.
16. Warren, *op. cit.* p. 76.
17. From the the *Dhammacakkappavattana Sutta* in A. Ferdinand Herold, Paul C Blum, trans., *The Life of Buddha* (New York: A. & C. Boni, 1927/1922), accessed November 15 2016, http://www.sacred-texts.com/bud/lob/lob26.htm.
18. Bhikkhu Sujato with Jessica Walton, trans, *Verses of the Senior Monks* (Sutta Central, 2014), accessed November 26 2016, https://suttacentral.net/en/thag12.1.
19. From the *Mahaparinibbana Suttanta* in T. W. Rhys Davies, trans., *Buddhist Suttas: The Sacred Books of the East: Vol XI* (Oxford:

Clarendon Press, 1881), accessed November 27 2016, http://www.sacred-texts.com/bud/sbe11/sbe1103.htm.
20. From the *Kaccayanagotta Sutta*, in Warren, *Buddhism in Translations*, p. 166.
21. Sylvain Chamberlain-Nyudo, *Nichiren Gosho – Book One* (Lulu Press, 2016), p. 9.

The Devil (15)
1. Waite, *The Pictorial Key*, p. 128.
2. Pollack, *Seventy-Eight Degrees*, p. 113.
3. Gardner, *The Tarot Speaks*, pp. 107-8.
4. Pollack, *op. cit.*, p. 112.
5. Gardner, *op. cit.*, p. 107.
6. See Joseph Fletcher, *Situation Ethics: The New Morality* (London: John Knox Press, 1966), esp. pp. 46-50.
7. Asvaghosa, *op. cit.*, 13: 1, 5.
8. *ibid.*, 13: 9, 16, 16-7, 55, 36, 58, 61.
9. Warren, *Buddhism in Translations*, pp. 80-1.
10. *ibid.*, p. 81.
11. Fausboll, *The Sutta Nipata*, pp. 330, 331, 330.
12. Implied in Asvoghosa, *Buddhacarita*, 13:5.
13. From the *Padhana Sutta* in Fausboll, *op. cit.*, 120-1.
14. Shaila Catherine, *Focused and Fearless: A Meditator's Guide to States of Deep Joy, Calm and Clarity*, ReadHowYouWant edition (MA: Wisdom Publications, 2010/2008), p. 135.
15. Stephen Bachelor, *Living with the Devil: A Buddhist Meditation on Good and Evil* (New York: Riverhead Books, 2005), p. 28.

The Tower (16)
1. Bill Butler, *Dictionary of the Tarot* (New York: Schocken Books, 1978/1975), p. 170.
2. Papus, A. P. Morton, trans., *The Tarot of the Bohemians* (London: Senate, 1994/1896), p. 169.
3. See illustration in Kaplan, *The Encyclopedia of Tarot Volume 1*, p. 51.
4. Katz and Goodwin, *Secrets of the Waite-Smith Tarot*, p. 180.
5. Waite, *The Pictorial Key*, pp. 135, 132.
6. Pollack, *Seventy-Eight Degrees*, p. 119; Banzhaf, *Tarot and the Journey of the Hero*, p. 174.
7. From the *Bhayabherava Sutta* in Bhikkhu Nanamoli and Bhikkhu Bodhi trans., *Teachings of the Buddha: the Middle Length Discourses of the Buddha: A translation of the Majjhima Nikaya* (MA: Wisdom Publications, 2015/1995), p. 105.

Notes

8. Mark Knickelbine, "The First Watch of the Night," accessed November 18 2016, http://secularbuddhism.org/2012/03/07/the-first-watch-of-the-night/.
9. From the *Bhayabherava Sutta, op. cit.*, p. 106.
10. Warren, *Buddhism in Translations*, p. 83.
11. Damien Keown and Charles S. Prebish, eds., *Encyclodepia of Buddhism* (London: Routledge, 2010/2007), p. 144.
12. Fausboll, *The Sutta Nipata* , p. 332, 335.
13. From the *Dhammapada* in Wagiswara and Saunders, *The Buddha's Way of Virtue*, accessed November 18 2016, http://www.sacred-texts.com/bud/wov/wov15.htm.
14. From the *Samyutta Nikaya* in Bhikkhu Bodhi, *In the Buddha's Words*, p. 365.
15. See Robert Beer, *The Handbook of Tibetan Buddhist Symbols* (Chicago: Serindia publications, 2003), p. 86.

The Return:
From The Star to The World

Introduction

1. Maurice Friedman, "Aiming at the Self: The Paradox of Encounter and the Human Potential Movement" in the *Journal of Humanistic Psychology*, Spring 1976, Vol. 16, No. 2, pp. 5-34 (p. 9).
2. Nichols, *Jung and Tarot*, p. 357.
3. See Carl A. Raschke, *The Interruption of Eternity: Modern Gnosticism and the Origins of the New Religious Consciousness* (Chicago: Nelson-Hall, 1980).
4. Muller, *The Dhammapada*, accessed November 13 2016, http://www.sacred-texts.com/bud/sbe10/sbe1003.htm.
5. From a BBC broadcast talk given by Jung in 1946, quoted in Petteri Pietikainen, *Alchemists of Human Nature: Psychological Utopianism in Gross, Jung, Reich and Fromm*, (London: Routledge 2016/2007), p. 106.
6. C. G. Jung, *Collected Works, Vol. 7: Two Essays on Analytical Psychology*, Herbert Read and Michael Fordham and Gerald Adler, eds., R. F. C. Hull, trans. (London: Routledge & Kegan Paul, 1953), para. 275.
7. Campbell, *The Hero with a Thousand Faces*, pp. 179.

The Star (17)

1. Papus, *Tarot of the Bohemians*, p. 172.
2. Jayanti, *Living the Tarot*, p. 259.
3. Waite, *The Pictorial Key*, p. 26.

Notes

4. See for example the still highly-relevant Marilyn Ferguson, *The Aquarian Conspiracy: Personal and Social Transformation in the 1980s* (London: Paladin, 1989/1980); or Ralph Metzner, "Age of Ecology" in *Resurgence*, November/December 1991, pp. 4-7.
5. Pollack, *Seventy-Eight Degrees*, p. 124.
6. Waite, *op. cit.*, p. 176.
7. Pollack, *op. cit.*, p. 123.
8. Papus, *op. cit.*, p. 171.
9. Asvaghosa, *Buddhacarita*, 15: 11-2, 52.
10. Campbell, *Oriental Mythology*, p. 276n.
11. From the *Ariyapariyesana Sutta* in Nanamoli Thera and Bhikkhu Bodhi, trans., *The Middle Length Discourses of the Buddha: A Translation of the Majjhima Nikaya* (Massachusetts: Wisdom Publications, 2015/1995), p. 260.
12. ibid., pp. 261-3.
13. Jack Kornfield, The Path of Compassion: Spiritual Practice and Social Action" in Eppsteiner, *The Path of Compassion*, pp. 24-30, (p. 25).
14. Gary Snyder, "Buddhism and the Possibilities of a Planetary Culture" in Eppsteiner, *op. cit.*, pp. 82-5 (pp. 82-3).
15. Michael Welton, "Can Buddhism Save the World?" accessed November 19 2016, http://www.counterpunch.org/2016/01/15/can-buddhism-save-the-world/.
16. See for example Kali Holloway, "Mindfulness: Capitalism's New Favorite Tool for Maintaining the Status Quo," accessed October 21 2016, http://www.alternet.org/personal-health/mindfulness-capitalisms-new-favorite-tool-maintaining-status-quo.
17. Sulak Sivaraksa, "Buddhism in a World of Change: Politics Must Be Related to Religion" in Eppsteiner, *op. cit*, pp. 9-18 (p. 13).
18. Michel Clasquin-Johnson, "Why are there so many Western Converts to Buddhism," accessed November 19 2016, https://www.quora.com/Why-are-there-so-many-Western-converts-to-Buddhism.
19. Welton, *ibid*.
20. Synder, *op. cit.*, p. 83.
21. See Dominique Side, *Buddhism*, esp. Chapter 21: *Buddhism in Western Society* (pp. 223-35).
22. Sivaraksa, op. cit., p. 16.
23. Tenzin Gyatso, "Hope for the Future" in Eppsteiner, *op. cit.*, pp. 3-8 (p. 8).

24. Wagiswara and Saunders, *The Buddha's Way of Virtue*, accessed November 19 2016, http://www.sacred-texts.com/bud/wov/wov05.htm.

The Moon (18)
1. Waite, *The Pictorial Key*, p. 140, 143.
2. Papus, *Tarot of the Bohemians*, p. 175.
3. Nichols, *Jung and Tarot*, p. 314.
4. A. E. Thierens, *General Book of the Tarot* (Philadelphia: D. McKay Co., 1930), p. 76.
5. Gail Fairfield, *Choice Centered Tarot* (California: Newcastle Publishing Co., 1985/1984), p. 99.
6. Rachel Pollack, *The New Tarot Handbook: Master the Meanings of the Cards* (Minnesota: Llewellyn Worldwide, 2012), p. 87.
7. Gardner, *The Tarot Speaks*, p. 123.
8. See illustration in Kaplan, *The Encyclopedia of Tarot Volume 1*, p. 40.
9. ibid., p. 54.
10. Starhawk, *The Spiral Dance*, p. 109.
11. Charles G. Leland, *Aradia: The Gospel of the Witches* (California: Ancient Wisdom Publications, n.d./1899), pp. 17-8, 18.
12. ibid., pp. 19, 20.
13. Eliezer Segal, "The Ten Sefirot: Shekhinah, Malkhut," accessed November 20 2016, https://www.jewishvirtuallibrary.org/jsource/Judaism/Shekhinah.html.
14. See C. G, Jung, *Collected Works, Vo 14: Mysterium Coniunctionis: An Inquiry Into the Separation and Synthesis of Psychic Opposite in Alchemy*, second edition, Herbert Read and Michael Fordham and Gerald Adler, eds., R. F. C. Hull, trans. (London: Routledge & Kegan Paul, 1970/1963), paras. 28-30. See also William Nicholson's *The Church Compared to the Moon* (1862), accessed November 20 2016, http://gracegems.org/Nicholson/church_compared_to_the_moon.htm.
15. From the *Ariyapariyesana Sutta* in Nanamoli Thera and Bhikkhu Bodhi, *The Middle Length Discourses of the Buddha*, p. 264.
16. Asvaghosa, *Buddhacarita*, 15: 117.
17. From the *Ariyapariyesana Sutta*, *op. cit.*, p. 265.
18. Asvaghosa., op. cit., 15: 112.
19. From the *Dhammacakkavattana Sutta* in Bhikkhu Bodhi, *In the Buddha's Words*, p. 78.
20. A poem by "Sumangala's mother" in Mrs. Rhys Davies, trans., *Psalms of the Early Buddhists: Psalms of the Sisters*, accessed

November 20 2016, http://www.sacred-texts.com/bud/pos/pos07.htm.
21. Ling, *The Buddha*, pp. 123, 124.
22. Paul Carus, *Buddha: The Gospel* (Chicago: The Open Court Publishing Company, 1894), accessed November 20 2016, http://www.sacred-texts.com/bud/btg/btg18.htm.

The Sun (19)
1. James Hillman, *Inter Views: Conversations with Laura Pozzo on Psychotherapy, Biography, Love, Soul, Dreams, Work, Imagination and the State of the Culture* (Washington DC: Spring Publications, 1991/1983), p. 25.
2. Sigmund Freud, J. A. Underwood, trans., *The Future of an Illusion*, (London: Penguin, 2008/2004), p. 5.
3. In words deeply appropriate for our times, Jung saw the repressed forces of religion bursting forth like some wild and misshapen beast into conscious life, provoking "international suicide." See C. G. Jung, *CW 10*, para. 32.
4. Gardner, *The Tarot Speaks*, pp. 125-6, 121.
5. See Owen Barfield, *Saving the Appearances*.
6. From Sophocles' "Root-Cutters," quoted in Sorita D'Este, "The History, Powers & Myths of Hekate" in Sorita D'Este, ed., *Hekate: Keys to the Crossroads* (London: Avalonia, 2006), pp. 20-38 (p. 27).
7. Harold W. Wood, Jr., "Modern Pantheism as an Approach to Environmental Ethics" in *Environmental Ethics*, Summer 1985, Vol. 7, No 2, pp. 151-64 (p. 156).
8. Starhawk, *The Spiral Dance*, p. 203.
9. Howard Eilberg-Schwartz, "Witches of the West: Neopaganism and Goddess Worship as Enlightenment Religions" in *Journal of Feminist Studies in Religion*, Spring 1989, Vol. 5, No. 1, pp. 77-95.
10. Nichols, *Jung and Tarot*, pp. 328-9.
11. Nicolas Berdyaev, "Salvation and Creativity: Two Understandings of Christianity" in Matthew Fox, ed., *Western Spirituality: Historical Roots, Ecumenical Routes* (Santa Fe, NM: Bear & Co., 1983), pp. 115-39 (pp. 115, 116, 118, 124, 123).
12. Fox, *Original Blessing*, pp. 165, 239.
13. Matthew Fox, trans., ed., *Meditations with Meister Eckhart* (Santa Fe, NM: Bear & Co., 1983), p. 88, 79.
14. G S P Misra, "Logical and Scientific Method in Early Buddhist Texts" in *Journal of the Royal Asiatic Society of Great Britain & Ireland*, Vol. 100, Issue 1, January 1968, pp. 54-64 (p. 64).
15. From the *Vatthupama Sutta* in Nanamoli and Bodhi, *The Middle Length Discourses*, pp. 120-1.

16. Davies, *Psalms of the Early Buddhists*, accessed November 22 2016, http://www.sacred-texts.com/bud//pos/pos17.htm.
17. From the *Kalama Sutta* in Bodhi, *In the Buddha's Words*, p. 90.
18. This story is retold in Edward Conze, *Buddhism: Its Essence and Development* (New York: Dover Publications, 2003/1951), pp. 104-5.
19. From the *Culamalunkya Sutta in* Nanamoli and Bodhi, *The Middle Length Discourses*, p. 535.
20. Ling, *The Buddha*, p. 106.
21. Carl Sagan, *Demon-Haunted World: Science as a Candle in the Dark* (New York: Ballantine Books, 1997), p. 278.
22. The Dalai Lama, *The Universe in a Single Atom: The Convergence of Science and Spirituality* (New York: Broadway Books, 2005), pp. 3, 13.
23. Batchelor, *Buddhism without Beliefs*, pp. 36, 37.
24. The Dalai Lama, *op. cit.*, pp. 66, 67.
25. Matthew Ricard & Trinh Xuan Thuan, Ian Monk, trans., *The Quantum and the Lotus* (New York: Three Rivers Press, 2001/2000), esp. pp. 63-9.
26. The Dalai Lama, op. cit., p. 63.
27. ibid., p. 133.

Judgement (20)
1. Cirlot, *A Dictionary of Symbols*, p. 166.
2. Fairfield, *Choice Centered Tarot*, p. 101.
3. Pollack, *Seventy-Eight Degrees*, p. 134.
4. Greer, Tarot *Reversals*, pp. 90, 91.
5. See Thomas S. Kuhn, *The Structure of Scientific Revolutions*, second edition, (Chicago: Foundations of Unity Science Series, 1970/1962).
6. Constance Cumbey, *The Hidden Dangers of the Rainbow: The New Age Movement and our Coming Age of Barbarism*, revised edition (Louisiana: Huntington House, 1983), p. 159.
7. Based on reporting by dpa, ITAR-TASS, and Interfax, "Russian Patriarch Says Gay Marriage 'Sign Of Apocalypse,'" accessed November 23 2016, http://www.rferl.org/a/patriarch-russia-gay-apocalypse-kirill/25052758.html.
8. This is a term used by Ralph Metzner to describe the contours of what he considers to be an emerging paradigm shift from an "Industrial" to an "Ecological" worldview, incorporating convergent trends across a wide spectrum of fields and disciples; including ethics, epistemology, science, politics, education, theology and religion. See Ralph Metzner, "Age of Ecology" in *Resurgence*, November/December 1991, No. 149, pp. 4-7.

Notes

9. Rosemary Radford Ruether, "Ecofeminism: Symbolic and Social Connections of the Oppression of Women and the Domination of Nature" in Carol J. Adams, ed., *Ecofeminism and the Sacred* (New York: Continuum, 1993), pp. 13-23 (p. 21).
10. Jung, *CW10*, par. 293.
11. Gardner, *The Tarot Speaks*, p. 129.
12. In this regard see Michael S. Howard, "Tarot and Alchemy: Two Parallel Traditions," accessed November 26 2016, http://tarotandalchemy.blogspot.co.uk/2012/04/star-moon-sun.html.
13. Cirlot, *A Dictionary of Symbols*, pp. 45, 46.
14. See C. G. Jung, *Collected Works Vol. 11: Psychology and Religion: West and East*, R. F. C. Hull, trans., second edition (Princeton: Princeton University Press, 1975/1958), para. 742.
15. Pollack, op. cit., p. 134.
16. From the *Agganna Sutta* in *Dialogues of the Buddha, Vol 3*, translated from the Pali by T.W. Rhys Davids and C.A.F. Rhys Davids, London, Oxford University Press, 1921. Vol. IV of *The Sacred Books of the Buddhists* series; at SuttaCentral.net, accessed November 26 2016, https://suttacentral.net/en/dn27.
17. Swami Prabhupada, *Srimad-Bhagavatam Twelfth Canto: The Age of Deterioration*, e-book edition (The Bhaktivedanta Book Trust, 2011/1984) 12:2: 19-20.
18. From the *Dhammapada* in Wagiswara and Saunders, *The Buddha's Way of Virtue*, accessed November 26 2016, http://www.sacred-texts.com/bud/wov/wov12.htm.
19. Bhikkhu Sujato with Jessica Walton, trans, *Verses of the Senior Monks* (Sutta Central, 2014), accessed November 26 2016, https://suttacentral.net/en/thag16.8.
20. *ibid.*, https://suttacentral.net/en/thag1.113.
21. *ibid.*, https://suttacentral.net/en/thag1.33.
22. Davies, *Psalms of the Early Buddhists,* accessed November 26 2016, http://www.sacred-texts.com/bud/pos/pos11.htm.
23. Sujato with Walton, op. cit., https://suttacentral.net/en/thag16.1.
24. *ibid.*, https://suttacentral.net/en/thag1.10.
25. Davies, *op. cit.*, http://www.sacred-texts.com/bud/pos/pos06.htm.
26. *ibid.*, http://www.sacred-texts.com/bud/pos/pos10.htm.
27. Kurt Spellmeyer, *Buddha at the Apocalypse: Awakening from a Culture of Destruction* (MA: Wisdom Publications, 2010), pp. 59, 35.
28. In that it appears to identify the "barbarians" with Islam.

29. Alexander Berzin, *Introduction to the Kalachakra Initiation* (Boston: Snow Lion, 2010/1997), p. 45.
30. *ibid.*, p. 46.
31. John Newman, "Escatology in the Wheel of Time Tantra" in Donald S. Lopez Jr., ed., *Buddhism in Practice*, abridged edition (Princeton NJ: Princeton University Press, 1995/2007), pp. 202-7 (pp. 203, 204).
32. Giuseppe Tucci, *The Theory and Practice of the Mandala* (Massachusetts: Weiser, 1970/1949), pp, 59, 60.
33. Berzin, *op. cit.*, p. 54.

The World (21)
1. Waite, *The Pictorial Key*, p. 156.
2. Banzhaf, *Tarot and the Journey of the Hero*, p. 221.
3. C. G. Jung *Collected Works, Vol. 18: The Symbolic Life: Miscellaneous Writings*, Gerald Adler, ed., R. F. C. Hull, trans. (Princeton: Princeton University Press, 1950/1980), para. 585.
4. Jeremy Yunt, *Jung's Contribution to an Ecological Psychology: Understanding the Psychic Roots of Environmental Issues* (Santa Barbara, CA: Barred Owl Books, 2009), p. 9.
5. Don Cupitt, *Solar Ethics* (London: SCM Press, 1995), pp. 54, 56.
6. Starhawk, *Dreaming the Dark: Magic, Sex & Politics*, second edition (London: Unwin, 1990/1982), p. 38.
7. Pollack, *Seventy-Eight Degrees*, p. 139.
8. Keller, *From a Broken Web: Separation, Sexism and Self*, 7, 205-6.
9. See Vivian Giang, "Transgender is yesterday's news: How companies are grappling with the 'no gender' society," accessed November 27 2016, http://fortune.com/2015/06/29/gender-fluid-binary-companies/. See also Sarah Marsh, "The gender-fluid generation: young people on being male, female or non-binary," accessed November 27 2016, https://www.theguardian.com/commentisfree/2016/mar/23/gender-fluid-generation-young-people-male-female-trans.
10. C. G. Jung, Collected Works 11: *Psychology and Religion: West and East*, Gerald Adler, ed., R. F. C. Hull, trans. (Princeton: Princeton University Press 1958/1969), para. 753.
11. Mary Grey, *Redeeming the Dream: Feminism, Redemption and Christian Tradition* (London: SPCK, 1989), see esp. pp. 27, 31, 36.
12. Gottfried de Purucker, "The Four Beasts of the Christian Apocalypse," *The Theosophical Forum August 1944*, accessed November 27 2016,

http://www.theosociety.org/pasadena/forum/f22n08p358_the-four-beasts-of-the-christian-apocalypse.htm.
13. From the *Mahaparinibbana Suttanta* in Davies, *Buddhist Suttas*, accessed November 28 2016, http://www.sacred-texts.com/bud/sbe11/sbe1103.htm.
14. *ibid*.
15. *ibid*.
16. Susan Murcott, *First Buddhist Women: Poems & Stories of Awakening* (California: Parallax Press, 2006/1991), p. 16.
17. See for example Nancy J. Barnes, "The Nuns at the Stupa" in Ellison banks Findly, ed., *Women's Buddhism Buddhism's Women: Tradition, Revision, Renewal* (Boston: Wisdom Publications, 2000) pp. 17-36 (p. 19).
18. From the *Anguttara Nikaya* 7:59 in Bhikkhu Bodhi, *In the Buddha's Words*, p. 123.
19. From the *Anguttara Nikaya* in Warren, *Buddhism in Translations*, p. 229.
20. Buddhismus Aktuell and Michaela Doepke, "Interview with the Dalai Lama about the Full Ordination of Women," accessed November 27 2016, http://info-buddhism.com/Interview_Dalai_Lama_about_the_Full_Ordination_of_Women.html.
21. See Karma Lekshe Tsomo, "Gender Equality and Human Rights" in Thea Mohr and Jampa Tsedroen, eds., *Dignity & Discipline: Reviving Full Ordination for Buddhist Nuns* (Boston: Wisdom Publications, 2010), pp. 281-9.
22. From the *Soma Sutta* in the *Bhikkhuni Samyutta* of the *Samyutta Nikaya*, from Mrs. Rhys Davies' appendix to her *Psalms of the Early Buddhists*, accessed November 27 2016, http://www.sacred-texts.com/bud/pos/pos22.htm#APPENDIX.
23. See Thanissaro Bhikkhu, trans., *Sannoga Sutta*, accessed November 27 2016, http://www.accesstoinsight.org/tipitaka/an/an07/an07.048.than.html.
24. Rita M. Gross, "How Clinging to Gender Subverts Enlightenment," accessed November 27 2016, http://www.inquiringmind.com/Articles/ClingingtoGender.html.
25. Lynn White Jr., "The Historical Roots of Our Ecologic Crisis" in *Science*, 10 March 1967, Vol. 155, pp. 1203-7 (p. 1206).
26. Stephen R. Kellert, "Concepts of Nature East and West" in Michael E. Soule and Gary Lease, ed., *Reinventing Nature? Responses to Postmodern Deconstruction* (Washington DC: Island Press, 1995), pp. 103-21 (especially p. 107).

27. From the *Mata Sutta* in Bhikkhuni Uppalavanna, trans, accessed November 27 2016, http://awake.kiev.ua/dhamma/tipitaka/2Sutta-Pitaka/3Samyutta-Nikaya/Samyutta2/14-Anamatagga-Samyutta/02-Duggatavaggo-e.html.

28. Joana Macy "The Greening of the Self" in Allan Hunt Badiner, ed., *Dharma Gaia: A Harvest of Essays in Buddhism and Ecology* (California: Parallax Press: 1990), pp. 53-63 (pp. 57, 61).

29. Joanna May, "Awakening to the Ecological Self" in Judith Plant, ed., *Healing the Wounds: the Promise of Ecofeminism* (London: Green Print, 1989), pp. 201-11 (p. 201).

30. See Bill Devall, "Ecocentric Sangha" in Badiner, *Dharma Gaia*, pp. 155-64.

31. From the Forres Eco-Sangha web-page, accessed November 29 2016, http://forresecosangha.net/?page_id=8.

32. Jim Deitrick, "Activist Women in Contemporary Buddhism" in Keown and Prebish, *Encyclodepia of Buddhism,* pp. 20-1 (p. 20).

33. Bill Butler, *Dictionary of the Tarot*, p. 5.

34. Bradford Hatcher, *Tarot as a Counseling Language: Core Meanings of the Cards*, Introductory Section (n. p.),